TWICE
AS HARD

TWICE
AS HARD

NAVIGATING BLACK STEREOTYPES
AND CREATING SPACE FOR SUCCESS

**OPEYEMI SOFOLUKE
& RAPHAEL SOFOLUKE**

DK LONDON
Publishing Director Katie Cowan
Art Director Maxine Pedliham
Senior Acquisitions Editor Stephanie Milner
Managing Art Editor Bess Daly
Copy Editor Renee Davis
US Editor Kayla Dugger
Proofreader Laura Caddell
Indexer Elly Dowsett
Jacket Designer Ciara LeRoy
Photographer Francis Augusto
Pre-production Manager Sunil Sharma
DTP Designer Tarun Sharma
Design Assistant Javana Boothe
Production Editor Heather Blagden
Production Controller Kariss Ainsworth

First American Edition, 2021
Published in the United States by DK Publishing
1450 Broadway, Suite 801, New York, NY 10018

Copyright © 2021 Dorling Kindersley Limited
DK, a Division of Penguin Random House LLC
21 22 23 24 25 10 9 8 7 6 5 4 3 2 1
001–323492–Jun/2021

A catalog record for this book is available from
the Library of Congress.
ISBN 978-0-7440-3993-1

Printed and bound in Canada

For the curious
www.dk.com

This book is a work of nonfiction based on the
life, experiences, and recollections of Opeyemi
Sofoluke and Raphael Sofoluke. In some cases,
names of people and places have been
changed solely to protect the privacy of others.

MIX
Paper from
responsible sources
FSC™ C018179

This book was made with Forest
Stewardship Council ™ certified
paper—one small step in DK's
commitment to a sustainable
future. For more information go to
www.dk.com/our-green-pledge

CONTENTS

To our parents, you have shown us that, despite the hurdles, we are more than capable.

To our children, we do this for you. Never let anything hold you back from running your race.

To our siblings, we're in this together. Thank you for always being there.

We love you.

"The issue of race is an issue we are forced to deal with; it is not our option."

–REVEREND AL SHARPTON[1]

LET'S GET TO WORK

*"THE ROAD AHEAD IS NOT GOING TO BE EASY. IT
NEVER IS, ESPECIALLY FOR FOLKS LIKE YOU AND ME.
BECAUSE WHILE WE HAVE COME SO FAR, THE TRUTH
IS THAT THOSE AGE-OLD PROBLEMS ARE STUBBORN
AND THEY HAVEN'T FULLY GONE AWAY."*
–MICHELLE OBAMA[2]

INTRODUCING ... OPEYEMI SOFOLUKE

I'd like to start by asking you two questions. First, if you could do or be anything, what would it be? In other words, what is your true passion? Second, have you ever felt that the color of your skin could present challenges on your way to fulfilling this goal? If you answered "yes" to the second question, you are not alone. For many of us, at some point in our lives, we have been told: "If you work hard, you can do or be anything you desire." Being the optimist I am, I had always believed that working hard, being committed, and striving for excellence would automatically equate to results. Yes, these qualities may have opened some doors of opportunity and have certainly helped me in my career. The reality is, however, that while we, as Black people, can aim to achieve success on our own terms, so long as we work within a system historically opposed to supporting, promoting, and advancing Black talent, then success requires more than just hard work. Essentially, environmental and systemic factors are more debilitating to Black people than their counterparts.

Growing up, my parents would often encourage me to aim to be the best. "Because when you're the best, *they* have no choice but to notice you," were words my Dad would often say to me. Life as a Black African man in the UK had taught him that expertise alone was simply not enough to make it. I recall evening conversations during our family time where my parents would share the challenges they faced at work every once in a while and, more often than not, those challenges were linked to the issue of race. Experience had taught them that as a Black person, you needed to be ready to jump over excessive hurdles to reach your goals. Promotion was possible, but seldom was it a straightforward process. They were all too familiar with the practice of working twice as hard as their colleagues just to meet milestones and three times as hard to maintain them. When they were building their careers and launching businesses, there was no handbook available to them detailing how to navigate predominantly white environments as a Black person. All they knew was the importance of going above and beyond what was expected of them, a dedication that was instilled in me from an early age. Setting affirmations and personal encouragement of "work hard and you will succeed," or, "you can do whatever you set your mind to" aside, what their experiences uncovered for me is that these statements do not address the fact that the world we live in does not reward a person just because they're good. No. For many Black people, there exists this overwhelming sense of responsibility to be great.

Repeating affirmations may motivate us to work hard, but they fail to address that many of the environments in which we work do not operate on a system of meritocracy; such statements assume that all people will be fairly judged and granted access or opportunity based on their abilities without the influence of class, gender, or race. But we know that is not always the case. The reality is that society consists of people—and, by nature, people are subjective. If you look carefully at the evidence, you will see that we are not on a level playing field. For example, in 2005, research found that people with white-sounding names were nearly twice as likely to get callbacks for jobs than people with ethnic-sounding names.[3] And sadly, 14 years later, in 2019, the numbers only worsened. A study by experts based at the Centre for Social Investigation at Nuffield College, University of Oxford, found applicants from minority ethnic backgrounds had to send 80 percent more applications to get a positive response from an employer than a white person of British origin.[4] Considering these facts, how does it make you feel to learn that your name alone could hinder your access to opportunity? The fact that there has been no improvement reinforces what many of us have experienced and know to be true: racial inequality remains an insidious disease that is still very much alive and kicking across professional institutions.

Let's return to the quote I shared at the beginning of this chapter from a speech Michelle Obama delivered to an audience of graduates from Tuskegee University, a historically Black university. Without trying to dampen their enthusiasm, Michelle Obama let the students know that the journey ahead was not going to be easy. She kept it real, calling out the many inequalities prevalent across the educational, professional, and social systems, addressing structural racism and the impact of it on Black hopefuls. As a Black woman, she could identify with the students and gave them the pep talk they needed to hear. In order to prepare them for the world they were about to enter, the pressure to perform was presented as something to be expected.

In a sense, many of us have been conditioned to accept that whether we like it or not, our race will play a part in how we are perceived and received. Until real change happens, the onus is on us to work "twice as hard." We're expected to be willing to push ourselves to the limit; exceed our own expectations, as well as the expectations of those around us; and be twice as hard—developing our mental, emotional, physical, and spiritual strength to persevere through challenges on top of distinguishing ourselves as individuals that display a level of excellence in our respective fields. While this pressure remains, I know hope is not lost, so my prayer is that this book equips you with knowledge, advice, and helpful tools to navigate the working world, how that affects your personal life, and all things in between.

INTRODUCING ... RAPHAEL SOFOLUKE

Entrepreneurship is not only important for creating wealth for individuals, but it often drives change in society through innovation. Garrett Morgan, Shirley Ann Jackson, and Frederick McKinley Jones are three Black individuals who have played major roles in shaping our world today.

Respectively, they are the creators of the three-light traffic signal, the technology behind Caller ID, and refrigerated trucks. These names may ring a bell to some of you, but for many readers, this will be the first time you have heard of these groundbreaking entrepreneurs. This is the case with many Black innovators throughout history. Today, things are a bit different; we are more aware of "successful Black entrepreneurs." However, as highlighted by the Toigo Foundation, a US career advancement organization for underrepresented groups, the rise of prominent Black entrepreneurs and leaders in the United States, such as Oprah Winfrey, Barack Obama, Robert L. Johnson, and Michael Jordan, creates "the illusion of inclusion."[5]

Leila Janah, founder of Samasource, said, "Talent is equally distributed; opportunity is not,"[6] a phrase which resonates with many Black entrepreneurs and professionals. This is not to say that Black entrepreneurs and professionals can't progress in the working world; instead, it is to highlight that the rate of progress and how many Black people actually make it to the most senior positions in corporations is far slower and more unlikely than some of their non-Black peers. With the rich array of successful Black entrepreneurs and professionals coming to the forefront in the UK, such as Edward Enninful OBE, Lewis Hamilton OBE, and John Boyega, just like in the United States, it's easy to be under "the illusion of inclusion." We only have to look at the diversity numbers of the executive boards in the UK's largest companies to see that despite all the talk of increasing and improving diversity at the top level of organizations, there are no Black chairmen, chief executive officers, or chief financial officers in any of Britain's 100 largest companies. Therefore, it is clear that there must be many instances in which invisible barriers have kept Black people from rising to senior levels—often described as the "glass ceiling."

As a soccer enthusiast and Liverpool F.C. fan, I would describe entrepreneurship for a Black person in the same way as starting a new season. At the beginning of the Premier League, 20 teams begin at 0 points; however, before a ball is even kicked, there are favorites to win the league. The favorites are normally based on previous league performance, transfer market activity (how much they have to spend or have spent), manager's ability, and how good the crop of first team players are. Although it appears that when a match starts, 11 players get on the field against 11 players and it is an equal contest, there is unfortunately a lot of activity off the field that generally determines the score of a match and the final league position of those two teams. As a Black entrepreneur, it is often difficult to get access to finance to spend on resources such as marketing and product investment, which in the soccer world would equate to transfer budgets for top players. Access to the right mentors and advice can also be an implication of not having the right budget and this, in the soccer world, equates to being able to pay for a top-flight, inspirational, world-class manager like Jürgen Klopp. It is also worth mentioning that regardless of how mentally prepared or fit a team of 11 players are, it is very hard to compete with a team who has the financial backing to acquire the best players or resources. Think about this in relation to entrepreneurs. As you can see, although on the surface it seems that at the start of the season all the teams have an equal chance to win the league, this is not the case; when other clubs have more money to spend on better resources, it generally has a direct implication on the final result. It is also clear that no matter how hard a squad of players train (or an entrepreneur works), it's very difficult to compete with others who have stronger financial backing behind them.

In 2017, I launched the UK Black Business Show to inspire and connect Black business owners and professionals working in various industries, but also to highlight some of the amazing Black entrepreneurs and professionals in the UK. Now the biggest event of its kind in Europe, the UK Black Business Show is an annual conference that attracts attendees who come to see business role models from the Black community. Representation creates an ecology of role models who in turn enable increased representation. From my experience, the more I have seen the plethora of Black entrepreneurs and professionals in the UK and United States, the more I have felt that I can achieve such greatness.

So what differentiates Black professionals who are successful from those who aren't? How have they overcome workplace stereotypes to be the person they are today? For me, mentality is the key to everything, and, fortunately for us, a positive mentality is something that can be built up and learned. Oprah Winfrey famously said, "The greatest discovery of all time is that a person can change his future by merely changing his attitude."[7]

Working "Twice As Hard" can drive many Black entrepreneurs and professionals to great heights. Yes, we have challenges and obstacles we must overcome, but with the right attitude, perseverance, and determination, there is nothing we can't achieve. I truly hope that there will be a time when Black professionals and entrepreneurs will be on a level playing field with everyone else, and it is down to us all to not only inspire the next generation, but to call out injustice and discrimination in business and professional spaces. May this book inspire you to do that.

INTRODUCING ... TWICE AS HARD

This book explores the struggles, barriers, and successes of Black entrepreneurs and professionals in order to inspire a change of attitude while showing others how to be better allies to their Black peers. Through interviews with leading Black executives, professors, innovators, influencers, musicians, athletes, comedians, actors, and more, we will draw on our own personal experiences and those of successful others to explore and share advice about how to establish yourself as a major player in your industry. By considering essential topics, such as personal branding, networking, mentorship, navigating white spaces, growth, money, mental health, and allyship, *Twice As Hard* will become the perfect guide to help you navigate your career and elevate your achievements to the next level.

For far too long, many people and organizations have shied away from discussing and tackling racism. Within our communities and organizations, there is still so much change to be made, but there has never been a better time to do it than now.

WHO DO PEOPLE SAY YOU ARE?

Building Your Brand by
Opeyemi Sofoluke

personal
/'pə:s(ə)n(ə)l/
adjective
relating or belonging to a single or particular person
rather than to a group or an organization

branding
/'brandɪn/
adjective
the promotion of a particular product or company by
means of advertising and distinctive design

WHO ARE YOU?

"Who do people say I am?" This is a question we should ask
ourselves on a regular basis. It is a question that encourages
self-reflection and an appreciation of how we are being
perceived. Ultimately, it is a question about our personal
brand. Pause for a second. Think about it. When you're not
in the room, what is the impression you leave behind?
What differentiates you from your peers at work? What are
your values? What is your "why"? Unpacking the answers

to these questions will help you understand the type of brand you currently have, prompting you to consider the brand you desire to create. This question is not limited to just personal branding—the same can be applied to businesses. Understanding the reputation of your business is valuable in enabling you to better serve your customers and identify ways to improve the product or service you offer.

The interesting thing about personal branding as a Black person is that we often find ourselves in environments where those around us already have preconceived opinions on who we are and how we are expected to behave. Let's run through a few examples to make sure we're all on the same page here. Have you ever been told that "You're so cool" by your white co-worker, and deep down you know that you're really not that cool? Because they associate Blackness and Black culture with being cool, you automatically fit the criteria. Or have you ever been in a situation when greeting colleagues and, instead of receiving a standard handshake, you are offered a fist bump? Worse still, have you ever been told that "you don't sound Black," or "you're actually quite articulate"? As if there is a homogeneous way for Black people to sound.

I've experienced all of the above and, believe me, it is frustrating to frequently find yourself in settings where people place you in a box based on the color of your skin. Be it in the school playground, the college cafeteria, the office corridor, or the business boardroom, Black people deal with this dilemma on a regular basis. We are under constant scrutiny and feel pressure to challenge stereotypical views others hold about us. This is especially important when considering how we develop our personal brands, because we are not afforded the luxury of starting from scratch. The issue we find ourselves battling surrounds perception. People's perception influences how they see us, subsequently playing a direct role in how our brand is interpreted. As early as primary socialization—when we first start to interact with people inside of our immediate family unit— humans learn the values, beliefs, and attitudes of their culture through the people they have close personal relationships with, such as their parents, guardians, and family members. If their parents have a stereotypical view about a group of people, it is more than likely that they will develop a similar view. If their parents have a fear of a group of people, again, it is likely that they will also develop a similar fear. Such values and beliefs can change over time and, if they do, it is a matter of unlearning what has been instilled from an early age. But if these views remain unchallenged from childhood to adulthood, they can have a negative impact on both the individual and the community in which they live. In the same way, people that are brought up to have a negative view about Black people will typically hold onto that view, particularly if it is reinforced during secondary socializations, such as learnings from school, society, and even the media. Now, if a person has a stereotypical view about an ethnic group as a result of socialization, it is most likely the case that their confirmation bias will make it difficult for them to see past their own views and see the person for *who they really are*.

In a professional and business context, the implications of being misinterpreted and misunderstood can have a significant impact on your career trajectory, which reinforces the need for us to be twice as good, take on twice as much, be twice as clear, be twice as calm, and work twice as hard. This is because a Black person simply cannot afford to fall short while working in a white environment, where we are underrepresented and therefore face the potential of being underestimated, viewed as our stereotypes, or scrutinized more closely than our peers. The same could be said on the basis of gender or age, but there are complexities to discuss when race is involved. With white professionals taking up 89.6 percent of the UK's leadership positions across both the public and private sector and Black people clutching onto a mere 1.5 percent of the 3.7 million leadership positions across the UK's public and private sectors, clearly we are not receiving the same opportunities[1].

We interviewed Bianca Miller-Cole—founder of The Be Group, serial entrepreneur, and personal branding expert—who shares a similar sentiment, explaining that as Black professionals and entrepreneurs, we essentially have to go an extra step when it comes to our branding because of the environments we have to operate within. "Being labeled means that you are essentially responsible for dispelling any stereotypes associated with the label you have been given," Bianca says. "Sometimes it isn't enough to just be great at what you do. You have to also think about how you come across and your style of delivery, when you're delivering that great work. Are you seen as approachable and personable? I feel like, as a Black person, there's an additional layer to building your reputation. So when we look at personal branding, while we're looking at the key characteristics that define your personal brand, we're also looking at how you're being perceived by the outside world. And so, you have to think about how you go about getting the job done when you're raising your reputation." Bianca offers some points to consider when building your brand.

"Whether you are in the corporate space or in the entrepreneurial space, you have to ask yourself, 'What does my personal brand represent? What do I want people to think of, or think about, when they think of me? What are the key points of value that I bring to this organization? What are the key problems that I solve?', so that people are very clear about where you add value. And that's on social media, networking platforms like LinkedIn, and in person."

I remember a conversation I had with my sister when she started a new job in the City and, after meeting her team, she realized she was the only Black person in her department. Being the only Black person on her team was not a surprise for her because, as we all know, in the corporate world, finding a team with more than one Black person is a rarity, and experience had taught her to have no expectations when it came to that. However, as someone who was relatively new in the organization, and being conscious of the fact that she was the only Black person her colleagues would be interacting with on a regular basis, she expressed that she felt this overarching pressure to be a good example and not reflect any of the negative labels typically associated with Black women. As someone who has spent the majority of my career in the corporate world, this notion my sister expressed was one I shared and experienced myself. As we spoke, there was something she said that resonated with me: "For a Black person going into a new working environment, your task is not to come in and prove that you can do the job. The task is disproving any stereotypes your colleagues may have about you, and *then* follows the proving that you can do the job." Her words highlight the challenges of operating in an environment that lacks an ethos of anti-racism. In such spaces, it's as if you have to prove yourself and at the same time be a good example in the hope of creating opportunities for other Black people that may come after you. This sentiment was echoed by business leader Herman Bulls. Herman has extensive experience as a board member on several Fortune 500 listed companies; is the Vice Chairman, Americas, and International Director at JLL; and also the founder of JLL's highly acclaimed Public Institutions Business Unit. With over 30 years experience in the industry and having served near 12 years of active duty service with the US Army, Herman is no stranger to being the "only one." Speaking to us via Zoom, Herman shares, "Many times, there is only one of me. So I do have that in my mind, because whether I want to or not, I'm representing. So, with that, there are things that I have to think about." Herman further explains, "As a person of color, your confidence could very well be perceived as arrogance, in one person's view. It's a kaleidoscope that's just so complicated that there's not a rule for it; there's just a set of rules, and you've got to be sensitive to each situation about how to use them."

Similarly, in a business context, establishing a strong brand and knowing who people say you are as a business can impact your achievement of success. Black-owned businesses face the challenge of disproving damaging stereotypes such as, "Black-owned businesses have poor customer service," "Black-owned businesses are always running behind schedule," or "Black-owned businesses are only for Black people."

These kinds of generalizations can impact how and whether a company thrives, and therefore it is vital for business owners to position themselves in such a way that reflects a strong brand or business identity by clearly highlighting:

- **The purpose of your business.** Why does your business exist? What problem is it trying to solve? What is the opportunity in the market you are trying to occupy? When you can succinctly answer these questions, you can begin to focus on clearly communicating ...

- **Your business identity and offering.** How do you want to be recognized by your target audience? How do you talk about what you are offering in a way that connects with your audience consistently across various media platforms? How will you communicate the value your business can add to its customers? What differentiates your business from its competitors? Getting a handle on these factors and understanding how to effectively get this message out will allow you to focus on ...

- **Your business strategy.** How will you authentically market your product or service to your target audience? How will you connect with your customer to build a loyal customer base? How will you test and refine your strategy to continue to effectively serve your customers?

Working on the above will not only help you to pay special attention to the business brand you are building, it will encourage you to think about the relationship you are building with your customer. The benefit of building a strong brand identity is that you build a strong community of customers who can personally identify with your business. This means that, as a brand, you remain recognizable, even in a market that may be oversaturated. Cultivating an authentic brand in an environment where you are a minority requires hard work, equally as a professional and a Black-owned business.

Let's explore how you can build your own personal brand in an environment where you are required to work around the nuances of unconscious bias and structural racism. Once you have discovered what you want your personal brand to be, we will take a look at some branding strategies that Black entrepreneurs have employed with the purpose of highlighting what has worked and what can be applied to achieve similar success.

PERSONAL BRANDING ... WHAT IS IT?

Simply put by Susan Chittron in *Personal Branding for Dummies*, "Your personal brand is your reputation, which is defined by your character. Your personal brand is also your legacy; it's the way others remember you through your actions, your expertise, and the emotional connections that you make. Your personal brand shows your authenticity from the inside out."[2] Effective and conscious personal branding should differentiate you from your peers and, going by the definition outlined above, it is the way you promote the distinct traits that belong to you alone. Branding creates an opportunity for self-discovery and allows you to highlight and draw on the attributes about yourself that you want people to see. So defining your personal brand requires you to be intentional about the way in which you differentiate yourself or your business.

Someone who knows all about this is award-winning leadership expert and executive coach India Gary-Martin.

Her 25 years of experience in the financial services industry proved how important it is to consider how to position yourself and your brand. Before establishing Leadership For Life (a global executive coaching, facilitation, and consulting practice), India held the senior position of Managing Director and Global Chief Operating Officer for Investment Banking Technology and Operations at J.P. Morgan, where she had multi-billion-dollar budgetary management responsibility for 15,000 staff in more than 40 global locations. You don't get to this position without successfully and effectively building a strong personal brand. Of course, one must deliver results and meet business objectives, but, as India has shown, doing so in parallel with building a reputable personal brand can yield positive results.

When speaking to us, India shared two factors to keep at the forefront of your mind when it comes to building your brand in an environment where you are a minority: "There are a couple of things. The first one, and the biggest, is being clear about what you want to be known for," she says. "That's really what it comes down to. If you can use what you want to be known for as your guiding star, then you never go 'off brand,' right? Because you're asking yourself, 'Whatever the outcome of this thing is, is that what I want to be known for?' And if the answer is 'no,' then that's not what you should be doing. You should act on those things and use them as your North Star."

Reflecting on this, on a personal level, and as a Black woman who has held a number of global c-suite roles in her career, India knows what it feels like to be the only Black female leader in a room of industry executives. She explains, "In terms of my own branding, there were certain things that I wanted to be known for. One was being really intentional about anything that I did. Early on in my life, I actually landed in banking in a very unintentional way, but once I decided I was going to be in that space, I became very purposeful about what my goals and objectives were. Intentionality is key as you build your brand," she says. This is particularly true for Black professionals.

Taking into consideration the importance of having goals and objectives as we build our brands, we asked Dr. Wayne Frederick, President of Howard University, scholar, and surgeon what advice he would offer Black professionals to best position themselves in order to establish a positive personal brand. Dr. Frederick is known for his academic excellence and has received multiple awards and honors, including recognition from Congress for his contributions in addressing health disparities among African Americans and historically underrepresented groups. Dr. Frederick advises, "Don't focus on yourself—focus on your mission. Emphasize your unique purpose and allow yourself to be defined by it. Who you are is less important than what you do and who you do it for."

Where possible, you need to be clear about your purpose and what you are trying to achieve, build the right work relationships, seek the necessary work experience and add value in order to raise your visibility in the workplace. In my experience, and the experiences of others that will be explored throughout this book, we will learn that Black people tend to face the simultaneous dilemma of standing out but being overlooked. Let's face it: Black employees are often not afforded the same privilege of establishing their brand, who they are, or what they want to be known for without bias. Research shows that we tend to be judged more harshly than our white counterparts.[3] Therefore, this notion of being intentional about how we come across is key to building our reputation and leads us back to that all-important question: *"Who do people say I am?"*

Generally speaking, in scenarios where the employer is part of the dominant ethnic majority group and the employee is part of the ethnic minority group, the employee will make an effort to influence the perception the employer may have about them. For example, when I started my first graduate role, I was keen to make a good impression. At the time, I did not know much about personal branding, but what I did know was that my reputation was important and it was necessary that I built a good one. I felt it was important that I displayed basic business etiquette and that I, of course, took the time to understand my role in order to perform. I was so grateful for the opportunity I had been given to start my career at a prestigious firm. I was aware that thousands of students had applied for the same opportunity but didn't make the cut, and the fact that I did was probably my biggest motivator at the time. People talk about getting a foot in the door, and there I was with more than a foot in the door—my whole body was sitting in a chair, at *my* own desk, with three monitors. Yet it didn't take long for reality to sink in.

In my first week of starting the role, my manager informed me of his expectation for the team to be in the office by 8 a.m. every day. This wasn't an issue for me—as the industry is one which tends to require early hours, it wasn't a ridiculous ask. I made sure to figure out the quickest route from my home to the office and even factored in time for potential delays. I typically arrived in the office by 7:45 a.m., which gave me enough time to grab a slice of toast and English Breakfast Tea, which I would eat and drink at my desk. As time went on, I began to notice that some of my colleagues would arrive after 8 a.m. and my manager seemed to have no problem with this. Nevertheless, I knew what was required of me and made sure that I was always on time. On one occasion, however, there were issues with the trains (which is typical in London) and, despite planning my journey with extra time, I knew that I would arrive at the office past 8 a.m. Considering the fact that the rest of the team would frequently turn up after 8 a.m., I didn't think being a few minutes late would be an issue. I emailed my manager to inform him of my delay but did not receive a response. When I finally arrived at the office, it was nearly 8:20 a.m. I remember rushing to my desk and greeting my manager, "Good morning," to which he replied, "Good afternoon." Shortly afterward, one of my colleagues arrived, and by this time, it was almost 8:45 a.m. I was sure that he would be scolded, too, but that was not the case. I told myself that there must have been a reason my manager was fine with my colleague(s) being late, but, even as I tried to justify his actions in my head, I could not come up with an excuse as to why most of my colleagues could show up after 8 a.m. or take multiple cigarette breaks throughout the day and not be side-eyed. I rarely took breaks and always ate lunch at my desk, yet still there was no grace.

A few weeks later, in a team meeting, my manager mentioned that there would be a team offsite and, as he provided details of the schedule for the day, he went on to say, "Opeyemi, did you get that? We'll need you to be *on time* for this offsite." I had only been late once, but still, I was the one being called out in a meeting in front of my colleagues. How was this fair? In that instant, I realized that if you are Black, you are judged more harshly than your white colleagues. A Black employee and a white employee could do the exact same thing, and in the white colleague's case, it creates no issue and is quickly forgotten. In the Black employee's case though, it becomes a mark against their character. Through that experience, I learned that we are not all measured by the same yardstick. Despite my lateness being a one-off, he held onto it as if it were a regular occurrence, and thus made it clear to me that he probably held a stereotypical view about Black people and their time management. His potential generalization of Black people subsequently influenced his perception of me from that point on. While he was not a bad manager with regard to the day-to-day role, the positive personal brand I had worked hard to portray had been tainted by his skewed perspective.

In their paper, "Racial Stereotypes: Associations and Ascriptions of Positive and Negative Characteristics," Samuel L. Gaertner and John P. McLaughlin from the University of Delaware explore the associations and ascriptions of positive and negative characteristics in relation to racial stereotypes. To no surprise, the study showed that while negative attributes may be equally associated with Black people (the outgroup) and with white people (the ingroup), negative rather than positive traits may come to mind first when thinking of Black people, while positive attributes may be more salient for the socially dominant white ingroup. The study concludes that racial stereotypes have not faded, but rather are more subtle and perhaps more complex.[4] Biases such as this, where superiors can be forthright in exacting personal opinions based on nothing more than exaggerated stereotypical falsehoods, mean that Black people cannot afford to be nonchalant in the area of personal branding. If you do not define your brand, others will define it for you. While we cannot control the stereotypes an individual may consider about us, it is imperative that we do what we can to direct the narrative of the variables that we can control.

Going back to the conversation with India, she shared that the second important element of establishing your brand is found in knowing who you are and being true to yourself. "In terms of how I made it through—integrity and being unshakable formed part of my personal brand," she says. "I know who I am, and so it didn't matter what anybody else said or did, I still knew who I was and I knew my value." India's words remind me of the self-awareness Black women have to carry. On a mental and emotional level, our journeys require twice as much strength and resilience as we push for progress in spite of the intersectional challenges that gender and race present. Of course, I do not want to suggest that Black men have it easy, because I know that is certainly not the case. I only have to reminisce on the numerous counts of racism my Dad experienced throughout his career in the corporate world to know that Black men face their struggles, too. But it is worth drawing attention to the dynamic of juggling not one, but two factors that cause you to be considered a minority—being both Black and a woman.

India provides a great starting point for personal branding with intentionality and integrity—both are vital as you work out and refine your brand. "When I experienced a whole bunch of crazy situations at work, it didn't shake me because I knew my value," she asserts. "It might have upset me in the moment, but, bringing it back to what I wanted to be known for and who I was, being really comfortable in my own skin was a big part of me being able to have the confidence to roll through my brand regardless. So when I think about branding, it's the confluence of both things: being clear about what you want to be known for, and being true to who you are."

Some of the key factors I consider important when it comes to personal branding are: appearance, work ethic, authenticity, and values and beliefs. Let's discuss.

APPEARANCE: IT STARTS WITH WHAT THEY SEE

"I AM NOT MY HAIR, I AM NOT THIS SKIN, I AM NOT YOUR EXPECTATIONS, NO. I AM NOT MY HAIR, I AM NOT THIS SKIN. I AM THE SOUL THAT LIVES WITHIN."
–INDIA ARIE[5]

Listening to these lyrics as a 14-year-old was truly empowering. Despite growing up in a relatively multi-cultural community, to hear a song on the radio that so explicitly challenged the perceptions people could have about me, based on my physical appearance, was empowering. Drawing attention to the negative stereotypes people tend to form around Black appearance, namely Black hair, Arie challenged her listeners to reflect on their own bias, asking questions like, "Does the way I wear my hair determine my integrity?" and with lyrics like, "Corporate wouldn't hire no dreadlocks." Arie's song, though uplifting, was a warning of the complex relationship between corporate environments and Black culture and identity. Growing up, natural afro hair felt like something that had to be tamed, controlled, and managed. The reality could not be more opposed to the truth—my hair is my crowning glory; so versatile and free. Yes, it requires time (deep conditioning), love (hot oil treatments), and affection (leave-in conditioner), but isn't that what we give in any relationship we want to see flourish and grow?

My journey toward embracing my natural hair started in my final year of college. Postgraduation, I found myself experimenting with different styles and products. I enjoyed the journey of discovery I was on and used the summer to try out new hairstyles. Whether rocking my afro or switching things up with a weave, I was beginning to embrace all of me. When summer came to an end, however, I began to mentally and physically prepare myself for the graduate position I had secured at one of the world's largest investment banks. A big part of that preparation was figuring out the best way to style my hair. Physical appearance matters more than we know, and in a business context, employers often make hiring decisions based on the appearance and attractiveness of the job applicants.[6] Having successfully made it through a summer internship, I was offered a graduate role. I was well aware of the environment I was stepping into, but I was still concerned with making a good impression on my new team.

As a Black female starting out in a corporate setting, one of my priorities was choosing the right hairstyle. One in five Black women feel societal pressure to straighten their hair for work,[7] so it should come as no surprise that many Black women go into work every day conscious that the style of their hair can result in awkward questions or microaggressions from nonblack colleagues. Passing judgment based on appearance is inevitable; however, the texture of one's hair, or complexion of their skin, should not influence how they are perceived. But unfortunately for Black women, in most cases, it does.

There are certain rules and unspoken expectations across the corporate community, and "looking the part" is one of them. This rule is embedded in office culture on a global level, and despite how progressive an organization may think they are, the majority of diversity and inclusion initiatives fail to explore and address the complex challenges faced by Black women across white-collar professions. It is sadly the case that for Black women, their white counterparts, in particular men, are able to take advantage of the gender and racial privilege they have been born into. A generational privilege that institutions have accepted and have become accustomed to. The career mobility of Black employees can be affected by their colleagues' feelings of familiarity or closeness with them,[8] and taking this into consideration, it is inevitable that appearance will play a part in building our personal brand, which influences how much our colleagues and managers feel they can relate to us. Many minorities are forced to adapt in an environment where homophily (the tendency of individuals to associate and bond with similar others) is bound to occur. "Similarity breeds connection"[9]— this is a statement sociologists Miller McPherson, Lynn Smith-Lovin, and James Cook wrote in their 2001 paper on the subject, "Birds of a Feather: Homophily in Social Networks," and it is a statement that rings true in social settings, as well as in workplaces. For Black professionals (in particular Black women) in the workplace, who are often

Frankly, as far as I am concerned, Black is beautiful.

"the only one," this raises the question: "How is my appearance going to signal what my personal brand represents?"

We are usually drawn to people based on what we see. According to research by Princeton psychologists Janine Willis and Alexander Todorov, it takes only a tenth of a second to form an impression after looking at someone's face for the first time.[10] Naturally, when we meet people, we form opinions that are influenced by the way a person looks, how well they are dressed, their body language, the sound and tone of their voice, so on, and so forth. As we take in this physical data, we begin to form social judgments about a person.[11] Based on our initial observations, and because these observations are made so quickly, there is no way we can form quick opinions that are not laced in bias. In a work context, some people are guilty of making judgments on an individual's competence based purely on how they look. The same goes for businesses and corporate brands. We can pass judgment on how professional or appealing a business may be based on how effectively the staff members reflect the business or how slick a website is.

Ultimately, appearance matters. We've all heard the saying, "You can't judge a book by its cover," but no matter how much we may try to apply this principle to our lives, most of us are guilty of allowing physical appearance to influence the way we interact with others. For Black people, it's our skin color, facial features, or natural hairstyle that often sets us apart. As a Black woman, I can confidently tell you that I love and embrace the person that I am, so if being Black makes me stand out, I am okay with that because, frankly, as far as I am concerned, Black is beautiful. What I am not okay with is being branded *the Black woman.*

Why? Because the color of my skin should not be my defining factor. My brand goes beyond my complexion and my hairstyle, and if you find yourself in an environment where you are referenced to as "the [*physical attribute*] person," take it as an indication that there is probably work to be done in the area of diversity and inclusion. I have experienced a number of encounters where it has felt like the perception of my brand was centered around my physical appearance. What's more, however frustrating it is, I know my experience is certainly not one I suffer alone. Angela Davis, civil rights activist, academic, and *Time Magazine's* 1971 "Woman of the Year,"[12] recounts her experience in a journal titled, *Afro Images: Politics, Fashion, and Nostalgia:*

> *One woman introduced me to her brother who at first responded to my name with a blank stare. The woman admonished him: 'You don't know who Angela Davis is?! You should be ashamed.' Suddenly a flicker of recognition flashed across his face. 'Oh,' he said, 'Angela Davis—the Afro.' Such responses I find are hardly exceptional, and it is both humiliating and humbling to discover that a single generation after the events that constructed me as a public personality, I am remembered as a hairdo.*[13]

Can you imagine? A whole Angela Davis, and all the young man could reference was the style of her hair. Sounds ridiculous, doesn't it? Sadly, the fact that so many Black people tend to stand out in professional spaces is confirmation that not enough work is being done to improve representation and to move the needle in a way that creates real change. Until workplaces and business environments push for diversity in every sense of the word and not just the "diversity" they are comfortable with celebrating, taking the time to understand and strengthen your personal brand will help you stand out for all the right reasons and not just for being Black.

Thinking back to when I started my career, I'll be honest, I didn't give my brand much thought. It was never mentioned in all the career workshops and graduate events I had attended while in college. The focus was mainly centered around building a strong record of work experience to enhance my employability and making sure my grades were on track to meet the entry requirements for the companies I was interested in. While this was helpful, it did not prepare me as a young Black woman making her first steps into a predominately white environment, where relatable role models were scarce. In as much as we are encouraged to be our authentic selves, I quickly learned that, in the working world, true authenticity is only acceptable from those who fit within the framework of the dominant culture.

When it comes to work attire, we understand that being smartly dressed whether you work in an office where suits are required, keep your uniform clean and pressed, or make sure your version of smart-casual is more smart than casual, there is a standard we have to set for ourselves. However, who constitutes what professionalism is when it comes to my physical appearance, specifically my hair? Surely, being dressed in formal work attire should be enough. For so many Black women and men, it just isn't. There exists this burden to conform to the mainstream view of "acceptable."

I remember too well the day I knew my hair played a part in how I was perceived by my colleagues. You see, as a Black woman, there is a lot we can do with our hair, and when I started out in my graduate job, I decided that single braids—my usual go-to protective hairstyle—would be appropriate. A protective style is any style that keeps the ends of the hair tucked away and minimizes manipulation. It is also a hairstyle that is easy to maintain and requires minimal time and effort to style. A few weeks into starting my new role, I decided that I wanted to change my hairstyle, this time opting for a weave, which I had styled into a side-part bob. This was the first time I had changed my hair in this environment, so I mentally prepared myself for the questions and the comments I knew would come my way. I received a few looks from people who were unsure whether to mention the obvious change I had made to my hair and, from those who were brave enough to say anything, I received a few compliments. There was one remark, however, that stuck out: "Opeyemi, I like what you've done with your hair … you look a lot smarter like that." I was surprised by this statement and sought further clarification, so I quickly responded, "What do you mean by smarter? Did I look less smart with my braids?" Realizing the blunder, my colleague tried to explain himself, and it became difficult to justify his comment. Amid the backhanded compliment, he highlighted what I already knew to be true—my appearance mattered. His unintended insult reinforced the fact that whether I liked it or not, my hair was a potential issue in the workplace. My appearance and subsequently my brand was considered "smarter" when my hair resembled white and white-adjacent styles.

I looked different, sounded different and no matter how much I tried to code switch, my strong south London accent still managed to escape. While I wasn't somebody who considered myself to be insecure, I certainly became more conscious of how I looked and how my appearance was interpreted by others. On top of the demands of starting my career in a top investment bank, I now had the added pressure of figuring out how to ensure my appearance positively contributed to the brand I was working to establish. This is a challenge faced by so many Black women in the corporate world who feel the need to "tame" their curls, coils, and kinks in order to be accepted.

Rondette Amoy Smith, Head of Diversity and Inclusion at Nomura, and also the co-founder of the Race2Rise podcast, which covers topics such as Black career development, relationships, mental health, and more, shares her experience of being a Black woman in a predominately white working environment with us. "I started at Goldman seven years ago, and I did not go natural until 2018—that's only two years of being natural. And that's because I felt I couldn't be. And every time I sort of teetered on the edge of 'Oh, let me wear my hair a little curly today,' someone's hand would just find its way into my hair. I don't think people understand how intrusive, and invasive, and distracting that can be. I don't think people fully understand. And I'm going to speak from a Black woman's perspective, but I think that there is an additional level and layer of pressure and preparation that goes into being a Black woman in the workplace." Rondette's experience is one I could totally understand and relate to. There are so many elements to being a Black woman in the workplace that we rarely explore. In addition to ensuring that we are prepared on a physical level, we also have to prepare on a mental level. Rondette further explains this: "You put on top of that, you know, how am I entering this space? How am I entering a room? Is someone gonna mispronounce my name? Is someone going to overlook me and think I'm part of the catering staff? So I think there's a lot of thought and preparation when we enter a space or when we enter a room—we always have to be prepared, we can't wing it. That pressure and that expectation, when I think about my role as an HR person, detracts from just showing up, and being excellent, and being yourself."

As we focus on the appearance element of personal branding, many of us grapple with the decision to bring out our natural self, or a more socially accepted version of ourselves, in order to build what feels like a more acceptable brand. Black men face a similar conundrum—despite being part of the gender majority, they still form part of the racial minority and are equally prejudged on the basis of their appearance.

In 2019, a popular campaign was launched throughout the UK with the aim of changing the perception of Black men.[14] The 56 Black Men campaign swept the nation, aimed at tackling the "dangerous" stereotype of "the Black man" and the negative connotations and stigma attached to the cliché image of a Black man wearing a hoodie.[15] The campaign consisted of powerful photographs of 56 Black men wearing hoodies, detailing their name and profession. The campaign was an effective way of directly addressing racial prejudice and challenging the negative narrative surrounding Black men, as it featured successful Black entrepreneurs and professionals from a range of industries. Labour Party MP David Lammy, who was included as one of the featured Black men in the campaign, highlighted the sad reality that a Black man in a hoodie has become synonymous with violence and knife crime. Sharing his personal experience in the *Guardian*,

Lammy recalls, "Having been stopped and searched in a hoodie myself as a young Black student, studying to be a lawyer at the University of London, I know that distrust of Black men in hoodies is endemic in the UK."[16] The 56 Black Men project was, in many ways, a public service announcement, educating and informing narrow-minded members of society of the fact that one piece of clothing should not define a person. Sadly, in the United States, we have seen extreme cases of how racial profiling based on clothing items such as hoodies can result in the deaths of innocent Black men. In February 2012, Trayvon Martin, a 17-year-old African American student, was shot and killed by George Zimmerman on his way back from a convenience store. Dressed in a hoodie, carrying a bag of Skittles and a bottle of juice, Martin was considered to be "dangerous." Although he posed no threat and was simply walking home, Zimmerman, who was armed and acting as a neighborhood watch volunteer, *perceived* him to be "a real suspicious guy," and on a call to the Sanford Police Department, he described the high school student as someone who was "up to no good, or he's on drugs or something." Despite receiving instruction from the police to not follow Trayvon, Zimmerman still pursued him, and this eventually resulted in Zimmerman shooting and killing Trayvon Martin. This heartbreaking case represents the fatal consequences of racism and discrimination. Though extreme, we can see that the most serious possible consequence of negative attitudes toward Black men concerns the ultimate questions of life and death.[17] The media has a role to play in the overall representation of Black men and influences public attitudes in relation toward them, hence why projects like 56 Black Men are necessary in challenging and changing the general public perception of Black men.

Relating this to a business context, stereotypical views of Black men can hinder their progression. I have literally lost count of the amount of times my Black male friends have told me that they have had to watch how they interact with others at work in order to not be perceived as "intimidating," and some of them are the calmest people I know. The Opportunity Agenda, a social justice communication lab dedicated to using communications and culture to shift narratives and tell stories that create opportunity for all, highlight that the distorted portrayal of Black men in the media influences public bias—both conscious and unconscious—against Black men. Inevitably, these biases can lead to real, practical consequences for them. Negative attitudes and perceptions of Black men can directly affect their likelihood of being hired or promoted or the chances of getting loans or investment. While we cannot control people's perceptions about us, supporting initiatives that educate and inform others to rethink and renounce their prejudice, like The Opportunity Agenda and 56 Black Men, can contribute to the promotion of more positive images of Black men in the community.

So how do we combat the negative stereotypes many have when it comes to "Black appearance"? While the aim is for there to be a time when Black men and women will be able to show up to a professional setting as their authentic self, I know we are not quite there yet. By ignoring ignorance, stepping out with boldness, and telling our stories, we are showing others that our appearance does not stop us from delivering results.

We spoke to Jay-Ann Lopez and Trina Charles, the founders of Curlture, an online platform which is purposed to empower Black women and publishes topics such as natural hair care, Black beauty, lifestyle, popular culture, supporting Black-owned businesses, and travel. With nearly 50,000 online supporters, Jay and Trina have successfully built a community where Black women are encouraged to embrace who they naturally are. Speaking with us about how to confidently express your personal brand through your appearance as a Black man or woman, Jay shares,

"You kind of have to give or take. The corporate world for the most part does not permit a lot of self-expression of Black women, or men, and that's just the reality, so it's either you show up or you don't. My advice is you show up, just take that step, take that leap to be yourself, so if that means showing up with your natural hair out, do it—deal with the questions, nip it in the bud, and set the precedent, because, if you don't, then you'll have to assimilate for the rest of your time there. If you don't set the precedent, it will be set for you. It's important to show up and be confident— even if you don't feel it. So whenever I show up to a job interview, my hair is out from the get-go. I had set a standard where they didn't have to ask about my hair in the workplace. I have experienced people touching my hair multiple times, even though I had told them not to, and that can be extremely frustrating. So it is important to find a workplace that has diversity you are looking for. I know that in itself can be a challenge, but look for a company with an inclusive culture that you can identify with."

Trina's experience working in the creative industry was slightly different. She says,

"Having a background in creative TV production, it's always been sort of cool to be different and have that freedom of expression. So I've never felt like I couldn't be my authentic self in terms of my appearance and so, I guess, I've been fortunate in that sense. However, I had conversations with people who would say, 'I can't go to work with my hair like this,' and I always ask them, 'Has someone told you that, or has someone made comments about what hairstyles are acceptable at work?' And often the response is, 'Oh, no, no one's actually said anything.' So it's really interesting, in terms of understanding why we often feel that way. I think there is a need for us to ask ourselves, 'where is this feeling coming from?' and, if it is based on our concerns of what others will think or if we are worried that our appearance may come across as unprofessional, we need to realize that we have the power to show up and be ourselves. It's about having confidence, and sometimes we have to adopt that 'fake it till you make it' vibe, and that's okay. It starts with stepping out."

I couldn't agree more with Jay and Trina. While we may not be able to control the perceptions others form about us based on our appearance, particularly if these perceptions are rooted in bias, we must continue to embrace our appearance as something to be proud of. When it comes to how you look, understand your work environment and dress appropriately to fit that culture. So, for example, in a corporate setting where you may be required to wear formal attire, dress accordingly. Similarly, if your line of work is in the creative industry and you have a slightly more informal dress code, again dress accordingly. While our places of work may require a particular dress code, that does not mean we need to leave who we are at the door. There are always ways to creatively express yourself through your appearance while following the office guidelines, whether it's through wearing a quirky tie as we have seen John Snow (English journalist and Channel 4 News presenter) do for many years or proudly wearing your natural hair out like BBC Radio 1 presenter Clara Amfo.

Let who you are shine through and learn to use our appearance as an asset. What do I mean by this? If we can bring our best selves to work, deliver in our day-to-day roles, add value to our organizations, and be recognized for positive attributes, then even if we do stand out because of our appearance, at least we will be remembered for what we do. Our brand will be less about how we look and more about what we bring to the table.

WORKING HARD AND MAKING NOISE

Growing up as a British Nigerian, if there is one thing my parents reiterated on a regular basis, it was "Hard work pays off." For the most part, this statement is true, especially if it is applied in an academic context. Those that focus, work hard, are committed, and are consistent usually achieve the grades they desire. However, the same cannot be said for the workplace. Hard work alone does not always cut it. Rather, hard work coupled with social capital is what can make the real difference, and this is something I had to learn over time. A strong work ethic should not just be about "the work." Time and effort should also go into building meaningful work relationships and knowing who should be aware of the value you bring.

In my own experience, I have seen that while it is great

to be diligent and deliver results, in order to progress and to be promoted or simply recognized, you must learn how to be your own cheerleader, and this, eventually, should form part of your brand. Questions you need to ask yourself constantly are: "How am I adding value to my organization?", "Who is aware of the value I add?", and "How can I better communicate the contribution I am making?" Your work ethic speaks to how much you value your organization and the quality of work you deliver. Indeed Career Development describes work ethic as "an attitude of determination and dedication toward one's job." Expanding that, "Those with a strong work ethic place a high value on their professional success. They exhibit moral principles that make them outstanding employees in any position."[18] An individual with a strong work ethic understands how essential it is in building and maintaining a positive personal brand. However, in an environment where managers may exhibit behaviors that suggest they hold stereotypes, hard work unfortunately has little impact.

Someone who has placed great value on hard work—be it in academia, the corporate world, or enterprise—is Asmau Ahmed, chemical engineer, strategy consultant, and founder of Plum Perfect, a groundbreaking visual search and advertising start-up. She nurtured the business from an idea to a recognized brand embraced by top retailers, major brands, and millions of consumers globally.[19] We spoke to Asmau about her early career experience of having a strong work ethic but still being overlooked as a Black woman:

"I'm an immigrant, so I came here for college and for the first couple of years I was in college, I was very naive, I did not see race. I just thought, get great grades in school. I

think as a Nigerian American, my parents instilled in me the value of education and, honestly, it made me believe I was a lot smarter than I was. And so I would not believe that anything was impossible. That naivete carried me through, that drive to work hard carried me through. And then I started working."

Asmau explains,

"I remember my first job. I had a boss that just did not like me. I couldn't fathom why he didn't like me. I don't know if it was race, I don't know what it was, but I could not succeed in his eyes. I would ask questions other people were asking and he would tag my questions as dumb. He actually said that, you know, "stupid questions." I remember a very specific incident in my team where all of us went out for a training program and I got a call from my boss's boss and he said, 'Where are you?' And I'm like, 'I'm at the training program, where everybody else is.' And he said, 'But your boss said you didn't show up to work today.' 'That's because I'm at the training program.' I replied. And then my boss's boss was like, 'Everybody's gone, why did he only notice that she was the only one gone?' But even with all of that—this is going to sound crazy—even with all of that, I did not see race. That was how naive I was.

This was in The South, where I would go out to the plant and people just wouldn't talk to me. I am grateful for that naivete, because now I see that naivete is a privilege, because it allowed me to skirt over the issues. But obviously, you know, I couldn't escape it for much longer. It was too glaring not to see; you would have to be stupid not to see it. It forced me to realize that this was not where I was supposed to be and that there were bigger things in store for me.

There was an experience where, in school, I graduated in the top 5 percent of my class, and then going into the work environment with some of my classmates and seeing them be perceived as smarter than I was, it was very discouraging. But I still had that drive. No one was going to tell me that I couldn't do anything that I knew I could do. And what I realized in my life, in my career, is that my superpower is being underestimated... And so that's how I see it. That's just how I see life. So, in my career, yes, I had to work harder.... I mean, look, you work harder, you work smarter as well. I've learned to do more of the latter as I've progressed through my career, but I've also built more credibility over the years."

Asmau's experiences remind me of the kind of discrimination my parents and grandparents faced during their careers. As a British Nigerian, the work ethic and drive Asmau refers to feels familiar, like a cultural attribute. A majority of the Nigerians I have grown up with value a strong work ethic. A common phrase used by many Nigerians is, "those at the top do not have two heads"—in other words, there is nothing stopping you from succeeding. Those who have achieved success do not possess a physical superpower—if they can do it, you can do it, too. I'll be honest and confess that a part of me agrees with this saying. Yes, there can be factors that negatively impact whether or not an individual reaches their goals, but I have always believed that what is for me will not pass me by. So even if the odds are stacked up against me; even if I have to deal with a manager that seems to hold stereotypical views and treats me differently; provided I put in the work and do my part, I *will* reach my goals.

We have already explored the challenge Black people face navigating stereotypes when it comes to their appearance and, as we have just discussed, the same is true when it comes to our work ethic. Stereotypes can influence the way our work is assessed, which subsequently influences the chances of promotion and how quickly we move up in an organization. Asmau's experience gives an insight into the complex work relationships Black employees can encounter when working with individuals who display their racism in subtle ways. Studies have shown that being white is considered a trait of the prototypical business leader. In the article, "The Historical Perspectives of Stereotypes on African-American Males," it is stated that the belief in white being right when it comes to leadership positions "may lead to biased evaluations of minority leaders, particularly African Americans (or Black) people who are stereotyped as being lazy and incompetent."[20] These stereotypical characteristics of a leader explain why Black people are often underestimated and overlooked when it comes to leadership opportunities, despite having strong track records. What these examples show us is that, regardless of a strong work ethic, if your employer holds racial bias and believes stereotypes about Black people's ability to perform, it makes it difficult for Black professionals to progress at the same rate as their white peers. Therefore, in a situation where a Black employee is able to marry the strong work ethic they have built as part of their personal brand with the ability to effectively develop their network and establish genuine work relationships, then there is more opportunity for professional progress. What active steps can you take to raise your profile at work and make your managers aware of the value you add?

Our work ethic must go beyond delivering results. While results are very important in any organization, an equal level of effort needs to go into building valuable relationships. An individual can work hard and build a reputation as the go-to person or the problem solver for their department, but if the individual is not considered to be a thought leader, or is not seen as someone who can drive organizational strategy, then an opportunity to progress can be easily missed.

Kenneth Gibbs, Forbes Council member and Head of Series Social at Amazon, shared some of the lessons he learned around branding and work ethic. Ken started his digital career in 2000, as part of the original staff of Africana.com (predecessor to TheRoot.com), and went on to hold leadership positions at AOL, Essence, BET, and ViacomCBS. Ken candidly shares with us how he learned that while having a strong work ethic is beneficial, it is important to effectively communicate the value you add.

"You have to have your brand in mind at all times. It is the most important thing. It was not something that was communicated to me by any of my mentors early in my career. But I also think because we're in different times now, social media wasn't what it is today. Social media allows for a different level of personal branding that just was not capable back then. And I'll tell you why it's important. As a result of me not going down that 'personal branding' path and being a natural introvert, early on, my

personal brand became about my 'hard work.' Like, that was it. When it came to working on projects, people would simply say, 'Just give it to Ken,' or 'Ken will handle it,' which gave me a lot of power and insight on things at work, but not a seat at the table that I was looking to be at. There were a lot of strategies that I was also implementing in that part of work, and many of the executives I was working with didn't understand the finer details. They would say things like, 'I don't need to understand that because Ken's got it.' But you need people to understand all that you're bringing to the table, as opposed to that things are simply solved if you're at the table. Back then I was more so focused on the solution piece, as opposed to me taking advantage of opportunities that I had due to my position, to make my own story about the strategies I had developed."

I am sure many of us can relate to Ken's story. Not everyone is comfortable when it comes to sharing the contributions they make at work, and I totally understand how that feels. For years, I didn't feel comfortable about self-promotion. I would lead strategic diversity initiatives, deliver on projects, and design and roll out global training programs in the hope that my managers would see the value I was adding. It sounds ridiculous when I think about it now, but why didn't I confidently speak up about all that I brought to the table? In an organization where you are the minority, you are more cautious to not appear as if you are overconfident, but the reality is blowing your own trumpet is something you have to learn to do. If you don't already, in your own way, learn to make noise about the amazing work you are doing. Ken shared how unnatural it felt to do this as an introvert but realized that it was something he had to do.

"Because I'm an introvert, that's just not me," he says "But that's not how you get the next gig in the c-suite and what have you. And that's actually what some people said to me, they were like, 'I know who you are, but you need to get out and start letting people know who you are, what you've done and what you can do.' Never assume that your work will speak for itself, especially in an environment where there is the potential to be overlooked. You need to be intentional about how you communicate the value you add to your organization."

AUTHENTICITY AND KEEPING IT AS REAL AS YOU CAN

When talking about personal branding, a common theme that always comes up is the importance of authenticity. For a business brand, I can agree that authenticity is key to connecting with your audience, but when it comes to personal branding in the workplace, it is necessary to establish what it means to be your authentic self. Authenticity is defined in the *Cambridge Dictionary* as: "the quality of being real or true."[21] "Truth" in and of itself can be seen as both objective and subjective. It can be a statement of fact or an expression of one's belief. Figuring out how to live out our truth in the working environment is a conundrum we are constantly faced with. It is a juggling act of bringing ourselves to work in a way that reflects our identity but also resonates with our colleagues. Based on this definition, being authentic suggests that we bring our real selves to work, and there are some who would interpret this as "bringing your *whole* self to work," which is a concept that I, personally, have never fully agreed with. As a diversity and inclusion lead, I have found that there are numerous trainings that promote the idea of bringing your real or whole self to work. While, in theory, this sounds like a great way to promote an office culture where inclusion, acceptance of others, and belonging reigns, if guidelines are not put in place, the idea of bringing your authentic self to work could actually be problematic, if taken literally.

Therefore, I am more so in favor of encouraging people to bring their best self to work—their authentic, best self. For me, it's about understanding the environment you are in and living out your real self within that framework. We each have multiple social identities, and how we draw on these identities is dependent on the environment and situation we find ourselves in. So, for example, as a Liverpool F.C. fan, when I worked in banking, I would not show up to the office in a soccer shirt and a pair of jeans, because I understood that there was a dress code and it is important to follow the organizational guidelines around that. However, if I really wanted to, I could find a more subtle way to share that I am a LFC fan by using my LFC mug in the office. Essentially, there is a time and place for everything, and being able to understand how to be your authentic, best self in the workplace can be effective in enabling you to build connections. Being my best authentic self has meant being confident enough to wear different hairstyles to work; it has meant learning to allow my personality to shine through; it has meant feeling free to bring jollof rice, rice and stew, or even stewed beans to the office for lunch (even if that means answering questions about what I'm eating). When asked, "What were you up to this weekend?", it means sharing that I went to Church and that I do so pretty much every weekend because my faith is a big part of my life. In a business context, it means giving enough of yourself for people to understand and get to know who you are. It is about being vulnerable, transparent, and true to you.

While I feel that I can bring myself to work, I do this in moderation. It is important to be in an organization that values diversity and is passionate about creating a sense of belonging for their employees. It was interesting to hear diversity and inclusion lead Rondette Amoy Smith's take on this:

"I don't think anybody is their full self at work, Black or not. Like, if you're LGBT, if you're a woman, even in your religion, you're probably not going to be your full self. I think as Black people, we're getting there, I don't think we can fully. The normal me talks like this, right, the normal me also speaks in Jamaican Patois, the normal me would probably be wearing a Lakers jersey right now. But, you know, you have to be a bit more professional. I remember my team, kind of jokingly, making fun of me and saying I was the only one that dressed up when lockdown[22] started, because people were coming on Zoom calls in t-shirts and every morning I would get up an hour before my first call, I would always make sure my face was decent, my hair was done, and my shirt was pressed. And I think that's because it's almost like I had to dispel the myth that I think exists, that Black people are lazy. I feel like I always had to go above and beyond. I have to keep this constant impression of professionalism and just an acute awareness

of knowing I need to garner respect. And so, to do that,
I felt I had to present myself in a certain way that, quite
frankly, my peers didn't. But I still think we're on
our way."

Bianca Miller-Cole, who is a specialist in personal branding and employability skills training, agrees with Rondette:

"In personal branding, we often talk about authenticity—
we say you can be your authentic self, but in reality, that
authenticity varies; it varies based on the culture of the
organization. You could be your authentic self and some
organizations would absolutely embrace that, and for
other organizations it's 'No, I don't want you to really be
yourself.' They want you to be your work self, and I don't
think we talk about that enough. We try to pretend you can
just bring your whole self to work, but the reality is very
different."

For me, building an authentic personal brand is about keeping it as real as you can in the context of your environment. It's about staying true to who you are but also letting parts of your personality and identity shine through; these are the things that differentiate you from others.

Similarly in business, authenticity is key to building a strong customer base. Building a strong company brand is, in many ways, a necessity in the virtual age we now live in. Tony Pec, Forbes Council Member, emphasizes that a "true brand is authentic to its core. The brand is formulated around the company or entrepreneur's values and builds on that foundation as it grows." In a time where social media plays a massive role in keeping brands engaged with their audiences, it is vital for businesses to build genuine connections with its customers.

Jay and Trina from Curlture share the importance of being authentic and understanding your audience when building a business brand. "How we established our brand is by making it authentic to us, so it doesn't feel like a chore to then create things through that brand," Jay says. "So any content that we make is something that we would do or say and look up to. It's not something that we have to put on or fake." For Jay and Trina, living out their truth is what enables them to create a brand that connects well with their audience. "We are very much authentic with our brand, which I think resonates with our audience." When Curlture launched in 2014, there weren't many platforms where two Black women would cover topics relating to Black women, popular culture, and hair in such a candid and honest way as it does. This approach was well received by an audience seeking content that was real and relatable. As Jay observes, "At the time when we started, the vocality around race that exists today wasn't there. So I will say that we in some ways primed the UK market to encourage people to speak more about culture and cultural appropriation when it comes to hair and beauty, by calling out white beauty standards more openly on a global platform without having to hide it behind frilly language." Having an authentic brand that is understood by their audience means that, for Jay and Trina, even when they update the aesthetic elements of their brand, their audience can still recognize them. Jay says, "So every time we sit down for a rebranding meeting, we keep the same thing at the forefront, which is Black women, and the fact that we might update our website, or rebrand the way our content looks doesn't matter, what we produce still stays true to our ethos." Trina added to this by highlighting the power in telling your story. "When it comes to being authentic, there is a great opportunity for storytelling. Even though we didn't plan it that way, I see that part of how we engaged our audience is through storytelling," she says. "We did that naturally from the beginning. Sharing about our upbringing and our experiences with hair and why we want to celebrate our natural beauty—that was all part of our storytelling, and that is what really connected us with people. It was the storytelling of two young Black women from London embracing themselves naturally—that was something fresh and new on the platform when we started, and it really highlighted our authenticity."

Being authentic requires businesses to:

- **Be transparent.** When you are open with your customers, they feel valued and also like they are a part of your journey.

- **Engage with your audience.** In this digital age, you can reach your audience in a matter of seconds through Instagram, Twitter, or Facebook, so brands can easily engage on a regular basis. Customers like to feel like you care, so staying in touch and staying relevant is important for businesses as they grow and develop. The more you share your brand identity, the more people can connect with the brand.

- **Tell your story.** Storytelling and having a personality builds connections. Be sure to see the value in building emotional connections with your audience through engagement.

Being able to connect with others makes a difference. Real connections can only be built when you are authentic. In being authentic with your brand, you will find that your values and beliefs naturally influence how you live; they add a sense of purpose to the actions you take in your business or your career. Therefore, as an entrepreneur, understanding who you are as a person and why your business exists will enable you to align your brand to your intrinsic values, which adds to the identity of your business.

Mark Maciver, the multi-award-winning barber and founder of SliderCuts, is the perfect example of someone who has built a brand that stays true to his values and beliefs. Businesses often start because entrepreneurs are looking to solve a problem, and this was most certainly the case with Mark Maciver. In his teen years, Mark could not afford to get a haircut at the barbershop, so his mom and older brothers would often cut his hair. But the basic cuts he was getting at home did not compare to the fades and shape-ups his peers chose. Mark finally decided he would solve this problem by learning how to cut his own hair, and that was the beginning of the successful business we see today. Mark has built a brand so respected that the likes of basketball player LeBron James, Grammy award-winning singer and actress Cynthia Erivo, and world heavyweight champion boxer Anthony Joshua have trusted Mark with their haircuts. Mark's brand is truly authentic, and he shared how he built a business that reflects his values and beliefs:

"So SliderCuts started off with me. It started off with my

ethics and my code of conduct, in terms of the way I live my life. People started seeing that and how it translated into my business. My honesty, translated into my business. Wanting to do right by everyone, translated into my business. Treating everybody fairly, translated into my business. But these were my core values because of my belief system as a Christian. Living that lifestyle meant that when people would refer to Slider, or SliderCuts, they had good things to say because of who I was as a person. You are an extension of your business, so, fortunately, my ethics in life were good before I was consciously building my brand. I had a good name around me. When it came to building my business and owning the studio, I knew what I wanted my personal brand to stand for, and the business had to reflect that. So when I'm speaking to people that are working for me, it's like, 'This is the standard, this is what I do, and this is what you guys have to do, too.' And that's how I've transferred my personal brand to the business brand."

As we see with Mark, an authentic business brand reflects the moral code, values, beliefs, and behavior of the entrepreneur. You are your brand, so be sure to ask yourself regularly: "Who do people say I am?"

BRANDING INSIGHTS FROM BLACK ENTREPRENEURS

We spoke to a number of successful entrepreneurs about building a business brand, and here's what they had to say:

Angelica Nwandu on Building a Successful Business Brand

Angelica Nwandu is the founder and CEO of The Shade Room, an Instagram-based media company that was founded in 2014 and has since grown to reach over 22 million active followers known as "Roommates." Angelica was listed in the 2016 Forbes' "30 under 30" list and is a leader in changing the way we receive celebrity news. Angelica shares,

> *"A key component is to disrupt an industry. At the time that The Shade Room came around, social media was taking over: people were spending their time there and getting their news from there. So, by posting directly to social media, we were solving an issue in bringing news to the people. Now, The Shade Room has become a part of the Instagram culture. Anytime you disrupt an industry, solve an issue, or present a solution, you're going to get the first fruits, or benefits, just for being the first to do something."*

Angelica has definitely been a trailblazer in this space. Building a platform with over 22 million followers has meant that Angelica had to maintain a clear vision, drown out the noise, and focus on building the brand—something that has not always been easy, as she explains:

> *"We've been focusing on the platform, and our aim is to constantly get better with the content that we have for our audience. As the business has grown, I had people advise me to get off Instagram, do conferences, do this, do that, you know? But with entrepreneurship, depending on the*

business you are in, you may not have a blueprint, right? And so, for us, we didn't have a blueprint on how to build a media company to something extremely big away from Instagram. So there were a thousand roads that I could take and everybody was like, 'You should take road A,' or 'You should take road B,' based on their own experience and what their interests were, they would project that onto me. They all meant well, but I had to focus on what felt like the right opportunities."

Angelica also emphasized the importance of differentiating yourself as a business and building a strong community in the process:

We offered originality. Not only was our content package very short and brief because we utilized Instagram, but also, we had a different voice. We had our own lingo and we had our own name for our audience. Once you name your community, you empower them, and they become more powerful than even the brand. And because of that, when you step into The Shade Room, it almost feels like a place rather than a page.

Mike Little on Confidence and Building Your Brand

Mike Little co-founded WordPress, the website-building software in 2003. WordPress is the world's most popular website builder and powers more than 38 percent of the web. Mike developed and continues to enhance the award-winning, "I'm a Scientist, get me out of here!" site for his client Gallomanor. He has worked on a number of UK government WordPress sites; most notably, he enhanced and supported the 10 Downing Street website for the Cabinet Office from 2008–2010.

As someone who is naturally an introvert, Mike shares the importance of being confident in your abilities as you build your brand and discusses his lack of formal education in software engineering as an obstacle to his career progress:

"Be more confident; put yourself out there more. I've always been an introvert, that's for sure. I definitely didn't put myself out there, especially in the early days. I was very much, and even used to label myself as, the backroom techie, hands on the keyboard, head down, and I don't think that helped me much.

I would apply for jobs, and they absolutely wanted a degree. Eventually, I got to the position where I understood that actually, and especially in the nineties and the early noughties, what you learned on a computing degree was nothing to do with the real world. By the time the Internet and the web hit, the real world was very, very different from formal university education. But, yeah, at the time, it seemed like it was a disadvantage not having that qualification. So I had to put myself out there. I have found that it is really important to have confidence and put yourself out there."

Part of building a brand is believing in yourself and your abilities. Mike's story is, in many ways, inspirational because despite his lack of formal tech education, his strong work ethic drove him to co-found a world-changing business.

Jamelia Donaldson on Building a Brand Customers Can Identify With

Jamelia Donaldson is the founder and CEO of TreasureTress, Europe's first and largest natural hair product subscription box, and also the co-creator of The Teen Experience, a personal development workshop for young, Black, and mixed race women. In 2019, Jamelia was recognized as an AdAge Woman to Watch in Europe.

Having seen the TreasureTress community grow rapidly since its launch in 2015, Jamelia knows the importance of understanding your audience and how they connect to the brand:

> *"When it comes to branding, you just have to be really clear about who you're serving, who your audience is, and you need to know what they want. As you continue to grow, you need to have an understanding of how your customers have evolved. It's important to be on top of who your customer is, pay attention to what they like, and give them more of that. Saying that, I also think a crucial part of branding and marketing is the fact that people don't actually always know what they want, and sometimes you have to give it to them before they know that they're ready for it. I think that that's key—being clear about who you're serving, why you're doing it, and what the greater purpose is. The brand is not just a logo, a name, and some colors."*

In my role as a diversity and inclusion lead, I have found that there is not enough coaching across learning and development training that speaks to the experiences of Black or minority ethnic employees in establishing themselves in professional working environments. Though helpful, the available resources often do not factor into our unique challenges of operating in a space that was not historically built for us. While this is currently the case, I hope that the recommendations, stories, and insights shared in this chapter provide you with things to consider as you build your brand— be it as an entrepreneur or professional. Ultimately, what matters is how you show up and what you do. Make sure you show up in a way that makes you feel proud.

NEXT STEPS AND REFLECTION

- List five adjectives that describe your current brand.

- Do you feel these words accurately reflect the brand you would like to have?

- What values shape your current brand?

- At work, or in business, what differentiates you from your peers?

- What do you want others to say about your brand?

- List three actions you will take over the next month to strengthen your brand identity, recognition, or development.

THE POWER OF YOUR NETWORK

Creating an Elite Circle by
Raphael Sofoluke

"NETWORKING IS MARKETING. MARKETING YOURSELF,
YOUR UNIQUENESS, WHAT YOU STAND FOR."
–CHRISTINE COMAFORD-LYNCH[1]

Building your network and creating valuable relationships are essential skills in business, yet it often presents itself as a daunting task. The phrase, "your network is your net worth"[2] has floated among professionals for years. It refers to the idea that the people you have in your business or friendship circle can be more valuable than what you have in your bank account. There needs to be more emphasis on not only increasing profits and revenue, but also on building strong networks and valuable relationships.

So why is your network valuable? According to Review42, "85 percent of vacant positions are filled through networking and 70 percent of people found a job through connections in a company."[3] According to Tech Jury, "80 percent of professionals believe that career success can be elevated through professional networking."[4] For the career professional, this means that, not only is networking important in getting a foot in the door, but it is also essential to being able to elevate yourself and climb up the corporate ladder. Dr. Wayne Frederick emphasized the importance of networking to us: "Networking is important. The more people you know, the more doors will open for you. It's also a critical way to explore opportunities and possibilities that you might never have known existed. However, it's not enough to put all of your energies on networking and avoid doing the work to better yourself and enhance your skills. Networking is a part of a strategy—it is not a strategy in and of itself." While Ken Gibbs adds, "I saw what working 'twice as hard' looked like in real time." Ken particularly noticed this when he attended West Roxbury private school, a very prestigious school in Boston. Realizing that his white peers were already ahead of him academically, Ken needed to get a tutor to catch up. It wasn't long before the reality that many of his white peers were well connected and had already been prepped on some of the lessons they would be taught, even before starting private school, dawned on him.

Ken believes that networking starts way before you land your first job. He relayed to me the harsh reality of how some of the biggest networks start through education systems and, in particular, private education. Private schools increase accessibility to networks to those from a high, generally white social class. This often creates elite circles, which tend to exclude those from Black backgrounds. In the United States, Private School Review reports that "the average amount of minority students in private schools is approximately 27 percent."[5] According to the *British Educational Research Journal*, "In private school with higher levels of educational achievement, children are more likely to go on to secure a high-status occupation and also have higher wages."[6] This means that those who are able to go to private schools are given an advantage over those who cannot afford to. An example of this can be seen in Eton College, an institution in the UK that has schooled 20 prime ministers, including our most recent leaders, David Cameron, and Boris Johnson.

Crazy, isn't it? A former student who went to Eton in the 1980s stated that "kids arrived there with this extraordinary sense that they knew they were going to run the country,"[7] and according to reports, the school puts a premium on individualism and encourages students to pursue any dream they might have. The encouragement given to those at private school as opposed to those in state schools creates the chasm of opportunity. This unfair disadvantage only serves to reinforce our point made earlier that "talent is equally distributed; opportunity is not."

For Ken, moving from a private school to a state school and realizing that the work he was given on returning was elementary was a shock. He says: "When I did get back to state school, I didn't encounter anything in the curriculum that I had been doing in 7th grade at private school until I reached the 12th grade in public school."

For entrepreneurs, networking is just as vital as it is for the working professional. A study on network development for entrepreneurs said that "an entrepreneur's personal network evolves from an identity-based network—dominated by strong ties—toward an intentionally managed one, rich in weak ties."[8] This study proposes that, in the emerging phase of their businesses and careers, entrepreneurs should rely primarily on strong ties, because those ties will usually provide resources. Later, in the early growth stage, entrepreneurs should expand their network to include weak ties. In the early growth phase, it is necessary to develop a diverse network that is rich in weak ties, as this will help in gaining information on new business leads.[9] Learning networking skills very early on in your career or in the development of your business can contribute to progressing more quickly. So, when creating your business plan, it's important that you actually devise strategies about how you are planning to build your network.

In my experience of attending business events, being the only Black person in the room made it harder for me to feel comfortable networking. This may not be the case for others, but, for me, the general nerves of networking combined with being a "minority" certainly had an effect on my confidence. In fact, walking into predominantly white spaces at networking events can impact the ability of even the most confident Black entrepreneurs and professionals!

"Being a Black professional is often to be alone,"[10] was published in an article written by Adia Harvey Wingfield in *The Atlantic*. Adia, a Professor of Sociology at Washington University in St. Louis, went on to say that most Black doctors, lawyers, journalists, and all of those in white-collar positions that may need special training and credentialing often have to work in environments in which they are in the minority.

When I speak with my Black friends and peers, they regularly mention the uncomfortable feeling of going to events and exhibitions and feeling that not only were there little or no Black people in the room, but also the speaker panels lacked Black representation.

I created the UK Black Business Show so that Black business owners and professionals could have a dedicated space for face-to-face networking, building meaningful connections, and formulating strong business relationships.

The UK Black Business Show allows Black entrepreneurs to network freely in a predominantly Black space while still inviting those from other backgrounds to attend, listen to stories, and be inspired by leaders from the Black community.

In the UK, the Association of Event Organisers reports that exhibitions contribute £11 billion ($15 billion) to the UK economy,[11] while UFI (The Global Association of the Exhibition Industry) reports that, globally, the exhibition industry generates "$325 billion in total output."[12]

As much as we are in an age where digital interaction has increased, it's important not to downplay the value of engaging with people in physical environments. Though not all networking can be done face-to-face, Forbes Insights found that, face-to-face meetings were more effective for persuasion (91 per cent), engagement (86 per cent) and decision-making (82 per cent).[13] These figures elucidate just how important face-to-face interaction and networking is and the direct implication on key business decisions it has. As an entrepreneur myself, I have experienced the benefits of networking, including gaining industry knowledge, learning from the success and failures of some of my peers, making new business connections, acquiring potential business partners, and more. In some ways, this book is an exercise in building your network—we've spoken to a multitude of entrepreneurs, professionals, and allies in the hope that it helps you gain from our network and utilize the advice from leading industry experts.

Jay-Ann Lopez and Trina Charles, founders of Curlture, as well as the founders of Black Girl Gamers, and the Curve Catwalk (the UK's first plus-size dance exercise class), offer us their advice. Trina spoke about the need to create these platforms because preexisting traditional spaces are lacking in opportunities for Black women to network in. She says: "Whenever I hear the phrase 'networking,' the first thing that comes to my mind is 'finding your tribe.'" What I liked about her description is that she hinted at how important it is to find networking groups and platforms that give you a sense of belonging.

When looking for groups to network in, you have to be deliberate—know who you want to speak to and what you want to get out of it. Are you looking for a specific skill set? Or do you simply want to be around like-minded people who share the same ethos as you? Whatever it is, approach networking with a sense of purpose. Trina consolidated this idea in my mind when she told me about the Curve Catwalk: "If I talk about the Curve Catwalk and the dance classes, it's something that relates to me and is something I am interested in. So, essentially, I am trying to find like-minded people who are interested in similar things or have experienced some of the same pain points [around exercising, not on the basis of aesthetic goals]. My pain point was that I couldn't find a space where I felt accepted, so I created my own, and I found other women that felt exactly the same."

Entrepreneurs are some of the biggest experts in turning frustration into creation. Frustrated with the constant back-and-forth emails that come with trying to schedule a meeting, Tope Awotona set about creating a platform to solve the problem. Calendly, a scheduling software that automated the process of arranging meetings launched in 2013, now has over eight million monthly users and in January 2021 was valued at more than three billion dollars.

Like the UK Black Business Show, the Curve Catwalk was built on the frustration of limited spaces and opportunities for people to network.

Jay has enjoyed playing video games since she was young and often struggled to find other Black women who were interested in gaming. After facing sexist and racist comments when playing video games online, Jay created a community for Black women to support each other while gaming. Launched in 2015, Black Girl Gamers now has a huge following on its social media platforms. Jay offers her own advice on networking and building a network which I found particularly interesting: "Find people who think differently but share similar values," she says. "You want to connect with people who understand what you are doing but can share a different perspective because, that way, you open yourself up to a new manner of thinking. It's always good to have more than one point of view on a single topic."

We often go into networking situations looking for people similar to ourselves. Yes, there are benefits to this; but, when you are trying to solve a problem, you need someone who thinks differently from you, too. Many of the successful people I've spoken to have intentionally gone out of their way to find people that are diametrically opposed in their thinking. Often, we gravitate toward people who remind us of ourselves, but there are actually great benefits in creating and building diverse networks. The benefits of diverse thinking can be seen in a study by Economic Geography in which they concluded that "increased cultural diversity is a boon to innovativeness."[14] The results also revealed that "businesses run by culturally diverse leadership teams were more likely to develop new products than those with homogenous leadership."[15]

Mark Maciver, founder of SliderCuts, offered an alternative view to networking during our conversation. He shares this piece of advice for entrepreneurs: "Stop trying to find the perfect places where you feel like your seeds are going to grow. Go wherever you've been invited, as you never know where your seed is going to land and be watered. Throw your seeds everywhere you possibly can." Mark's analogy vividly paints the picture that you may not see an immediate response from networking and that, ultimately, it could be considered a numbers game until you make the right connections.

As someone in the sales and events industry, I know that the number of calls or emails made directly from me is positively correlated with the likelihood of completing a deal. I learned very early on in my career, when I started as a telesales executive, that if I made more calls than anyone else, then there was a high probability that I would get more "yeses" than anyone else. Of course, there were times where I would get "nos," but that didn't faze me; I was resilient and would keep trying until something positive would come through. But as Mark described in his analogy, it is ultimately a numbers game. You can't always find the perfect event or environment for networking, but just being in the right spaces and speaking to people enhances the potential for opening doors you didn't know were available.

Opeyemi and I spoke with Mathew Knowles—author, professor, lecturer, music executive, artist manager, and the father of superstars Beyoncé and Solange. Praised as the man who turned Destiny's Child into a global phenomenon, he boasts an impressive portfolio of 450 million worldwide record sales. In his early career, Mathew spent 20 years in corporate America working for Xerox.

During our Zoom chat, Mathew told us about one of the defining moments in his career. When Beyoncé lost the TV talent competition *Star Search*, he decided he would venture into the music industry himself, feeling that he needed to go back to college because, as he concisely put it, "knowledge is power." Mathew expands on his reasons for going back to college: "One of the traits of failure for entrepreneurs is that they don't have the knowledge. So I went back to college to get as much knowledge as I could, and I went to every seminar in the music industry about business, and I began to build relationships." Looking at the initial steps Mathew took to begin his music career, we see that first, he acquired knowledge, and second, he began to build relationships. Building relationships can only be done through successful networking, and it is clear that it's one of the most important things to do when starting a business. In our conversation, in reference to Solange and Beyoncé's albums, Mathew jokingly tells us that he wanted to "have *A Seat at the Table* and drink *Lemonade*,"[16] and he certainly got his seat through patience and seizing opportunity when it arose.

Reflecting on his time at Xerox, Mathew says he knew the importance of not only creating his own opportunities, but also how valuable just being "in the room" was to discovering opportunities. Mathew would intentionally get to work early and pick up the one newspaper his branch manager would read. He knew that if he kept on doing that, it would at some point lead to a conversation with him. It did, and Mathew was later invited to shadow his manager in some key meetings. What was significant about this was that Mathew reported to a sales manager who reported to the branch manager, and sales reps generally never interacted with branch managers. Mathew tells us, "I would go to these meetings with my manager, and the room would be full of older white men. I didn't know who they were, and they would ask me to get the coffee and do photocopying for them." Mathew continued to attend the meetings and to carry out these tasks until his opportunity came 3–4 months later, when they finally asked him a question, and, not only that, they reacted positively to his answer. Describing this experience, Mathew said, "I used to sit behind their table, but then they said: 'Matt, come here and sit at the table,' and I can only tell you, seated there were the President of Exxon, the President of Shell, and the President of Pennzoil." Mathew is a great example of someone having patience and seizing their opportunity when it arises; the more he attended those meetings, the more he increased his chances of building positive connections.

Research shows that "people tend to prefer things they're familiar with—whether people, objects, or other stimuli,"[17] so by constantly going to networking events or spaces or just making yourself visible to senior leaders, you are enhancing your chance of finding a new opportunity or building a valuable relationship.

We spoke to the impressive Omar Wasow, an Assistant Professor in Princeton's Department of Politics. Omar focuses much of his research on race and politics, protest movements, and statistical methods. He was also the co-founder of BlackPlanet.com, a social network established in 2001, which grew to over 3 million active users. It was sold in 2008 for $38 million. BlackPlanet was one of the first social media platforms to bring celebrities and regular consumers together, and it is even reported that Myspace, the largest social media platform between 2005 and 2008, took inspiration from it.

"Being visible will always give you an advantage over those who are invisible."

As one of the pioneers of social networking, Omar believes that networking has been really important in his career, but he also likens it to low probability bets. Omar says, "You go to a conference, you mingle, you meet people, and then six months later, somebody's like, 'Hey, I've got this opportunity you might be a good fit for,' and you can't plan for that, you just kind of have to be visible." Visibility and patience are two vital components to networking that we witness in successful people.

Omar continues, "It may come six months after that particular event, or it might not come at all, but being visible will always give you an advantage over those who are invisible." Omar also compares networking to success in the music and film industry: "You might have one hit for every nine failures, but that hit can be good enough to make your business profitable."

As we further discussed the importance of networks and networking, Omar highlighted two strategies which he believes the majority of people use to network: the "explorer strategy" and the "exploit strategy." He says, "In explore mode, you are seeking opportunities, you're trying to grow your business and find new clients, so it's important for you to be visible." Omar describes exploit strategy as much of what he was doing for the first 15 years in his career: "I was digging deep in a particular area and I was not high profile. I was doing some networking and going to conferences, which helped with jobs and other things, but it was very narrow." The need to have the right trade-off between profile-building "explore" work versus the more narrow "exploitation" work is paramount for success. Each tactic has its own value attached to it, and one can sometimes preclude the other, which means there is caution to be taken in balancing the two modes. It's important to know which networking strategy is the best to start off with. As a working professional, the networking you do in a new job would begin within your team, management line, and business stakeholders. As you progress through your career, you should put more emphasis on speaking with your senior leaders and getting their buy-in, thus strengthening your network within the company.

According to Smart Insights, more than half of the world now uses social media. A staggering 4.57 billion people around the world now use the Internet, and 346 million new users have come online within the last 12 months.[18] With the emergence of social media platforms and deliberate networking platforms, such as LinkedIn, accessibility is no longer the issue. Now, more than ever, it is even easier to reach out to those who you would like to build a business relationship with. However, even with the different forms of digital connection, we can see that the forms of interaction (such as video calling, emailing, and phone calling) all have different levels of intimacy—a phone call offers a different type of intimacy and could potentially be more effective than a video call or email given the scenario.

Whether speaking face-to-face or digitally, creating the right lasting, strategic, worthwhile relationships is still a difficult task for a professional or entrepreneur to master. There are some that enjoy getting out and meeting people, contacting potential "colleagues" out of the blue, and establishing a good rapport, while there are others who feel anxious at the thought of a cold approach. Whether it's something you enjoy or not, you must learn these skills to be successful in any capacity. John Donne's famous quote, "No man is an island,"[19] sums up networking and building a network perfectly. Humans are social creatures, so we work better in a community rather than in isolation. Reaching the top of any career will require some sort of help at some stage.

THE CHARACTERISTICS OF A GOOD NETWORKER

*"THE CURRENCY OF REAL NETWORKING IS NOT GREED, BUT GENEROSITY." –*KEITH FERRAZZI[20]

The characteristics that a good networker must have is not often discussed. Whatever medium you choose to make your initial approach, you must ensure that you are coming across as sincere, authentic, and collaborative.

When I asked Ken Gibbs about the importance of networking, he said that "networking is invaluable, and you have to go into it with an actual focus." Whether it's time or money, people only invest in people they trust, so it's essential that they buy into you right away. Keep it simple— your initial introduction does not need to be lengthy. Introduce who you are, what you do, why you want to connect, and maybe anything else that differentiates you from the other people interested in connecting with them. You have to ensure your behavior in social settings and also online does not push people away from connecting with you. Ask yourself, are you an approachable person?

Let's discuss some of the tactics you can employ to become a good networker.

Have Confidence

Whether it's sending that initial email or finding the courage to speak to someone at an event, we all need a little confidence boost. As a young Black man, I used to think, "Why would they want to speak to me? What's the point in messaging this person or going up to that person?" But once I built up my confidence, all of that changed. Whenever I feel nervous, even with my developed confidence, I think about an inspiring quote by Wayne Gretzky, who says, "You miss 100 percent of the shots you don't take." Without trying to shoot, you cannot score, so if you let fear hold you from taking aim, you will never get the chance to succeed. Those who try constantly and fail are still better off than those who do not try at all, simply because they are building their confidence and learning from each failure.

Prepare and practice what you would say at an event and conduct research on the industry of the event you are going to. Understand what challenges the companies face, what the latest trends are, and anything else which may help you in conversation.

Listen

All great relationships start with listening. When two people are able to listen and find out more about each other's needs and wants, the more likely they are to establish a good rapport. As much as talking is important, there is a reason the Greek philosopher Epictetus said, "We have two ears and one mouth, so that we can listen twice as much as we speak."[21] When you listen openly without speaking, you are able to hear about opportunities, gain knowledge, learn lessons, and much more.

Be Authentic

People respond to genuine people. The people with the biggest networks and strongest relationships are those who show authenticity in their interactions with others. *Psychology Today* says that authentic people act in a way that shows their true self and how they feel, expressing their whole self genuinely rather than showing people only one particular side of themselves.[22]

When speaking with our contributors in researching and writing this book, authenticity was a quality that was constantly brought up as one of the key things they look for when speaking to new people. According to research, within the first seven seconds of meeting, people will have already made an impression of who you are.[23] Other research suggests that all it takes is a tenth of a second to start determining traits like trustworthiness. You should not be too pushy in first interactions, messages, and conversations. They should flow naturally to create a genuine bond.

We sat down with DJ and presenter Trevor Nelson, MBE. Trevor, who was born and raised in Hackney, Stoke Newington, UK, started his broadcasting career in 1985 as "Madhatter" on Kiss FM (originally a pirate radio station that gained its legal license in 1990). He began to DJ with Soul II Soul, promoted numerous club nights, worked in A&R at Cooltempo and EMI and was instrumental in building the careers of D'Angelo, Mica Paris, and Lynden David Hall. In 1996, Trevor moved to BBC Radio 1 to present the first ever national R&B show, "The Rhythm Nation." A year later, he began a Saturday afternoon program, which gained him a MOBO Award for Best DJ in 1997.[24] Trevor Nelson is a pioneer of UK Rap and R&B, and also showcased some of the biggest American artists to the UK scene. Today, Trevor remains a DJ on BBC Radio 2 and BBC 1Xtra and continues to hold influence in and advocate for the music industry.

Trevor epitomizes authenticity. I followed his career for years, and when we met, he came across exactly how he appears on radio and in the media: friendly, sincere, and humble. When speaking about networking, Trevor said he actually stopped attending events, because everywhere he would go, someone would step in front of him and ask for his email or number as a route to get into the industry. This is an example of where "explore" mode expires.

Those in the public eye may not enjoy having people come up to them asking for things; it can be rather exhausting. The same applies to online networking attempts, too. So be thoughtful about how you behave in face-to-face networking settings with people who already have the added pressure of being well-known.

Be Impactful

Trevor offers some advice for those trying to be better at networking, particularly those in the music industry. "No matter how small it is, what are you great at? What have you done that is worth talking about? I always say to people, don't give me 10 demos, give me your best song, and if you don't know what your best song is, you're in the wrong industry," he says. "Don't overload people. What's your best attribute? Just focus on that. People often get swamped, so have no patience or time."

Even with his words of advice, Trevor is concise and straight to the point. Some people at networking events may have a limited time to speak, so it's all about impact. In those few minutes, you must come across confident to make your point without being too pushy. It's also worth mentioning that no matter how hard you try, you may not create a bond with some people, and that's okay. There are enough people to network with and who you can create lasting relationships with.

Collaborate

"NETWORKING IS AN ENRICHMENT PROGRAM, NOT AN ENTITLEMENT PROGRAM." –SUSAN ROANE[25]

Networking isn't all about you. In any relationship, two people have to offer something to each other for it to be beneficial.

Do not go into a networking scenario if you are not open to being collaborative. It can be draining on the other person to always give and not receive. As much as you want to grow, so does the other person, so ensure that you are able to listen and spot areas where you could potentially help them. David McQueen, entrepreneur, professional speaker, and executive coach, described his view on networking and the importance of relationships and collaborations. When asked about his thoughts on the key elements of being a good networker, David says, "Networking is reciprocal, and it has to be genuine. There are people who reach out to me to set up a call, but I don't have a relationship with them, so I'll ask them to send me an email instead. You have to build relationships with people and have a connection. You don't always have to give to receive, but I've had people who I've given stuff to, and maybe five or six years later, they reciprocated with something else that's life changing for me."

We also spoke with Pamela Hutchinson, Global Head of Diversity and Inclusion at Bloomberg, who is cited as one of the most recognized thought leaders and vocal advocates for diversity across the private sector, with more than 20 years' experience in managing diversity across engineering, financial services, technology, and media. Pamela emphasized the importance of collaboration. "I think it's really critical to have a network. Utilize your network but not just to progress yourself," she says. "For me, networks are a two-way street: you give and people give back."

Follow Up

Have you ever met someone at an event or show, had a great conversation, collected their business card, and added them on LinkedIn, but taken a month or two to follow up? Don't worry, you're not the only one. In most cases, taking a month or two to follow up with someone is too long. To avoid this, I would suggest an initial message along the lines of, "it was great to meet you, and I look forward to connecting with you in the future." Gathering 50 business cards and doing nothing with them is similar to not spending money you have converted for a vacation and taking it back home. Yes, you may have the opportunity to use the money again, but in some cases, with time, the value of that money is not what it was when you received it, and by the time you do decide to use it, it may not be worth what it used to be.

Nurture Your Network

All good relationships are developed over time and, like a plant, they need to be watered often for them to grow. The relationships that are watered over time have stronger roots, and those that are left alone with little or no water at all eventually die. A good networker knows how to keep a relationship alive and growing. The importance of this characteristic mustn't be taken for granted; it is possible for you to have all the above characteristics but fail to nurture your network. Like a plant, nurturing your network is essential to growth, and if one of the ways you feed your connection is missing, it will die.

Have Integrity

In business, integrity and respect are fundamental attributes, not just in networking, but in every day. Integrity has helped a number of successful entrepreneurs and professionals in being able to network well throughout their career.

Adrian Grant spoke with us to share his story and advice on business. Adrian is a producer, director, and writer who has worked in the entertainment and media industries for over 30 years, producing magazines, books, records, videos, television, concerts, and theater shows. Adrian's career started in 1988, when he published the Michael Jackson fanzine *Off The Wall*, which, within a couple of years, grew from a circulation of 200 to 25,000 copies, distributed in 47 different countries.

This led to an amazing 20-year working relationship with the "King of Pop." He created *Thriller Live*—a theatrical show now seen by nearly 5 million people worldwide, and the twelfth biggest West End show of all time. Adrian also produced the West End show *Respect La Diva* and the recent

UK tour of *The Aretha Franklin Songbook*. Currently, Adrian produces the annual Visionary Honours, which celebrates inspirational culture, media, and entertainment that has influenced social change and debate.[26]

For someone who was able to have such longevity in a creative industry, one that thrives on constant networking, Adrian admitted that it's not something he really enjoys. It made me ask how he has managed to grow a successful network. "Integrity and having a good name in business is highly important," he says. "Making sure that you're just respectful and deliver what you say you're going to deliver will ensure that good word-of-mouth publicity will spread. *Thriller* has traveled internationally, so people know my work, and this has helped to grow my network."

Adrian continues, "Whether it's going to a meeting on time or giving people what they've asked for, follow through so that people will want to work with you again. They're going to recommend you, which will help you grow your network."

Golden Advice for Networking

- **Find your tribe and locate your audience.** Put together a business plan; you should know who your target audience is and the types of people you need to connect with to grow your business or venture. You need to do your research and find where these people are going to be. You need to narrow it down to specifics.

- **Prepare before any interaction.** Have in mind the end result that you want to achieve when you meet and speak to people in any medium. Though you can't predict exactly how a conversation will go, your objective should be to exchange business cards or details with a view toward setting up a further interaction.

- **Take your time and make the effort.** Networking requires time, effort, and long hours. It's not just about going to one event or sending a few LinkedIn message requests at once. It needs to be something that you allocate time in your calendar to.

NETWORKING STRATEGIES

"NETWORKING IS A LOT LIKE NUTRITION AND FITNESS: WE KNOW WHAT TO DO, THE HARD PART IS MAKING IT A TOP PRIORITY." –HERMINIA IBARRA[27]

Black professionals who are able to stay at a company and climb the ranks are employees who have successfully figured out "how to navigate white spaces," something which we will go into in Chapter 4. They are also people who clearly display great networking attributes with their peers and senior leaders at their company.

Building relationships and networking as a professional starts as soon as you walk through the door. My advice for a Black professional joining a new team or role is to remember that regardless of your color and ethnicity, you can still find people within the team who you can gel with and with whom you share similar interests. Where possible, make a conscious effort to have an individual conversation with everyone on your team; this could be in the office or going out for a lunch. Good working relationships start at work but are often built and developed through outside engagement.

When I started my career (and some of you reading this may be familiar with debating with yourself whether to attend social gatherings at all), I felt a bit anxious about going to work socials. The thought of being in another environment where I would be forced to talk about something other than work made me feel a bit awkward. I would have to talk about myself, and I didn't feel comfortable with sharing the details of my personal life. The pub wasn't a place I would usually go to on the weekends, but drinks in the pub is something that is heavily tied to white British culture. I knew this would have to be something I would need to adapt to if I wanted to fit in.

To get more knowledge on networking as a professional, we caught up with the passionate and articulate Rondette Amoy Smith. Born and raised in Brooklyn with her little brother, her parents both being teachers meant that education was a really important part of Rondette's upbringing. As an adult, Rondette studied in Trinidad for a year but also spent three years working in Hong Kong. On leaving Hong Kong, she had visited around 50 countries through activities she carried out with work. In 2017, Rondette moved to London and spent seven and a half years at Goldman Sachs before moving to Nomura to become Head of Diversity & Inclusion for EMEA.

Rondette spoke to me at length about her journey through the corporate world and offered some fantastic advice on networking, which she believes is crucial for getting to the top of your career ladder. "There's a certain point in your career that it's no longer about what you know, but who you know," she says. If you're a career professional reading this, have a think about who in your network would be able to vouch for you in terms of recommending you for higher positions and roles. If you cannot think of anyone, it may be time to start improving your networking skills at work.

Rondette describes herself as an introvert but also acknowledges the fact that as introverted or awkward a person may be, they will not be able to get far enough in the corporate world without being a good networker. "When you're a junior in your career, it's about proving what you know—your technical skills, enthusiasm, your depth and your knowledge—and then, when you move up, it's about how much of every little thing you know, who you know, and how you are connecting to other people." Rondette decided that she would teach herself the essential skills of networking through reading books and watching tutorials on YouTube.

It's important to remember that not everyone can be good at networking, but as it is an essential skill in life, you have to make a conscious effort to practice and to learn how to do it. What I found even more fascinating in our conversation was her "board of directors."

Rondette created her own board of directors outside work with peers she had met throughout her career. This board comprises of junior and senior roles, white men, Indian women, Chinese men that she met during her time in Hong Kong, and people from many other walks of life. Rondette clearly sees the benefit of surrounding herself with diverse people. The importance of this can be seen in recent studies, which suggest that diverse teams are 87 percent better at decision-making than less diverse teams. Teams of different genders and races, as well as an age gap of at least 20 years, were recorded as making better business decisions [28].

Because of the diversity of her board, Rondette is able to gain different types of knowledge and apply it when networking in different spaces. Some of the things Rondette does to prepare for networking events include figuring out who is going to be there. This way, she can draw from her own personal skills and the attributes of her personal board of directors and decide on the specific traits she needs to exhibit at these events. One of Rondette's biggest assets, however, is her exceptional memory. She uses this to remember the smallest things about people after their first encounter—whether it's the name of their child, partner, or dog—as a means to build relationships. Adding a personal touch to networking is a different technique to those we've discussed already, but being a good networker requires you to draw on one of the tactics I mentioned earlier: being a good listener. Meeting someone who remembers the tiny details about you makes you feel like they have genuine interest in not only the things you do as an entrepreneur or professional, but also you as a person.

Being a connector, or what she refers to as a "conduit," is another trait that Rondette displays in networking. "If I meet one person, and I think they're super dope, and they could benefit from meeting my friend or someone I know, I'm so open to saying 'Hey, you know, I think you should really meet so and so,'" she says. Being able to connect and collaborate in this way shows you are genuinely interested in helping the person and not only in what they could possibly do for you. In the working world, Rondette says, "Being a conduit helps to pay it forward and sideways with my peers. It shows people who are more senior than me that I have the ability to recognize intelligence, innovators, thinkers, creatives, all kinds of good qualities in people. It shows that I can recognize good talent and that I'm able to bring people together."

Entrepreneurs and professionals who are not networking are missing out. Building a great network takes time, intention, and effort, but adopting some of these strategies will make it easier and improve your chance of success.

DIGITAL NETWORKING

With the rise of social media, digital platforms, and networking apps, there has never been a better opportunity to network online. These spaces have given us the opportunity to connect with individuals from across the globe.

Visibility is one of the most important aspects of networking. Staying at the forefront of someone's mind is why some entrepreneurs are considered luckier than others. In fact, by simply being, and most importantly, *staying* visible, they are given more opportunities.

Platforms such as LinkedIn, Instagram, and Twitter are great for keeping your business and your name at the front of people's minds. Regular posts on business activity, talks you may have done, and work updates help you communicate to a large number of people without having to meet them. Social media allows you to gain genuine supporters of your business or personal brand. I have often spoken to entrepreneurs who receive more support from some of their social media followers they have never met than they do from actual friends and peers. Aim to create a following and network of people who will speak about your brand positively for you.

Social media platforms also allow you to engage with people who have a keen interest in you but may not be people who you might meet at a social event; for the introverted entrepreneur who prefers not to attend social events, this could be a more preferable option. Being able to network online gives you the advantage of engaging with those who are less likely to attend a physical event but may still have some value to add to your network.

Angelica Nwandu, CEO of The Shade Room, told us that she does not enjoy networking but realizes the power of it. Angelica's way around this was to go out and hire people who have great networking attributes, because when referring to her own networking prowess, she says, "It's not a strong suit for me, so what I've done is hire people who it is a strong suit for. I have 'personalities' that go out there and create relationships. I also have my ad team go out to create relationships." This tactical form of networking has seen The Shade Room create ties with leaders and celebrities such as current President Joe Biden, Lizzo, and DJ Khaled, to name a few, all of whom have personal relationships with Angelica's staff.

We know that a combination of face-to-face and digital networking is essential for today's Black entrepreneurs, professionals, and Black business owners, and Angelica clearly ensures that she can do both well through careful management of her and her staff's skill sets.

On networking, Mathew Knowles added, "In my age, there wasn't an opportunity to speak to everyone across the world. There is no excuse for your generation; you have the advantage, so take it." He's absolutely right. With the technology that we hold quite literally at our fingertips, we really have an opportunity to reach out to almost anyone, anywhere. So who are you online? What does your profile look like? Does it represent your values? Is the design and content consistent across your platforms? Aim to be genuine and consistent across all your platforms, and you will certainly reap the benefits.

Face-to-Face Networking

In Chapter 1, we discussed personal branding and the best ways to market yourself. Networking at events and venues is the most common type of networking.

A pause on event-based networking due to the global restrictions on movement in 2020 made businesspeople, businesses, and media companies think about new ways to network through social media or by video calling. There was a boom in multimedia platforms like Clubhouse and Lunchclub that are dedicated to making digital networking easy. Face-to-face networking in real life or on screen can also be described as a way of marketing yourself, with the main aim being to find and build new business connections and relationships.

Face-to-face networking requires a number of the skills already examined in this chapter. Confidence, for instance, is a characteristic that is more pronounced in face-to-face environments. When you go for a job interview, as much as you may be nervous, it's important to try not to show your nerves outwardly to the interviewer. Hiring managers may sympathize with a nervous candidate but are very unlikely to hire them if a person seems like they are unable to deal with the pressure of an interview. This is not to say you can never be nervous again, but you should practice control over your nerves so that you are able to perform at your best.

As someone who now regularly speaks at events and to audiences of all different sizes, I use my nerves to help me prepare. Because I overprepare for things, people perhaps overestimate how confident I actually am. Just like an employer would favor a more confident candidate in a job interview, people naturally gravitate to confident people. A confident person is memorable. Many of you reading this have at some point been the person at an event waiting for someone to come up to you—you want to speak to people, but you're too nervous to make any approaches, and then the anxiousness of standing by yourself while other people are in groups only adds to that pressure. Having an aim and goal of what you wish to achieve from attending the event will give you some security and a plan to fall back on, thus helping you control your nerves better and allowing you to be more confident. We all know that those who prepare and study for an exam will always have an advantage over those who just show up and take the test. "Fail to prepare, prepare to fail"—a cliché statement, but if it weren't true, it wouldn't be said so often, and this adage definitely applies to networking.

Preparation is key, but one thing that you can't always prepare for is awkward conversations. With some people, you'll start speaking and instantly hit it off, rarely even thinking about what you will say next as the conversation just flows. Whereas with other conversations, you'll find yourself scrambling to prepare the next question in your mind as soon as you are speaking. Both situations are perfectly normal, and it's important that when going into any networking event, you embrace it and be prepared for potential awkwardness.

Listening in face-to-face environments presents itself slightly differently than listening online. Because you are in the moment and the chance to go back over an email or message is not available, it is important to follow the conversation keenly and pick up the learnings as you go along. Paying attention and listening to others during networking will build your relationships, as well as help you spot opportunities for yourself and opportunities to help others, all while keeping the conversation flowing. When you are truly listening and paying attention, you will not need to worry about what you say next, as questions will automatically come into your mind.

For me, authenticity is the key thing to take into a networking environment; this is not to assume that everyone is not authentic or genuine, but the manner in which you may approach someone must come across as authentic.

MAKE MEANINGFUL CONNECTIONS

Building a strong network is strategic. Once you make the connections, how you maintain them is just as important as how you've acquired them.

When considering how you build your network, there are a number of components that will help you build a strong one. As a starting point, focus on the right people. As much as speaking to and handing out your business cards to everyone in sight may potentially increase the chance of you gaining a good connection, your time can be used more productively if you make meaningful connections as opposed to multiple connections. Focus on the people who you know can make a difference for you. Be deliberate about who you want to connect with, target them, and put more energy into the networks that you feel will enhance your objectives.

As Rondette Amoy Smith advocates, being a connector is essential to making lasting, meaningful connections. Utilize your social media to build your network and check out who the people you admire are following as a way to meet new people. Use these platforms to connect and stay engaged with people already in your network. It may be a simple comment on a picture or a reply to a post, but doing these small things will keep you at the forefront of your connection's mind.

As well as discussing personal branding with India Gary-Martin in Chapter 1, we also spoke about building a network. India feels that it's disingenuous to wait until you need something before messaging a contact. She explains the importance of following up quickly. She says, "Building a network is about building your relationships, and not necessarily worrying about what you might need it for, but also treating every single person that you meet as important. When I was getting business cards, I would always email the people on every single card I received to say, 'Hey, nice to meet you. Let's keep in touch,' because it means that I can go back to them later and say, 'Oh, remember we met at this place.'"

Remember the analogy Mark from SliderCuts used— seeds need to be watered in order to grow, and the action of "following up" is the water to the seed of networking. Asmau Ahmed, founder of Plum Perfect, also gave some great advice on how she built her network. Asmau has led corporate strategy and digital innovation in a number of industries, including financial services and consumer retail. With experience in both corporate and entrepreneurial leadership, Asmau honed her skills in assessing the business viability and risk profile and in leading innovation in enterprise, finance, and technology. Being one of a small pool of Black women to have raised more than $1 million in VC funding is indicative of the fact that Asmau must have some enviable networking skills. For Asmau to be able to raise this amount of money, she would have to have met and gelled with the right investors. Like so many of the entrepreneurs we've spoken to, Asmau considers herself an introvert. Speaking on networking, she says, "I like my personal space and time. Just going out and meeting people makes me nervous."

Discussing how she uses her digital skills to make connections, Asmau says that she utilizes emails more than anything. She walks us through how she managed to build and maintain great relationships with some of her investors. "I have a networking spreadsheet which I keep track of as much as a sales log. This sheet can include some of the investors I've met, the dates I've reached out to them, as well as the people that introduced them to me. I always remember to say thank you to people, and always think of ways that I can circle back and say 'hey.' The sheet will also include how conversations have gone, whether it went well or bad, if it was a great event, and also the next steps I hope to make."

As you can see, there are many ways to stay organized and build a strong network, use the tools around you that you feel most comfortable with, and remember to stay in contact as much as possible but ensuring it's not too overwhelming when doing so.

Byron Cole on Being a People Person

Byron Cole is an award-winning serial entrepreneur, public speaker, investor, philanthropist, and mentor to entrepreneurs and students. He runs the BLC Group, an umbrella company that looks after his many business interests.[30] Byron speaks about how his trait of being a people person has helped him when networking: "It doesn't matter whether it's the janitor or the loo man [plumber], I will talk to anybody. I love talking and I love people. I don't care who you are or what you do, I will talk to you."

Ronke Lawal on Building Relationships

In 2004, Ronke started her PR business and, as part of her 10-year anniversary, she rebranded to launch Ariatu PR, a public relations agency that is geared toward representing clients in a variety of industries, including entertainment, fashion, lifestyle and beauty, food, and luxury goods. She has a wealth of PR and marketing communications experience in the high-growth start-up sector, as well as working for corporate clients in a range of industries. Ronke speaks on how building relationships has helped her with networking: "Networking is central to building relationships and building community. I've got social media channels that I use for myself and another for my business and use them all very intentionally. I use them to attract not only my network, but also build relationships offline."

Herman Bulls on Connecting

Herman Bulls, founder of JLL's highly acclaimed Public Institutions Business Unit, shares why connecting is his key: "Networking is something you should think about substituting with 'connecting.' Most people look at networking as transactional; I propose connecting with people. Connecting is when you will do something for someone without regard to what you will receive in return. If you can say, 'instead of me being the sponge, I'm going to be the giver,' you will reap the benefits of this. If you connect consistently, over 50 years like I have, you will end up with a network that is very powerful and very strong."

Glenda McNeal on Being Strategic

In 2020, Glenda McNeal made history as the first Black woman to be on American Express's executive committee. President of Strategic Partnerships, Glenda has served at Amex for more than 30 years leading significant partnerships and negotiations with key clients including Delta, Marriott, Hilton, PayPal, and Amazon for co-branded credit cards and marketing initiatives.

Glenda spoke about being more targeted and strategic when looking to network:

"When you network and you're trying to find role models or mentors, it's important to know what it is you want. What is it that you're looking for out of that network? What is it that you're looking for out of that mentoring relationship? You want to network with that person because you think that they have shared values and that they are on a path that you'd like to be on. Focus on people who are like-minded, who you admire, and who might serve to be a role model for you. Focus more on those relationships."

NEXT STEPS AND REFLECTION

- What part of networking do you find the hardest?

- What steps can you take to overcome this?

- What interpersonal skills do you need to improve on?

- What advice can you take from the chapter to better build your network and the relationships within it?

RELATIONSHIP GOALS

Thoughts on Mentorship
and Sponsorship by
Opeyemi Sofoluke

"SHOW ME A SUCCESSFUL INDIVIDUAL AND I'LL SHOW YOU SOMEONE WHO HAD REAL POSITIVE INFLUENCES IN HIS OR HER LIFE. I DON'T CARE WHAT YOU DO FOR A LIVING—IF YOU DO IT WELL, I'M SURE THERE WAS SOMEONE CHEERING YOU ON OR SHOWING THE WAY. A MENTOR."
—DENZEL WASHINGTON[1]

"Relationship goals"—a phrase we often see floating around social media, hashtagged underneath cute photos of attractive couples. The term is used to describe what society perceives to be the "desirable" romantic relationship. But actually, it's a term that could be applied to any relationship—family, friends, work, you name it. In a professional context, I have found that there are two types of relationships that could be considered "relationship goals": mentorship and sponsorship. Mentorship is typically defined as a relationship between a senior or more experienced individual (mentor) and a more junior or less experienced individual (mentee). Mentorship is designed to provide guidance, support, knowledge, feedback, and opportunities for whatever period the mentor and mentee deem necessary.

Business articles often reference the importance of having a mentor when it comes to advancing in your career. In my personal experience, the mentors I've shared a relationship with have added significant value to my personal and professional development. Similarly, having a sponsor—someone who is at a senior level of their career and is willing to use their influence to advocate for you—also carries a positive impact. Both mentors and sponsors are very valuable in offering developmental support, but as put ever so succinctly by Allyson Zimmerman, Executive Director of Catalyst Europe, Middle East, and Africa, "While mentors may be seen as career developers, sponsors are considered to be career accelerators."[2]

For India Gary-Martin, leadership expert and coach, mentors and sponsors have very different roles. "So a mentor is somebody that you go to, to help you think through what you're doing. Whatever the current business issue is, or maybe what your future thing is," she says. In many instances, mentors also take on a coaching function. "Teaching, advising, and supporting people with the skills and toolset to be able to navigate and/or step into whatever the next thing it is they're trying to do, it is a strategic function. It's about skills and development." Sponsorship, however, carries a different kind of weight. "A sponsor is somebody who is actively your voice when you're not in the room. Sponsorship is doing something on somebody's behalf when they're not there to elevate them," India says.

Ultimately, these two relationships serve different purposes and address different needs, so the combination of having both mentors and sponsors can be a real sweet spot in your career or business journey. Having an understanding of the difference between these two relationships will enable you to effectively utilize your network to gain the necessary guidance and support to aid you in your journey. It can equally aid you as you seek to offer guidance to others.

TYPES OF MENTORS

The role of a mentor is primarily to advise, coach, and teach. Through sharing their experiences, mentors can fulfill what psychologists Kathy E. Kram and Lynn A. Isabella refer to as career functions and psychosocial functions:

> *"Mentors provide young adults with* career-enhancing *functions, such as coaching, facilitating exposure and visibility, and offering challenging work or protection, all of which help the younger person establish a role in the organization, learn the ropes, and prepare for advancement. In the psychosocial sphere, the mentor offers role modeling, counseling, confirmation, and friendship, which help the young adult develop a sense of professional identity and competence."*[3]

While their description makes reference to the mentee being a young person, it is worth noting that being a mentee is not limited to age. A mentor can be older or younger than their mentee, and as such, a mentee can be older or younger than their mentor.

For me, the key part in this description is that a successful mentorship is "career-enhancing." What comes to mind when I think of this phrase are my days as a child playing Mario Kart 64. I can almost hear you saying "What is the relevance?", but stay with me for a second. In Mario

Kart 64, all the characters begin the race together, and during the course of it, there are various objects that pop up that can have a positive or negative impact on a player's performance. Some of the good items include: "the mushroom," which temporarily boosts your speed; "the triple mushroom," which provides you with three temporary speed boosts that can be used anytime; and "the super star," which for a limited time makes you invincible. All of these items enhance the race for the player, giving them an advantage that the other players do not have. Similar to "the mushroom," mentors can assist in boosting their mentees career through the guidance, support, and insight they offer. In the same way that "the super star" acts like a shield, mentors can protect their mentee, helping them avoid career potholes and offering advice on how to navigate challenging scenarios. Having a mentor can mean that the mentee moves ahead faster than their peers as a result of their career-enhancing relationship.

Ultimately, the matter of mentorship is about the value the mentors' knowledge and experience can bring to the mentee. As described to us by Omar Wasow, Assistant Professor in the Department of Politics at Princeton and co-founder of BlackPlanet.com, "Creating opportunities for people is in some ways the first act of mentorship. It's giving somebody a chance to learn, grow, and develop expertise and skills." This sentiment was echoed by Christina Okorocha, co-founder of VAMP, a digital talent and entertainment PR agency, who explains, "With experience comes wisdom, so having someone who is able to guide you, give you advice, and bounce ideas off is always valuable. But, I must say, mentorship is not just about taking from your mentor; you should also be thinking about how you can give back. I think that's very important; relationships cannot be one-sided."

Mentorship can take a number of forms, and next, I have listed a variety of mentoring relationships I have encountered in my career.

The Traditional Mentor

As one of the most common forms, this mentoring relationship takes a top-down approach where someone more senior or advanced in their career mentors someone who is at a junior level. Therefore, they can offer advice and insight based on their level of seniority and experience. Usually, in a traditional mentoring relationship, the mentor can transition to be a sponsor, as they have a level of influence that can be used to advocate for their mentee.

Adrian Grant, writer and producer of *Thriller Live*, is very familiar with this form of mentorship and the particular importance of mentoring for students. He explains to us, "About seven years ago, I started mentoring students through an organization called Urban Synergy. They're a great charity in London, and we go to schools across South East London to mentor kids from the age of 11 to 16. It's amazing to see how many successful Black professionals there are from so many industries—engineers, doctors, scientists, air pilots. The kids get inspired and get to hear talks from these people who are succeeding in their line of business. I never had that when I was at school," Adrian continues. "I never had that kind of person to look up to. But now, thanks to the work of organizations like Urban Synergy, it's possible, and kids who are at school can see that there are pathways and opportunities for people like them to succeed beyond what we were told at school. So mentorship is really important. If I had a mentor or somebody to guide me or to teach me certain things when I was growing up, I wouldn't have made as many mistakes as I have done."

Someone who is also a big advocate of the traditional mentoring approach is Mark Maciver. Having not had any formal mentors as he built SliderCuts, Mark shared with us how he had to observe and learn from everyone around him. "Having a mentor is very important. I never had a mentor, so when I got to a good position, and knowing all the things I know now, I realized that there were actually a bunch of people above me who could have saved me from making some of the mistakes I made. If I had someone there who had been through it to talk to, it would have made a difference," Mark says.

Mark's experience has influenced his own approach to mentoring. "For me, it is very important to be in a position where I mentor people and I give them all the information, so they don't make the mistakes I did. They say, 'a wise person learns from their mistakes,' but I believe that an even wiser person learns from the mistakes of others. So mentoring is basically trying to do that—it's about saying, 'Listen, don't waste your money on this or that .... I lost my money this way, but you don't have to.' It's really important to share because you can affect people's lives and the direction they're going in."

Mark further shared that, for him, mentorship is about giving and not looking for anything in return: "I generally don't look for anything because if I am mentoring someone, it's not about me, it's about them. Just like if a teacher is teaching in a class, it's about the students, not themselves."

The Peer Mentor

Peer mentors offer an important alternative to traditional mentoring relationships. Where traditional mentoring tends to have a more hierarchical construct, peer mentoring takes on a more lateral form. As the name implies, "peer" mentoring refers to relationships among individuals that are at the same or a similar position in terms of experience or organizational level and are able to share their knowledge and skills with one another. In a peer mentoring relationship, it is common that the mentor has slightly more experience and knowledge than the mentee, and so will offer guidance to the mentee, but their level of experience is still close enough to enable a sense of familiarity.

I once had what I would consider a peer mentoring relationship with a friend of mine. Our friendship actually began as both of us started our careers in investment banking. My friend was a couple of years ahead of me and though she worked at a different firm, she had gone through a similar graduate program to me. During the early years of my career, we would catch up on a monthly basis and I was able to ask her for both general and technical advice on anything pertaining to work. Having her as a mentor was great. As two young Black women finding our way in the City, we were able to relate to one another and share our similar experiences in a way that would have been different if I was being mentored by a more senior colleague.

The Reverse Mentor

The reverse mentoring model is one where the mentee is someone who is at a more senior level in their career than the person they are being mentored by. Reverse mentoring, partners junior or entry-level employees with employees who are in positions of leadership or at an executive level, thus promoting learning among senior staff. Such pairings allow for the mentee to gain insight on latest trends and create a sense of connectedness between junior and senior levels of an organization.

In our conversation with senior strategy executive Asmau Ahmed, she touched on the value she gets from reverse mentoring. Asmau explains, "For me personally, my mentors are usually people that are younger than I am and earlier in their careers. I'm constantly learning, and often they don't even realize that they're my mentors, but they are. I'm learning about new technologies, new ways of thinking, and new approaches," she says. "I don't think we realize that as we get older, we can have all of these 'constraints' that are really just constraints of our experiences and may not necessarily be real, so it's just refreshing to talk to someone younger."

The Virtual Mentor

Virtual mentoring allows for mentorship to take place between two individuals or more without ever meeting in person. Virtual mentoring makes mentoring more accessible and enables people to make connections beyond face-to-face interactions. This means that mentors and mentees do not have to be in the same geographical location to connect and learn from one another—they can connect using online platforms, such as email or video calls. In a world that relies so heavily on technology, virtual mentoring has become much more common, and people are no longer restricted to finding mentors they can only meet in person.

Speaking with Byron Cole, entrepreneur and business mentor, he shares the benefits of virtual mentoring: "People are used to being in the room, and traditionally that's the way they learn. However, technology has caused the mentoring scene to adapt for the better. Now you can access your mentor or mentee in a much easier and faster way. So, for example, we used to have people from different countries who couldn't access our mentoring classes because of location, and we had people based in the UK that could access us but were traveling an 8 hours round-trip to do so. Being virtual has meant that we are able to reach a larger audience and they're also able to reach us. It definitely has opened up a different realm for us as mentors, but also for the mentees." Reflecting on the power of technology, Byron says, "Being able to connect with people internationally at the click of a button is a phenomenal thing. You can have a 10 a.m. session with someone in London and on the same day have a 2 p.m. session with someone in Germany."

The Group Mentor

This form of mentoring consists of a group of individuals who all benefit from mentoring one another or are being mentored by one individual but in a group setting. In this form of mentoring, members are often interchangeably the mentor and the mentee. Each group member is able to use their experience and expertise to advise other members of the group. As the group members tend to be at similar levels, group mentoring can often create a strong sense of community.

June Angelides, founder of Mums in Tech, the first child-friendly coding school in the UK, touched on the psychosocial benefit that can be gained through group mentoring. She explains: "I found myself as a mentor to every single mum in Mums in Tech, and we had about 250 women go through the program. They all became my friends, but also, they were all on a journey, so I found myself wanting to support them. And I guess there was the structure of the program to help with that," she says. "We had Slack channels, we had different cohorts, and we would interact as frequently as they wanted to—but I was conscious of helping them get to the point where they reached their goals."

The Mentor That Doesn't Know They're Your Mentor

Essentially, this form of mentoring allows you to choose absolutely anyone to look up to as a mentor. You may not know them directly, but you can learn so much from them. My personal experience has taught me that even if you are struggling to find a mentor in the traditional sense, you can identify individuals that inspire you. Such individuals can become "unofficial" mentors, and you are able to apply what you learn from them to support your professional development without any personal interaction at all. Whether it's through listening to podcasts, watching YouTube videos, or joining Instagram and Facebook Live sessions, technology allows us to hear from people we admire through many media. I can recall so many amazing authors, bloggers, preachers, and motivational speakers who I've never met that have offered me some of the best pieces of advice. From Michelle Obama to Myleik Teele, Michael Todd to Sarah Jakes Roberts, I have a whole bunch of mentors who do not know I exist. The mentor who doesn't know that they're your mentor could work in the same company as you, they could be someone you simply go to for advice but have not put a label on your relationship or connection. Do you have any mentors that come to mind who don't know they've mentored you?

Arlan Hamilton, Founder and Managing Partner of Backstage Capital, identified with this approach of mentoring. She told us: "I don't necessarily feel like I had a very specific mentor-mentee relationship along the way. But I pulled from all kinds of books, podcasts, and interviews and crafted my mentorship in that way."

PR and communications consultant Ronke Lawal also offers us some sound advice when it comes to utilizing social media platforms to find mentors. Reflecting on her experiences as she built her career, Ronke explains, "We're in a different age. Back then, we had forums, and books, and TV, but we didn't have social media. Now, I can follow the people I admire on Twitter or Instagram without ever having met them. Use that. You don't have to constantly 'collect' mentors—you can literally follow and pay attention to the wisdom that's out there."

Ronke is right; today's technology makes it so easy to learn from people, whether they are on the other side of the world or in the same office as you.

SHOULD BLACK PEOPLE HAVE BLACK MENTORS?

In my experience, finding mentors and sponsors has not always been easy. The majority of my career has been in financial services, specifically technology within banking, and has been a predominantly white and male environment. As a result of these dynamics, I have a very limited pool of ethnically diverse leaders to choose from. For some of you

It makes a massive difference to get advice from someone who understands and knows what it feels like to be in your shoes.

reading this, you may wonder why a person's race should matter when it comes to mentorship. Well, it matters for the same reason we have mentoring programs where women mentor other women. In the article, "The Case for Women Mentoring Women," Betty Ann Block and Tara Tietjen-Smith argue that it is important to have access to gender-based guidance and support. In such mentoring relationships, the mentor is able to help the mentee process situations based on the entire context of the female lived experience rather than relying on an objective and logical approach.[4] Similarly, it makes a massive difference to get advice from someone who understands and knows what it feels like to be in your shoes. While it is not "a must," having a Black mentor can be extremely valuable.

As the President of Howard University, the number one Historically Black College University (HBCU) in the United States, we were eager to hear Dr. Wayne Frederick's thoughts on how important having Black mentors is. He was very clear in his response:

"Vital. I don't know where I would be today without the support of my mentors—Dr. LaSalle D. Leffall Jr., Vernon Jordan, and many others. As a Black individual from Trinidad and Tobago who suffers from sickle cell disease, most mentors would have focused on what I can't do rather than what I could do. But I was fortunate to find people who instilled within me the confidence that I could do anything. And, in Howard University, I found an environment that insisted on nothing short of my best. Black mentors can instill confidence in a way that someone of a different background would not be able to. That's what our young people need to succeed."

Whether it is a conscious or unconscious thing, race tends to play an underlying role in how individuals connect. Research shows that Black employees, as well as those from ethnic minority groups, tend to find it more challenging to find effective mentoring and sponsorship relationships at work.[5] This goes back to the theory of homophily among co-workers and managers referenced in Chapter 1; people are more likely to associate with individuals that are similar to themselves. According to the Joseph Rowntree Foundation, marginalized groups tend to miss out on these formal and informal relationships, and as a result, Black employees tend to have unequal access to opportunities for development. Often, they lack insight and information on training opportunities or progression routes within their workplaces. You can see how this can be compounded if progression relies on opaque processes or informal networks. If there is a lack of Black role models or mentors at senior positions within corporations who might offer support and advice, or if there is a gap between equality and diversity policies and practice in the workplace[6], how will Black employees ever be on a level playing field?

Race in and of itself is not a key determining factor in whether or not a mentor and mentee establish a strong relationship, but there may be instances where having a shared or similar cultural identity adds value. Tommy Williams, Forbes 30 under 30 entrepreneur, shares his views with us, saying, "I don't think that just because someone is Black it always means that they're going to be a good mentor for you, but I do think it helps if they are. The most important thing is that the person genuinely cares about the progression of your career."

Senior digital marketing executive Ken Gibbs expressed how important mentorship has been in his career and, had it not been for some of the mentoring relationships he had built, he could have missed opportunities. Nepotism in the workplace is still very much in existence and often only benefits white people. Having a mentor who can support your career journey through sharing their experiences and advice can make such a difference. Ken emphasizes, "Unless your parents happen to have a career in the same field, nothing is more important than mentorship. My pops was a bus driver and my mom was a nurse, so for me, the mentors have always been far and wide, Black and white."

Ken tells us about his current mentor who he says has had a significant impact on his career. "He's a white man called Michael Wilson, and I've known him for over 12 years. I'll say, I didn't recognize his early approaches at mentorship, and maybe it was because of his culture and race. I was replaying some of our interactions over the years, and there were so many opportunities that were available to me, but because they were just so foreign, I didn't even recognize them as that. Michael was someone who had been in a similar career to me but had the family background, knowledge, and experience to know what those opportunities looked like when he was my age."

Mentorship is key in providing guidance that a mentee would not have received otherwise. Ken recalls,

"I remember there was a time when Michael took me into a room at AOL. I was less than 25, and at that stage in my life and career, I was just getting on with it. He asked me: 'What do you want to do?' And in my head, I'm thinking, 'Keep working and not go back home.' I didn't know what to say. But really, in all honesty, my dreams and goals

weren't fully fleshed out at that point because I didn't have a thorough understanding of the landscape to put them in. I was literally looking at everybody, trying to understand what they did, whether I wanted to be in that position, and how I could get there. I just had no idea. And, you know, I think one of the things people don't realize is just because someone has made it to a certain level, it doesn't mean they understand everything about getting there."

Despite Ken getting to a level in his career that others considered to be an achievement, having a mentor who offered guidance, asked the right questions, and highlighted career opportunities proved to be truly invaluable.

As has been established, most of the senior positions in corporate organizations are held by white men and so, from a practical point of view, the solution is not to simply suggest that Black people should look for only Black mentors. The few Black leaders in organizations are already inundated with mentor requests, so instead, we need to start seeing true allies rise up across organizations and build genuine connections with Black talent. Bianca Miller-Cole, co-author of business book *Self Made: The Definitive Guide to Business Startup Success*, explains to us,

"I don't necessarily think that as a Black employee, you need to only find a Black mentor. The perception is often 'okay you're Black, so you need a senior Black mentor.' Well, yes, it is good to have visible Black leaders. It's good to see that it's possible for you to reach those kinds of upper echelons of the corporate world, but I don't think your mentor needs to be Black. You need to find someone who maybe had a similar career path and approach that

person to find out the route they took and what they suggest you could do. In the corporate space, you could actually have more than one mentor. You could have your peer-to-peer mentor and you could also have a senior leader who may actually only be able to meet you once a quarter because they're so busy. Or you could connect with someone who's a middle manager and has more time for you. It all depends on what you need."

One of the best mentors I have is a woman named Anna Doherty. I worked with Anna during my time at J.P. Morgan. While Anna isn't a Black woman, she is an ally. She cares, and she is the type of person that uses her position to advocate and influence. We have very different backgrounds, but something that I think connects us is our passion to drive change. Our relationship has always been organic and, come to think of it, we've never explicitly put a title on it. But Anna has played the role of a mentor and sponsor and has taught me a lot about navigating the corporate world. She's the kind of person who has a natural ability to weave anecdotes and practical advice into conversations. Aside from teaching me the importance of being self-aware, the value in learning to read the room, and the power of having a voice; she taught me that as one of the few Black women in my department, my voice would be remembered, and how it was remembered was down to me. She would regularly tell me to "be bold, be brave, be yourself." Our racial differences did not make our mentorship less meaningful, and our ability to connect was the key to building a trusting relationship.

It is through my lived experience that I understand the various challenges we as Black people can face in acquiring mentors and sponsors. However, learning to network effectively and embracing who you are as a Black person trying to climb the corporate ladder can make a major difference in the approach you take when it comes to building relationships with senior colleagues. Similarly, for those in leadership positions, being active and intentional about supporting and mentoring Black employees is just as important. Networking works both ways.

ELEMENTS OF A SUCCESSFUL MENTORING RELATIONSHIP

Mentoring requires a level of investment in one's career journey and cannot be approached in a half-hearted manner. At its core, traditional mentoring is relation-based and is rooted in the mentor supporting the mentee to achieve a desired goal. Whether it is to develop leadership skills, enhance knowledge of a particular specialty, or facilitate personal or professional growth, a mentor plays a role in guiding an individual from one level to the next. Research shows that mentoring has a positive effect on the mentee's performance and overall success in organizational settings. Mentees receive more promotions, have higher salaries, exert greater influence, have more opportunities, and are more satisfied with their jobs and careers than individuals who are not mentored.[7] If you have ever had a mentor, you will know that mentor-mentee relationships tend to thrive when connections are organically built. The importance of the interpersonal dynamics in these relationships cannot be overlooked.

Successful mentoring is rooted in both parties being able to authentically and openly engage with one another.

As Glenda McNeal explains, "'Can you mentor me?' is not the conversation you want to have. Build the relationship, build the friendship, build the trust, and people will want to see you succeed," she says. "People will want to believe in you, people will want you to demonstrate that you're capable. So the mentoring comes as a result of people wanting to give you guidance."

Knowing what a good mentoring relationship looks like can help as you review or create your mentoring "relationship goals." The following five considerations can help you in this process.

1. Understand the Dynamics of Your Mentoring Relationship

While there are benefits to both formal and informal mentorships, I have found that informal mentoring allows for both the mentor and mentee to create a partnership on the basis of the connection they have forged. Formal mentoring, on the other hand, often occurs in companies or on structured mentoring programs and the process is one whereby a mentor is selected and paired with a mentee for a specific purpose over a predetermined time frame. The mentors are volunteers, and the mentees are assigned. In such partnerships, it is likely that the mentee and mentor may not voluntarily choose each other[8]; nevertheless, such relationships can still be effective and a personal connection can develop over time. If you are a mentee, to get the most out of your mentoring relationship, it is ideal, and also important, that you understand the type of mentoring relationship you have entered. Consider the relationship boundaries and how the mentorship is going to be structured;

this will help you effectively manage your expectations. Whether formal or informal, mentorship requires that a mentor gives up some of their time to focus on the mentee and how they can aid the development of the individual being mentored. Depending on the type of mentoring relationship you are in, how this is achieved may vary.

Where an informal mentoring style may mean that your mentor is happy for you to reach out to them outside of your agreed meeting times, formal mentors may prefer that communication primarily takes place during mentoring sessions. Either way, in any mentoring relationship, having an understanding of what each party is expected to contribute will help set the relationship off on the right foot, and this starts by setting out the goal of the relationship. Having an understanding of this will enable mentees to inform their mentors of the areas where they need advice or support and will help the mentors know how to tailor the sessions in order for the mentees to get the most out of it. Of course, the relationship goals can develop and evolve over time, but establishing this earlier on creates a focus for the partnership, as well as a sense of accountability for both mentor and mentee.

For Trina from Curlture, her first mentoring relationship was part of a formal mentoring program organized by The Prince's Trust, a youth charity that has helped over 86,000 young people start their own businesses. Being part of such a formal program meant that she was assigned a mentor. She explains, "It was such a good experience because I was partnered with someone so different from me."

Trina joined the enterprise program as she was building the Curve Catwalk[9], and, as there was nothing like this in the UK at the time, she experienced the benefit of having a mentor who could approach her business idea from an objective point of view. She smiles as she says,

"Here I was, talking to this more mature white woman about plus-size women jiggling their stuff, but she loved it, and she was amazing. I think it was great to have someone that was so far removed from that world, as she was very strategic with her feedback and advice. And actually, I found it very helpful that she didn't know anything about the world of dance. The mentoring was strictly from a business point of view and the goals of the relationship were very clear. She was a no-nonsense kind of woman, so it was more about results and less about mollycoddling."

Trina points out,

"If I had the chance to choose, I never would have chosen a woman like the mentor I had, because we did not have much in common. But I found so much benefit in having a mentor that was so far removed from me because she just saw my business idea from a completely different viewpoint. At first, I was not a fan of hers, but after some time, I thought, I need a woman like this in my life, because she just got me into gear. She was straight-talking, and I was quite happy to take feedback on board from someone I had no kind of relationship with. We would meet up for our sessions and that was it. Having a mentor that I probably would never have met anywhere else was actually a really cool experience."

In Trina's experience, having a clear understanding of the format in which the mentoring relationship would be taking place meant that she did not expect anything that her mentor could not provide; the mentor-mentee relationship was strictly about addressing the goals of the business plan, and it achieved that purpose.

About the structure of her current informal mentoring relationships, Trina says,

"I have actually just chosen mentors that really inspire me and that I feel more connected to. They are two Black women and I was quite specific with that because they are people who have gone before me doing great things. That familiarity and representation empowers me. The structure of our relationship allows for me to literally pick up the phone and have conversation, so I feel a bit more supported. There are still those boundaries of a mentor-mentee relationship, but I also have a friendship with them. So learning from the dynamics I had with female entrepreneurs as my mentors, I now mentor two young Black women who want to start a business."

Clarity around what is expected of both the mentor and the mentee means that everyone starts on the same page, and this helps avoid feeling disappointed with the outcomes of the relationship. As part of determining the structure, it is also useful to be clear on commitments, such as frequency of communication, duration of meetings, modes of communication, and whether the mentee is required to complete tasks ahead of sessions. Setting out these guidelines will enable you to be clear on how to best utilize the time you have together.

2. Make Sure You Communicate

Good communication is integral in building a successful mentoring relationship. Cultivating meaningful conversations is a necessary and important part of any growing relationship, which is why we often measure the quality of our relationships by how well we communicate. For a mentor or mentee to establish any sense of closeness or relatability in their mentorship, it is essential for both to consider the ways in which they can build a rapport that allows for open and honest communication. Communication runs two ways and involves the ability to clearly convey a message, as well as the ability to actively listen. Our ability to communicate has a direct impact on how well we connect with an individual. It is a hallmark of effective mentoring relationships.[10] Through my mentoring experiences, as both a mentor and a mentee, I have witnessed how open and effective communication achieves at least three key outcomes in mentorships. It ...

1. Helps build trust between the mentee and the mentor.
2. Enables both mentor and mentee to develop reflective listening.
3. Creates a teachable environment where honest and constructive feedback can be given and received.

The most successful mentorships I have are those that have developed organically. Do you have a go-to person whom you reach out to whenever you find yourself in need of practical professional advice? Is this someone slightly more experienced than you who you can be open with about work, business, or life in general? If so, the likelihood is you're being mentored without the label. When good communication exists in the scenarios similar to the one I have just described, you can find yourself being mentored without even realizing it.

In our conversation with businesswoman and Fortune 500 board member Shellye Archambeau, she shared how, in the early days of her career, she had mentors without knowing it. It was not until an official mentorship program was introduced during her early years at IBM that Shellye was able to recognize the impact of maintaining good communication and building genuine connections. She explains,

> *"As part of the mentoring program, instead of assigning mentors to mentees, I was asked who I would like to be mentored by. So I picked a guy I knew who was a couple levels above me—his name was Roland Harris. Well, several days later, I got a phone call and it's Roland. He said, 'Shellye,' and I said, 'Hi, Roland.' He says, 'Shellye, you put my name down to be your mentor.' And I'm thinking that he doesn't want to be my mentor, when he goes on to say, 'Shellye, you've got me. Go get someone else.' I was like, 'Oh.' So that situation taught me a bunch of things. One in particular was that the person I wanted to be my mentor was my mentor already and I didn't even realize it or know that I could tap into him in that way."*

As a result of their already established relationship, Roland viewed Shellye as his mentee—someone he could invest time in and offer advice to.

Another key part of communication in mentoring is learning how to deliver and receive feedback. It is the obligation of the mentor to support their mentee in developing their strengths and abilities. But this cannot happen if a mentor is not listening to the mentee to understand how they can grow. Similarly, if the mentee finds it difficult to share and receive feedback, then the mentor cannot fully serve their purpose. Therefore, it is important to get comfortable with the idea that sometimes feedback may make you feel as though you are being criticized, and this is where perspective comes in. Recognizing that the feedback being given is to help build your strengths is so important. For the mentor, be sure to be thoughtful about your delivery. Feedback allows a mentor to highlight their mentee's achievements and at the same time encourage their mentee in areas they could improve on. In a mentorship where communication is open, mentees will know that they do not have to put a guard up when the discussion of growth comes up. Mentorship has an objective, it is the role of the mentor to provide guidance and, in order for that objective to be met, the mentee must welcome constructive criticism to support them on their journey.

3. Take Time to Connect

When I started my graduate job, I was assigned a mentor who, according to the graduate handbook, would be someone I could reach out to for advice and guidance as a new analyst in the firm. Based on previous peer-mentor initiatives I had taken part in at college, I knew that formal assigned mentor-mentee relationships could be hit or miss, and unfortunately in my case it was a miss. My mentor was a few years ahead of me on the program, and we were expected to connect on a monthly basis. Initially, the idea of having a mentor who had a few years' experience was reassuring. On paper, he was the ideal person to be my peer mentor. He worked in the same business area but on a different team, had been recruited through the same internship program I had been on, and was involved in volunteer initiatives at work—something I was interested in—so he looked like a good match.

We scheduled our first catch-up to take place during my second week of the program. I recall us grabbing a coffee from the office Starbucks and settling down in the seating area. My mentor was a young white man, in his mid-20s, who grew up in Derby. Honestly, in the first few minutes of meeting him, I could tell that the connection just wasn't there, but thought I would give it a go anyway. We spoke about basic details such as where I studied, what I studied, and what I hoped to get out of the graduate program.

He shared a bit about his role and used more acronyms than I could keep track of to explain what he did in the company. Trying to be as engaged as a new graduate could be, I nodded along and wrote notes. I asked questions about his experience, and any tips he could offer me as a new joiner. After around 30 minutes, the conversation wrapped up, and we went our separate ways. Despite the whole situation feeling forced, I followed up with an email thanking him for his time, but I received no response. A month later, I took the initiative to reach out to schedule another catch-up—again, there was no response. Clearly, the pairing did not work. It lacked a genuine connection and, as a result, the mentoring relationship was extremely short lived. The poor communication from my assigned mentor meant that the pairing could not develop into anything meaningful. This encounter taught me that one of the most important factors in a mentor-mentee relationship is communication—genuine, open, and regular communication.

When embarking on the journey of mentoring, it is important for both the mentee and the mentor to be patient when it comes to building connection. The connection may not always occur during the first meeting, so be sure to give yourselves an opportunity to get to know one another. However, if, after giving the mentorship a good try, it still seems that no connection is formed, then please be transparent with your mentor or mentee. In mentoring relationships with no rapport, it becomes very difficult for the mentor and mentee to feel invested and provide the level of engagement required to make the relationship a beneficial one. There is no need to stay in a mentorship out of obligation; however, there is a need to respectfully inform the other party and exit the mentorship gracefully. Such an approach is often received well.

4. Build Trust In Your Relationship

Trust is essential in building mentoring relationships, and it is something that must be earned. Because trust is earned, it may take some time to build, but, once established, it allows for openness and honesty. To effectively explore and understand the importance of trust in interracial mentorships, it is necessary to first understand the role of cultural mistrust among Black and white communities. By definition, "Cultural mistrust is a tendency to distrust whites based upon a legacy of direct or vicarious exposure to racism or unfair treatment by whites."[11] Psychologists

Francis Terrell and Sandra Terrell developed the Cultural Mistrust Inventory (CMI) in 1971, which identifies four domains in which cultural mistrust of white people may exist. These are: education and training settings, law and politics, work and business, and interpersonal and social settings.[12] Be it overt or covert, in one or more of the settings Francis and Sandra Terrell outlined, most Black people will be able to recount at least one time in their life where they have experienced racism. Even in instances where one may not be able to recall personal encounters of racism or racial bias, the history of racism and racial oppression in the United States and the UK toward Black people is significant enough to be a reason for cultural mistrust to exist within the community. Such encounters can negatively impact the level of trust Black people have toward white people.

As already discussed, effective mentorship is rooted in the readiness of mentors and mentees to authentically interact with one another, demonstrating a willingness to share experiences. However, developing trust can be further complicated when mentors and mentees cross lines of race, particularly in a formal mentoring relationship where partnerships are assigned as opposed to being naturally formed. People often trust individuals they can relate to. Therefore, it is the role of the mentor to build trust with the mentee and create a space for sharing experiences. Generally speaking, we, the Black community, experience the world differently than those who are not Black, so it can often feel easier to trust the advice of someone who is similar to us or more likely to have gone through situations we can identify with. The benefit of having Black mentors when considering trust cannot be overlooked. Jamelia Donaldson, founder and CEO of TreasureTress and former

BlackRock analyst, explained that if she were to do anything differently during her time working in the corporate sector, she would look for a Black mentor. "I would tell myself to find a mentor that looks like me, but in a different firm," she says.

There is a sense of relatability we experience with people from our community and the freedom to express ourselves on a level of realness that we tend to hold back on when interacting with non-Black peers. This sense of connectedness allows for trust to be more easily built. Jamelia continues, "I did have mentors who are really great people, but they were white men. They gave me good advice, and most of them were very honest. A lot of the time, they would say things like, 'Jamelia as a young Black woman, I'll be honest with you, you need to do this or that ...,' but then we didn't have the shared experience, which I think is really important."

Though the shared experience may not have been present, Jamelia's mentors offered advice and recommendations that were useful and factored in the racial and cultural dynamics at play. They were what popular culture would call "woke." They weren't ignorant of the injustices and biases that could occur in the work environment for a Black woman, and their approach to offering advice was reflective of it. Their awareness of the nature of the work environment is an example of how trust can be built between a mentor and a mentee. Rarely have I heard of non-Black mentors offering advice or openly discussing the challenges in the workplace that occur as a result of race. Jamelia's mentors' ability to show an appreciation of her reality is what enabled trust to be built in their mentorship. Part of successful mentoring across cultures is an acknowledgment of different lived experiences within the corporate environment. According to the *Harvard Business Review*, mentees report that, to build trust and successfully launch relationships with them, mentors need empathy, genuineness, and approachability.[13] While a mentor's experiences may bear little to no parallels to that of their mentee, being able to demonstrate empathy by considering how best to offer advice to someone whose circumstances may be completely different can cultivate and build trust in the mentorship.

Another aspect of trust in mentorship is being completely confident that your mentor has your best interests at heart. Mentors may give you advice that pushes you outside of your comfort zone; however, this is usually to stretch and challenge you in ways that encourage growth. Where this is the aim, experiencing discomfort is not necessarily a bad thing. Once you get past the fear of being outside of your comfort zone—where things feel safe and secure—you can begin to experience learning and its by-product, growth. Omar Wasow shares an interesting perspective on this. As an academic and teacher, his approach to mentoring is similar to the approach his grad school advisors took with him. Omar explains, "Life is full of moments where you have self-doubt, and with one of my advisors, what I'm really grateful to her for is just having faith in me during the times where I was a little bit lost in the ocean. She'd tell me, 'no, no, no, you've got what it takes to do this.'" Having someone to provide encouragement and reassurance in seasons where we are being challenged is a benefit of having a mentor. Omar continues, "That's a lot of what I try to do in my own work now, to help students see past their doubt to possibility." Omar shared another example of an advisor that pushed him toward reaching his goals, even if that meant putting him in situations that challenged him: "There's one other person who's a kind-of academic mentor, and what she's done at times is set deadlines for me. So while sometimes mentorship means being a coach who can help somebody have faith in themselves, there are other times where it might mean putting somebody in a slightly ...," Omar pauses. "You know, there's a term I love called 'hard fun.' And the idea is if something's too easy, you quit because it's boring. And if something's too hard, you quit because nobody wants to fail all the time. So what you're trying to do as a mentor, or a coach, or a teacher, is to help get people to the place where they're challenged so they're pushing themselves, but are not so challenged to the point where they feel despondent about not being able to succeed."

Creating a perception of risk and challenging people to move outside of their "comfort zone" is seen as an integral feature for growth.[14] Therefore, in a mentor-mentee relationship where there is trust, if a mentor is pushing you, it is not to break you, but to build you.

That said, in the event that you receive advice that you are not comfortable with, it is important that you ask yourself "why?" If your unease is because you think the advice is wrong, or it goes against your personal values, then in such situations, you should do what feels right to you. However, if the advice makes you uncomfortable because following it will stretch you, this is what I would call a good kind of discomfort—the kind that enables you to fight your fears and overcome personal challenges. This kind of discomfort ought to be welcomed if growth is going to take place.

5. Be Proactive

In a mentorship, mentors like to see their mentees use initiative. Using initiative and being proactive demonstrates that you care about the mentorship and also about your growth. How frustrating would it be for you to invest time in someone, offer them advice and guidance, only to see them ignore it or show up to meetings unprepared? Basically, no one likes to feel as though they have wasted their time, so here are some points to consider when it comes to being proactive in a mentor-mentee relationship:

- **Figure out what you need as a mentee.** Self-evaluation is a powerful thing. It enables you to be more self-aware and cognizant of the areas you require coaching or advice in. Naturally, your needs will change over time, but in order to get the most out of your mentoring relationship, regularly evaluate yourself. Not all aspects of this self-evaluation must pertain to your career, so depending on the type of mentorship you are in, complete a personal, professional, or business SWOT analysis[15]. Seek to understand what your strengths, weaknesses, opportunities, and threats are. Having a better understanding of the skills you want to develop or the knowledge you desire to build will help you identify your mentoring needs and can lead to a more productive mentorship.

- **Take the lead.** It is likely that you are not your mentor's only mentee, so taking the lead when it comes to scheduling time with your mentor will demonstrate to them that you are conscious of their time, that you care, and that you are not waiting on them to drive the relationship.

- **Ask for feedback.** The purpose of mentorship is to provide guidance and advice, but it is also a way to learn more about yourself, so ask for feedback. This will enable you to be aware of how you are progressing, as well as find areas you can continue to work on.

- **Understand that you have something to offer.** Mentors are able to learn from you, too! You offer a different perspective to their work and often, through sharing your experiences, your mentor can learn a lesson from you. There are always teachable moments for both mentor and mentee in a mentorship.

THE MISCONCEPTION ABOUT MENTORS

It is also worth highlighting that having a mentor is not imperative. Many people feel that without mentorship, things will develop at a slower pace. However, Omar shared with us that, while mentorship has its benefits, "it is not essential for career development." Omar continues, "I think it is certainly helpful. And I think certainly in a large organization where there can be lots of knowledge that is not explicit, having somebody who is an insider to help you navigate that matters a lot. But there are also lots of examples of women, women of color, and people of color who have made it in organizations without somebody ahead of them."

So if you don't have a mentor, that's okay. Having a mentor is not the be-all and end-all, but if you truly believe a mentor will support your personal and professional growth, then identify the kind of mentor you feel would be suitable for you at this current moment in time and go for it!

WHAT ABOUT SPONSORS?

Sponsors are equally as important as mentors, and some would argue that in certain circumstances, they are more critical for success than mentors. I think that having someone in your corner who is willing to put your name forward for opportunities, link their reputation to yours by vouching for you in front of senior audiences, advocate for you when you are not in the room, and use their political and social capital to get your work in front of the right people is a powerful person to have. This, right here, is the kind of relationship goals we could all do with. For Black professionals, having a sponsor or senior leader in your corner who is willing to clear away systemic roadblocks in order to propel your career forward is invaluable.

Can You Choose a Sponsor?

A sponsor in a hierarchical structure is an established leader, executive, or entrepreneur who intentionally invests in a junior talent that they see as outstanding. Sponsorship often happens informally because, over time, the senior talent identifies qualities in the junior talent that makes them want to support their career. As Glenda McNeal puts it, "sponsors find ways to advance your career; they can really help you move your journey to greater distance, higher heights, and that's what you want. What we have to do is make sure to effectively utilize those relationships."

I don't think sponsorship is something that can be forced; you can't just go up to someone you don't know very well and ask them to be your sponsor. It just doesn't work that way. Sponsorship is rooted in relationship. Rondette Amoy Smith, Executive Director at Goldman Sachs working in Diversity and Inclusion, offers a great perspective on a sponsor-protégé relationship: "When I think of a sponsor, I always say '*a sponsor chooses you.*'" Can we just let that sink in for a minute: a sponsor chooses you. Listening back to the conversation we had with Rondette, I actually clicked my fingers and nodded in agreement when I heard this again. I think so many of us have it wrong in thinking that we need to go out looking for a sponsor in the same way we look for a mentor. While I don't think there is anything wrong with having a desired sponsor in mind (in fact, this is a good thing), we must recognize that in successful sponsor-protégé relationships, the sponsor takes a liking to the protégé. So, if you do have someone in mind when you think about sponsorship, the first thing you should ask yourself is "How can I build a relationship with this person?" It is important to get to know them first and explore whether a rapport and connection exists between the two of you.

Another thing to consider when it comes to the topic of sponsorship is how you get that senior person to see you. Pamela Hutchinson, Global Head of Diversity and Inclusion at Bloomberg, emphasizes, "The thing about sponsorship is, you're more likely to get a sponsor, in my view, if you're well-networked and always giving back. If you're a help to somebody else and you're known to be someone who supports and shares their best practices, you're likely to be well-known in the organization for that. And particularly, if you've helped a senior leader with a problem or challenge, they are the ones that are more likely to be your sponsors." Pamela also reinforces the importance of making sure your contribution is being seen: "Visibility, a can-do attitude, and putting your hands up are all things that lead to people wanting to support and grow you."

What Do Sponsors Look For?

Sponsors look for a number of traits and behaviors in their potential protégé. I have decided to focus on three of these and to make them easy to remember as the three Ps:

- Performance
- Potential
- Passion

Performance

First, sponsors analyze performance. It is difficult to advocate for someone if you do not know how they are performing. So, if you want to be recognized, you need to be bringing your A-game. You are likely to get the attention of sponsors and senior leaders if you are contributing to the organization in a tangible and meaningful way—in a way that demonstrates your impact. Impact creates room for influence, and your performance will directly influence whether leaders want to support you.

As music mogul Mathew Knowles put it, "I always strive to be the best. When you're number one, you can tell people what you really mean and you don't have to have a filter. If you are number two, you've got to play the game. But when you're number one, you don't have to play the game—*the game comes to you.* So the question is, do you want to play the game, or do you want the game to come to you? I prefer the game to come to me."

Referencing his book, *Racism: From the Eyes of a Child,*[15] Mathew reflects on his time in corporate America and why performance is so much more important for Black employees, "I was at Xerox for 10 years, three of those years was at an elite medical division of Xerox, and I was the number-one sales rep worldwide. If I was the number-two sales rep, they probably would have gotten rid of me."

Mathew's performance meant he was noticed by senior executives for the value he brought to the company. Your performance is a way for others to see the value you can add, and the quality of the work you produce can directly impact whether you are a candidate for sponsorship. A sponsor needs to be confident in the person they have invested in, so it is paramount that the protégé is actually delivering results. If you want to get on the radar of your potential sponsor, make sure you are maintaining a consistent level of excellence in the work you do. A sponsor will not use their influence to support an individual who is not considered credible or who could negatively impact their reputation, so maintaining a good standard of work will support you in this area.

We spoke to Danielle Prescod, a writer and former Style Director at BET. During her years working at well-known fashion magazines, such as *ELLE, InStyle,* and *Teen Vogue,* Danielle recalls how impactful sponsorship can be, especially in an environment where you are a minority. "I've been really lucky in meeting the people that I've met, but I am also a really, really hard worker," she says. "The people that I've met have noticed that, and appreciated it, and wanted to make sure that I was advocated for, promoted, and paid adequately for my hard work."

Danielle's experience reinforces why anyone seeking sponsorship needs to be diligent in their work. Danielle's diligence meant that her sponsor had a case when the time came for her to advocate for Danielle. Reflecting on an early career experience, Danielle shares, "One of my first bosses, in one year, doubled my salary. She was like, 'Danielle needs to get paid this much more' and you know, I'm so grateful because she really let me see how much she was fighting for me and that she valued my work. I had a lot of friends who were in similar jobs and they were told, 'at these magazines, you can get a title change, but we cannot give you a raise.' So you get more work, you get a fancy title, and you're still making the same amount of money you were two years ago."

A sponsor is someone who sees the value you bring and seeks to close the gaps if you are not being appropriately recognized or compensated for your performance.

Potential

Second, sponsors look for potential. When a sponsor decides to invest in you, they do so because of what they believe you can be, and not necessarily because of what you are today—they see a greatness in you, and it's that greatness that they want to nurture. Remember, in order for your potential to be seen by a sponsor, a relationship needs to exist first. How can you be sure someone has potential if you never met them or barely know them? Sponsors support individuals they believe in. We caught up with June Angelides on this. She shares what it means to be sponsored by the inspirational Jacqueline de Rojas, someone she describes as a "Titan of Tech," and having a sponsor that believes in you: "The way Jacqueline has sponsored me—I don't even understand why. She's put me forward for things where I'm like, 'Wow, this woman is my guardian angel.' But it's because we're aligned. We have a conversation and we're on the same page. She sees something in me, and that had to happen naturally."

As you may have noticed, the common theme to building relationships when it comes to both sponsors and mentors is the need for these relationships to be genuine. June emphasizes this point: "You can't force these things; it has to be a very organic interaction. When it comes to sponsorship, just find someone that you connect with, someone that shares similar values to you. I feel like there's so many mediums to try to get to know people, but take your time with it. The sponsor will feel your energy and will want to support you when you're aligned."

Passion

Finally, sponsors choose to sponsor people because of their passion. They need to know that you believe in what you can bring, and this starts by being driven by what you truly enjoy doing. When I started my career, I worked as a Trade Support Analyst in the Global Equities and Equity Derivatives Group business. I was not passionate about the work I was doing, but I was passionate about learning and, honestly, that was my saving grace. It wasn't easy. I worked long hours and often felt out of my depth, but I gave it my all because it was my first role and I was keen to start well. I was raised to always give my best, and on days when I lacked motivation, I would remind myself of a Bible verse that stuck with me throughout college: "Whatever your hand finds to do, do it with your might."[16] Yet passion can't be faked. I would put effort into investigating failed trades, I would put effort into creating monthly governance reports for external regulatory boards, and I would put effort into learning more about the financial products—but I was not passionate about the work. I struggled to find mentors, and sponsors definitely struggled to find me, because I lacked passion for the area. When you are passionate about something, it shines through. I recall meetings with senior leaders to discuss my development as a trade support analyst, they often felt pointless because deep down I knew it was an area I wanted to move away from, and as much as I tried to be enthusiastic, I'm pretty sure they could see through it. If you are looking for someone to sponsor you, they need to know and see that you are passionate about whatever it is your hand finds to do. Whether it's your business, your job, or your personal growth, if a sponsor can see your passion, it is more likely that they will want to help open doors that support your passion.

Mathew Knowles explains that, "Passion tends to coexist with work ethic. Passion is that thing that motivates us, inspires us, and enlightens us. It's that thing that wakes us up in the morning early and that we go to bed at night dreaming about. And so when you find those entrepreneurs, or intrapreneurs, that have passion, you'll also find that they have these incredible work ethics, because the two coexist. And it's that passion that can open doors for you."

The combination of the three Ps—performance, potential, and passion—will help you on the journey to sponsorship.

As you continue in your journey as an entrepreneur, intrapreneur, or professional, be sure to position yourself to build the relationship goals that will help you along the way.

NEXT STEPS AND REFLECTION

For a mentee/sponsoree

- Before looking for a mentor, what are some of the resources you could use to support yourself as you build your career/business?

- If you could connect with a dream mentor, who would that be? Have you built a relationship with them?

- Write down three actions you will take over the next four weeks to connect with your potential mentor.

For a mentor/sponsor

- How can you use your expertise to support someone who is junior to you?

- If you are not a mentor or a sponsor, do you have the capacity to positively impact and support the career of a Black professional or entrepreneur?

- Write down three actions you will take over the next month to give back by becoming a mentor or sponsor.

NAVIGATING WHITE SPACES

How to Survive and Thrive by *Raphael Sofoluke*

navigate

/'navɪgeɪt/

verb

1. plan and direct the course of a ship, aircraft, or other form of transportation, especially by using instruments or maps

2. sail or travel over (a stretch of water or terrain), especially carefully or with difficulty[1]

References to white spaces are alluded to as circles predominantly excluding those from other ethnic minority groups, often presenting themselves in business and professional settings like the workplace.

As the above definitions highlight, navigation becomes more difficult in choppier conditions, and it reflects well the task that a Black professional may face when "navigating white spaces." Black professionals often have to "plan and direct the course of their ship"—the ship being their career, and the instruments or maps being the behaviors they must exhibit to successfully navigate the terrain or landscape. The second definition emphasizes "carefully or with difficulty," a great reminder to us all that, often, navigating white spaces has to be done with caution, in doing so making it an arduous task for the many Black professionals within the space.

Growing up in Surrey Quays and Bermondsey, I knew all too well what it was like to exist in predominantly white spaces. In elementary school, between the ages of 7 to 11, I was one of four Black boys in a class of 30, along with one Black girl. In middle school, I saw more Black people in my year, but it was still not as many as would be expected. However, it was at high school and college where I felt like I could network and liaise with a larger number of Black students and not feel like "the only one in the room"—a term often used by Black professionals feeling alone in white spaces. After I left university and started my career, the realization that the corporate world is a "white man's world"—an idiom describing the prominence of white faces in the office and professional spaces—dawned on me very quickly.

One instance that has made an indelible mark on my memory is one of a former colleague who changed her name on her resume from Tolu, her traditional African name, to Tallulah. On making this change, she received callbacks within days from the same companies who had not given responses to her application months previously, when she had used her real name. Now maybe it was a coincidence, and maybe the companies just didn't have vacancies when she applied under the name Tolu, but when it's three or four companies who have previously not responded, it starts to look a bit peculiar.

Interview processes are fascinating. When you think about it, you're competing against people that you don't know, nor do you know how smart they are or how well their interpersonal skills are. In spite of this lack of knowledge, the aim is always to outperform them. Whenever I talk about the term "twice as hard," I always explain my belief that the only way for me to get a job is to prepare twice as much as anyone else. I have always held a notion that preoccupies my mind, which is that if at some stage my interviewer has to decide between two candidates, myself, a Black man, and another candidate, a white person, the interviewer is more likely to choose the latter.

This is not to say that overt racism is always the reason for such an occurrence, but naturally people tend to gravitate to others who remind them of themselves. This can have a negative effect when the basis of hiring decisions should come from a pure assessment of ability and capability, but rather are mixed with added subconscious bias.

By preparing myself extremely well for interviews, even if there was potential that they might relate more to the other candidates, I would make sure I was so good that the interviewer would have no other choice but to hire me.

Now I know this chapter is about navigating white spaces and the struggles actually within those environments, but it's equally as important to highlight the challenge of actually getting into these spaces. With so much unconscious bias; lack of support from senior leaders; and unfair interview processes, which might often be carried out by white middle-aged men, the barriers to entry for Black professionals into any white spaces are somewhat limited.

Gillian B. White in *The Atlantic* states that "There's data that demonstrates the unfortunate reality: Black workers receive extra scrutiny from bosses, which can lead to worse performance reviews, lower wages, and even job loss."[1] We hear a lot about being your "authentic self" at work, yet with the added pressure on Black employees to simply stay in their job, it's hardly surprising many Black professionals don't feel like they can be truly real at work.

The article further states that "employers invest more heavily in monitoring Black employees, this could be everything from instructing supervisors to closely watch a new hire, or more directly monitoring job performance."[2] Because Black workers are more closely scrutinized than their non-Black counterparts, the chances that error, whether large or small, will be caught and magnified by employers increases.

Research shows that it's more likely that a Black employee would be fired for minor errors than a white employee.[3] With the margin of errors being much smaller for Black professionals than their white counterparts, it is no surprise that there are not many Black professionals at senior-level positions in companies in the United States and UK.

Looking back at my own career, something that I always remember was when a former white manager of mine who hired me said: "When you started at the same time as Chris (a white man), we really thought he would be the better one out of the two of you." He didn't offer any further explanation and, thinking about it now, maybe I should have pressed him for one. Nonetheless, one thing I did know was that Chris was a white, posh male with blonde hair, and he spoke exceptionally well. What wasn't exceptional though was Chris's work rate—he sat next to me and would watch *Suits* all day.

Chris had been at the company for six months and had not made a single sale, and I would always wonder if I would have been given the same amount of time to deliver on my targets. Probably not.

We spoke with Shellye Archambeau, Fortune 500 board member, advisor, author, and former CEO of MetricStream. Shellye is an experienced CEO with a fantastic track record of accomplishments building brands, high-performance teams, and organizations. As a Black woman who is a board member at four companies in one of the most underrepresented sectors in the world (technology), Shellye is well placed to be able to accurately share her insight into the challenges of navigating white spaces.

Shellye spoke of her experience of how she made her voice heard among predominantly white males in her industry. "So when I first started serving on boards, not only was I the only Black person, I was the youngest by probably a decade," she says. "I got my first public board seat at 42 years old, so I was pretty young. I show up, the youngest, Black, and a woman, and, initially I did feel that I wasn't necessarily being heard, and so I drafted allies to help me."

Allyship and finding allies is something we will delve deeper into in Chapter 8, but the definition of "allies" in the context I'll be using it here is generally to describe someone from another race who is supportive of your goals and uses their position of privilege to vouch for and help you in ways in which you are unable to do for yourself.

Shellye tells us that she drafted allies and utilized them in meetings when she had something really pertinent to say. She would reach out to one of her allies on the board prior to meetings and say, "Hey, based on what's going on, I'm planning on raising these points in the meeting. What do you think?" If her ally believed it was a good idea, she would say, "Great. When I say it in a meeting, if you would just reinforce it, I'd appreciate it."

Shellye did this a few times and, after a while, people listened to her because they believed in her work, not just because it was being co-signed by one of her white allies.

The majority of the time, it's not that you don't have good ideas or solutions—it's just that sometimes people are used to listening to a certain type of person, maybe with a certain type of voice. Shellye told us that to navigate white spaces, you have to learn how to communicate in different environments, as different cultures listen differently.

The Muller-Lyer Illusion,[4] Figure-Ground Perception,[5] and Dynamic Decision Making[6] are three models that explain how mental, and sometimes emotional, processes that happen within a certain culture are influenced by the experiences we have *living* in a specific cultural environment. Therefore, although we think we make unbiased decisions, it is in fact cultural experience stored in our brain that makes the decisions. We may not be aware of it, but cultural influences shape how we see the world, the decisions we make, how we approach problems, and how we solve them.[7] Shellye's understanding of these concepts helped her become a force to be reckoned with in her industry.

Mathew Knowles also shared similar views, and referencing his book *The DNA of Achievers*,[8] explains that he has looked into the exercise of navigating white spaces; "There is a cultural difference between Black people and white people. How we approach critical thinking is different, and being around white people at a young age allowed me to understand their communication process and the way that they critically think, which helped me and taught me to navigate corporate America."[9]

When we spoke with Trevor Nelson about the highlights of his career, he explained how his personality was key to navigating white spaces. He also speaks about how he continues to be a success in a predominantly white industry: "I think your personality is so key to this. There are some genius Black businesspeople who don't have social skills. If you're a white genius and you don't have social skills, you can probably still make it, but it's more difficult if you are Black. I have a big personality, which is everything, and if I didn't have it, I think work would be very tough for me."

As an entrepreneur, you may not be working in predominantly white spaces, but it is still very likely that those you might need to engage with externally, such as other companies, partners, banks, or other institutions, are more likely to have majority white representation than not. Sadly, the reality is that the corporate world is a white one, and whether you are a working professional or entrepreneur, it is essential to learn the skills to navigate these spaces.

There are many challenges that come with navigating these spaces, but in this chapter, we hope to give you some practical advice about how to do it while also addressing many of the problems. If you are a non-Black person reading this, I hope this chapter opens your mind up to the many struggles your Black colleagues and Black entrepreneurs encounter while at work or in the business world.

CHALLENGING STEREOTYPES

According to the *Harvard Business Review*, challenging stereotypes threatens people's status and relationships with supervisors and co-workers.[9] Speaking up has also been directly related to negative performance evaluation, undesirable job assignments, and even job termination.[10] Not only is it difficult to speak up, but according to what is referred to as the "bystander effect," when a person is in trouble, those who are present often fail to intervene in a situation where someone or something is discriminatory and people don't call it out, either because they assume other people will or because they think it's not their place to act—and the more costly the perceived effect of intervening is, the less likely they are to do so.[11]

India Gary-Martin, leadership expert and coach, told us, "It's really hard to stand up in spaces that are tied to your livelihood because you know you need money to support yourself and your family and to be happy."

As you can see, it's not as simple as you think to just challenge stereotypes and to speak out against injustices at work or in business. When I've spoken to professionals who have challenged stereotypes or who have challenged the status quo, it often resulted in them leaving the company (by force or choice), or no further action was taken to resolve the problem that they boldly spoke out against.

In one of my previous roles, I raised that I was being treated differently by my white South African line manager—I was pretty distressed when I spoke to my director about the treatment I was suffering and, honestly, it was probably one of the toughest working moments I have experienced. When I told my director about what had been going on, I prepared a letter with all the facts, time stamps, and people who had also seen or witnessed my manager's discriminatory behavior, and in the end, for some reason, this exchange ended with me being put on a performance review, despite the fact that I was actually performing well at the time. I had made a complaint about something that wasn't right and nobody had complained about the efficiency or quality of my work, but it was me who was punished. This is a clear-cut example of my experience of being brushed aside and disregarded by senior management in the workplace, and unfortunately, I know I am not the only Black person who will have experienced something like it.

Hearing about outcomes like this gives others little confidence to challenge some of the most audacious comments, microaggressions, and stereotypes displayed at work. Speaking to some of our contributors made me realize that, although it is difficult to speak out or challenge stereotypes, it is necessary for progress and there are a number of ways to do so successfully.

When we talk about stereotyping, one recent incident comes to mind: on May 25, 2020, in Central Park in New York, a white woman by the name of Amy Cooper called the police, falsely accusing an African American man called Christian Cooper of threatening her life after he asked her to leash her dog.[12] Thankfully, the incident was recorded. It went viral online because it displayed such a clear example of everyday racism. This particular case brought up other incidents of racism to the forefront of common consciousness where many white people had treated Black people unfairly in the United States. Some of these experiences included white people calling the police to report Black people for doing regular day-to-day activities, such as jogging and swimming.

The issue with Amy Cooper also highlighted another area of concern that many Black professionals face—it is very difficult to prove incidents of racism when there is no tangible evidence. Amy Cooper was Head of Insurance Investment at Franklin Templeton, a global leader in asset management at the time of the incident. It's a scary thought to think that someone who has openly exhibited such racist behavior could be in such an influential position of power. Fortunately, in this instance, the world was able to see her behavior, but unfortunately there are many people like Amy Cooper in the corporate world who have not made overtly racist comments, but instead display such behavior at work through microaggressions and unconscious biases. In the corporate world, there are people who have unfairly denied Black professionals the chance to be promoted or to advance their career simply because of the color of their skin. Amy Cooper was eventually fired from her job at Franklin Templeton, but it's important that we examine this situation as an example of how some white senior leaders can have such negative opinions of Black people based on stereotypes.

When we spoke with Omar Wasow, an Assistant Professor in Princeton's Department of Politics, he too also mentioned the Amy Cooper situation, expanding on some of the workplace stereotypes for Black men. He says, "Everybody has different challenges that are specific to their case. So, you know, I'm coming to these questions as a man because they're clearly different to the challenges that women face." Omar then discussed the stereotype and assumption that follows many Black men and women throughout their career: "Black men can be perceived as angry in a way that is not at all reflective of what they might be feeling," he says. Stereotypes such as this can and do have many extreme and often dangerous consequences for Black men and women outside the workplace. According to research, "aggression" and "violence" is probably the strongest stereotype that is associated with Black men.[13] In the workplace, Black men being labeled as aggressive can be very problematic and often leads to them being unable to be truly comfortable expressing themselves at work.

"The angry Black woman" stereotype is also something that you may be familiar with. Shellye spoke with us about how she deals with situations in an attempt to avoid it. Shellye ensures that she does not come across "angry" specifically when challenging biases in the workplace, regardless of what has been said or done to her; she takes an approach of asking questions, which causes the person she is engaging with to reconsider whether what they have said is appropriate.

"Ask questions in a very nice way, like: 'I don't understand?' [or] 'What do you mean by that?' People usually get it, but they can't accuse you of being angry, right? Or aggressive, or anything else," she says.

Further to what Opeyemi discusses in Chapter 1, Shellye considers the idea of what hairstyles are deemed "professional" in the workplace. "They're used to seeing white women's hair that is usually straight. So they think straight hair is 'normal hair,' which they think is neater, which is another way of calling it 'professional,' right?"

Having experienced microaggressions in reference to her hair, such as "Let's make sure everybody looks professional tomorrow," Shellye reiterates the importance of asking questions like, "What do you mean by that?" After asking those questions, in an attempt to not make the other person feel uncomfortable, Shellye turns the situation into a joke. She believes it's important to make light of the situation so as to not create an "ongoing awkward thing" at work, and so that the other person also doesn't feel awkward every time they see her.

Shellye adds, "They realize, 'oh, gosh, that was probably not the right thing to say,' then it's really easy to come back with 'like yeah, one of the cool things about having this hair type, is that I can change it all the time.'"

Comfort is important at work, and regardless of the confrontation you have or the stereotype you challenge, I feel that it is important that your colleagues still feel comfortable around you and you do around them. It is important to realize that there are white people who are genuinely interested in learning about you and may not know how, so give them a chance. With that said, it's also important to call things out when necessary; it may create an unsettling feeling among your colleagues, but those conversations need to be had. This was backed up by Christina Okorocha, whose business was the first agency to focus solely on the representation and development of Black talent in the digital industry. VAMP is recognized for generating sales through impressive marketing for film releases in the UK, including *Blank Panther, Girl's Trip, Queen & Slim,* and many more. Christina says, "I think that it's so basic to tell someone to ignore these things that affect their everyday life. I know it's difficult to do, but honestly just keep believing in yourself and don't let it affect your performance."

India Gary-Martin shared a similar idea to Shellye with regard to not making anyone feel uncomfortable. "I would tell any Black person in these spaces not to assume others know anything about your culture, because they really don't," she says. "If they know nothing, this makes understanding you challenging."

Talking about white people who are trying to understand our experiences but may not know how, India says, "Many white people are shocked and appalled by our experiences but do not have the language to discuss it, so I say—grant them some grace for not having the language right now."

India makes an interesting point. Sometimes, when we don't understand things, our words may come out in the wrong way—especially when it comes to race. It's okay to not understand and maybe sometimes get things wrong. What's important to me is that the person is open to correction and learning. Unless we start to have more conversations with one another, we will never truly understand each other's cultures. It is also important to highlight that you need to be aware when someone is clearly making an insulting comment and when someone is truly trying to understand your culture. If they are trying to better understand your Black heritage, then use this as an opportunity to educate them. We will go into this further when we discuss microaggressions.

Not only do we have to face the battle of being discriminated against because of our features, background, and natural attributes, we also have to deal with the issue of colorism. India was very honest in telling me that because of her "lighter" complexion, she was much more palatable than darker-skinned women. She recognizes that she has a degree of privilege when it comes to speaking up at work compared her darker-skinned colleagues. Referencing colorism, India says, "It started in slavery and colonialism. Colonizers favored the people who looked more like them and they treated people who looked less like them very badly. While that isn't a practice that is exposed in the same way today, it's still in the DNA of our societies. People want to put the blame on Black people for colorism, but it's not something that we created."

"For white people, I am much more palatable," India continues. "Both of my parents are Black, but because of my lighter complexion, I'm closer to what white people see as being acceptable. People will accept what I say and my being more angry than they will accept a darker-skinned woman saying the same things."

Because of the respective privilege that her skin tone awards her, India tells us that she has made it her mission to continually speak up for Black women of all shades. I find this truly admirable.

Rondette Amoy Smith tells us of an experience with a senior member of staff at a previous job who said to her,

"You're really good at what you do, and you're safe." Rondette responded, saying, "What does that mean?" In response, the lady said, "Well, you know, you're smart, and you're pretty, and you're not like the others." Rondette continued to dig for answers: "Not like the other who?" The lady replied, "You're not Black Black."

In shock, Rondette suggested she and her colleague grab a coffee and go for a walk to have a deeper conversation around what was meant. Rondette found out that colorism was actually at the root of it all. Because Rondette wasn't "darker" and perceived to be loud, confrontational, aggressive, or angry—all the negative stereotypes associated with Black women—her colleague believed she was "safe" in her role.

Though scary in the way it was articulated, Rondette actually feels that the situation with her colleague taught her something. "It made me realize that there are dozens of other senior members of staff who think that way and don't say it," Rondette says. "I was actually proud of her for owning up to that because it meant I could teach her what was wrong in what she'd said."

"But equally, it made me feel terrible for darker-skinned Black women and those who potentially have names which are perceived as more complicated than mine because they aren't getting opportunities because of their skin color or their origin."

Jay-Ann Lopez, co-founder of the online platform Curlture, shares her frustration with people relating to her in a way that she doesn't relate to them, such as stereotypical greetings like "fist bump" and "hey gurrrrl." Jay's straightforward advice is to under no circumstances endorse this behavior.

"I think letting certain behaviors slide is more harmful than actually pulling someone up on the brand that they've

A lot of the struggles in navigating white spaces is that there is already a brand identity which was created for you before people even get a chance to truly know who you are.

tried to 'create' for you—whether it's your business or who you are as a person," she says.

We talked about personal branding in Chapter 1 and actually, a lot of the struggles in navigating white spaces is that there is already a brand identity that was created for you before people even get a chance to truly know who you are. You're already "the angry Black girl," "the aggressive Black guy," "the cool Black guy," the one they fist bump instead of shake hands with, and this is extremely problematic. Thinking of my own experiences, I've had many people attempt to fist bump me, but instead, I leave my hand out for a handshake. I don't fist bump at work, so why do you assume I do? After a while, people began to notice that it wasn't something I appreciated, especially when it was only done to me.

Trina Charles, fellow co-founder of Curlture, reflects on what she would do in similar situations: "'In some situations where I haven't needed to necessarily say anything, I give blank stares instead. Sometimes you will really just get 'that look' from me."

This works for Trina, as constantly saying something can be draining. If you're able to master "the look" like Trina has, it can also be an effective nonverbal way of getting your point across.

IMPOSTER SYNDROME

I'm sure you're familiar with the term "imposter syndrome." If you're not, let me break it down for you before we get into it. Coined by psychologists Pauline R. Clance and Suzanne A. Imes in 1978, the term describes, "A collection of feelings of inadequacy that persist despite evident success. 'Imposters' suffer from chronic self-doubt and a sense of intellectual fraudulence that override any feelings of success or external proof of their competence."[14] Now, of course, imposter syndrome is not limited to those from the Black community, but I certainly can echo Jolie A. Doggett's statement in her *Huffington Post* article, where she said, "For people of color, imposter syndrome isn't just an imaginary voice in our heads. We receive almost daily messages from society that we don't truly belong."[15] The feeling of imposter syndrome is something that definitely resonates with the Black entrepreneurs and professionals we have spoken with.

The feeling of not being good enough, or worthy enough, to be in a certain position is a horrible yet common feeling. Studies show that everybody feels imposter syndrome at some point, and women feel it more than men. Shellye Archambeau, who sits in the boardrooms of companies like Verizon, told us about her battle with imposter syndrome and how she continues to overcome it. "I have been fighting with imposter syndrome forever—my whole life—and still do, and that's what I tell people because it isn't something that goes away," she says.

Explaining further, Shellye says, "First thing is to realize that you're in great company, to take nothing personal—it's not just you." Shellye compares the feeling of imposter syndrome to headaches when she says, "Remember, everyone gets one; it's just something you have to overcome and deal with because when people offer you a job or invite you into the room, they do so because they believe that you're capable. Believe them, and remind yourself of why you are there. There was something special about you that made you a better candidate than ten others interviewing for the role."

Trevor Nelson echoes this sentiment—he states, "As long as you know that you merit being where you are, that's where the power comes from. BBC Radio 2 is massive and I believe there's a reason I'm here."

Take Shellye's advice, who says, "Put your shoulders back and say, 'Okay, today, I'm a Fortune 500 board member and I'm going to play that role, and eventually, I'm going to figure out what I'm doing.'"

Hyping yourself up is important. Having an awareness of where you are going to be and the sort of persona you need to adopt in certain environments is key to not feeling overwhelmed in big spaces, such as boardrooms, on stage, and around mostly white people.

Get yourself some cheerleaders. Through singing and dancing, we can all see the energy and positivity cheerleaders give to a sports team when they are entering the field. Shellye emphasizes how important cheerleaders are to her. "I'm a big believer in cheerleaders because honestly, the world tells us every day in so many ways how we are not quite smart enough, not quite technical enough, not quite financially astute enough, not quite pretty enough. So we need people around us to say 'yes you are,' to remind you of all the things you have done and all that you've accomplished."

I particularly loved this advice; it's something I've never thought of, and in fact you may find you already have cheerleaders in your life. Embrace these people when you need that boost of confidence or that reassurance that you deserve to be in these spaces as much as anyone else.

MICROAGGRESSIONS

Microaggression, a term first coined by Harvard psychiatrist Chester M. Pierce in the 1970s, can be directed at members of any marginalized group. For the purpose of this book, we will be discussing it in relation to race and the Black community. We will break it down into three categories: microassaults, microinsults, and microinvalidations.

Microassaults

Microassaults are overtly discriminatory actions that are intentional. With microassaults, the person committing the microaggression is acting intentionally and knows that their behavior might be hurtful.[18] Using a derogatory term to refer to a person of color would be a microassault.

Rondette Amoy Smith was able to give us a clear example of a microassault she experienced in one of her previous roles. "I was leaving a work party and I hadn't been drinking, but all these senior people around me had. I was heading home because I didn't feel like networking at the time. As I was leaving, this super senior white guy was like 'Where do you live?' I told him I lived in Brooklyn and he said, 'Oh, good luck dodging the bullets on your way home.' He said this in front of 15 people, and they all had their glass in their hand just laughing and chuckling—I just remember being mortified."

This sort of microassault is very common in the workplace and is often disguised as being a joke when it certainly is not. This scenario was totally out of order and left Rondette really embarrassed about where she came from.

Opeyemi once shared an example of a microassault she experienced at work with me. She says,

"I was in the office pantry and my colleague, a white man, began a conversation with me. He asked me where I lived

and before giving me the chance to reply he started listing areas in London that are considered Black areas: 'Peckham, Camberwell, no you're probably a Brixton girl.' I was so shocked at the way he spoke but I was also keen not to give him the reaction I felt he was looking for, so I just replied, 'No.' He clearly didn't get that I didn't want to entertain this conversation and went on to ask me whether all my friends were in gangs. He thought this was funny. Honestly, by this point, I was actually angry that he felt comfortable to be so overtly racist but I made sure I didn't show how I felt."

People often display microassaults under the guise of a joke, but such behavior is unacceptable and is certainly not funny.

Microinsults

Microinsults are defined as "verbal and nonverbal communications that subtly convey rudeness and insensitivity and demean a person's racial heritage or identity."[16] Common examples of microinsults are comments about how someone is not like others of their ethnicity, or how articulate or well-spoken someone is "given their race." It can also include touching a colleague's hair without permission (a regular occurrence for Black women specifically), not attempting to say someone's name correctly, and offering a more Anglicized nickname. There are many more.

Asmau Ahmed, founder of Plum Perfect, spoke about some of her experiences of microinsults and remembers times when she would ask questions that would be labeled as "dumb," or "stupid," but other people would ask the same things, and it wouldn't be received in the same way. We have already discussed how Asmau graduated in the top 5 percent of her class yet found herself facing microaggressive behavior when she entered the working world alongside some of her classmates, who were perceived as smarter than her just because of the color of their skin. Can you imagine how discouraging that would be?

Asmau instead showed courage and decided that she would use these microaggressions as her motivation to succeed at work.

Microinvalidations

Lastly, microinvalidations can be described as "communications that subtly exclude, negate, or nullify the thoughts, feelings, or experiential reality of a person of color."[17] An example of this would be a white person telling a Black person that racism does not exist.

Though they are often so subtle, keeping your eye out for microaggressions in your working environment is very important. If you are a senior leader and these things are reported to you, it is important that you listen to those describing their experiences and do not dismiss them.

BEING YOU IN WHITE SPACES

Over the past few years, there has been a lot of talk about bringing your authentic self to work and making workplaces more diverse and inclusive. But in reality, within environments catered heavily toward a particular race, how is that even possible?

As much as it may be difficult, I would encourage you to bring your authentic self to work as much as you can. This helps you figure out what sort of organization you actually work for. The ones that accept you and your culture are organizations you will enjoy working in and feel comfortable adding to their success. Employees should be allowed to be themselves at work and not have to hide or cover up the differences that make them unique. It's important that you understand where you are working.

We spoke with June Angelides about being yourself at work. On the point of navigating white spaces, June recommends, "See it as an opportunity to educate and help people understand your culture." June offers a couple of ways to do this successfully in the workplace, including bringing in food that reflects your culture or suggesting that you have a culture-themed day to help those from outside your race better understand your heritage.

Reflecting on her time in the corporate world, Jamelia Donaldson explains, "I didn't really feel like I was restricted. I just felt like I couldn't be bothered to bring my full self to work and always answer questions. I wouldn't bring my leftovers in because I just felt like it was going to take this extra amount of energy to answer questions posed by my colleagues and I couldn't be bothered." For many Black professionals, it often feels like too much hard work to have to explain things about our heritage, which explains why many people opt to avoid these types of situations altogether.

For me, "being yourself" is an important step toward being truly comfortable with being in white spaces, but it can involve breaking through your fear, and the onus should be on the organization as well as individuals to make all their employees feel like they can be themselves at work.

CODE SWITCHING

Code switching is one of the key mechanisms in which Black professionals and entrepreneurs navigate white spaces. It may be something you do but didn't actually know there was a term for it. Code switching is defined as "the process of shifting from one linguistic code (a language or dialect) to another, depending on the social context or conversational setting."[18] Language, however, is only one element of code switching. Today, the term includes any behaviors we exhibit to fit certain social circumstances or into an environment.

You may remember the video of former President Barack Obama entering a US basketball locker room in 2012.[19] The clip was very popular, as it showed how he greeted Black staff differently to white staff. Although it's amusing to watch, this is a clear example of how many Black professionals adapt their behavior toward their white counterparts and, in general, in white spaces. When we code switch, we adjust our behavior, appearance, and speech in ways that will make others feel comfortable. Sometimes we do this consciously and other times we do this subconsciously in an effort to gain fair treatment and increase employment opportunities in these spaces.[20]

Dave Chappelle, a hugely successful comedian who often integrates a "white voice" into his stand-up routines, once said that: "Every Black American is bilingual. All of us. We speak street vernacular, and we speak job interviews." Here, Dave emphasizes the fact that we have to be able to switch it up—it's almost an essential skill to be able to survive.

According to research, code switching often occurs in spaces where negative stereotypes of Black people are present. As much as the Black professional may see it as a skill to be able to successfully code switch, it emphasizes the clear disparities of inclusivity within the workplace.

Work drinks are especially an occasion where the Black professionals I have spoken with felt that they had to code switch for long periods. Though we may have interactions with other colleagues in the office, it's limited, whereas during work drinks, you are required to speak and interact with your colleagues without breaks and it can really expose the differences between cultures for a Black professional.

If a company was truly inclusive, then there would be no need for Black employees to code switch. I visited the Legacy Centre of Excellence in Birmingham, Europe's biggest Black-owned event venue, and the feeling entering it was very different from what I was used to in London. It was only after I had left and reflected on the experience with my colleague that we noticed how big the difference was.

In this space, we didn't have to suddenly change our behavior to adapt to our environment—there was no awkwardness, the music was of Black heritage, the drinks behind the bar were popular to our culture, and all the staff were Black. It reminded me of a trip to Nigeria in 2017, when I visited for the first time as a 27-year-old man. Going from being in a country where I was in the racial minority to Nigeria, where I was in the racial majority, was a new feeling that I can't even describe. It was really refreshing.

The same feeling can be compared to when you enter the UK Black Business Show; here, you find a space where there is no need to code switch, there is no tolerance for microaggressions, no feeling of imposter syndrome—just Black professionals hungry to learn, network, and promote their brands.

UNBALANCED RELATIONSHIPS AND "THE NOD"

We all know that building good relationships takes time; they require honesty and opening up to each other. When Black professionals are in white spaces because of the problems we mentioned earlier, such as imposter syndrome, code switching, and challenging stereotypes, it's sometimes very hard for us to also be our full selves, which limits the opportunity to develop strong relationships. Relationships that are unbalanced are generally described as those where one party is more invested than the other. Surface-level relationships rarely go any deeper than trivial conversations and may be because both parties are not interested in developing a strong relationship with each other.

When I say "strong relationships," I mean a relationship with a colleague who you would speak to on the weekend—someone who you would genuinely consider a good friend. Now for an ally who believes that maybe their relationship with a Black colleague is surface level and wants to improve it, I would make a few suggestions. Ask questions, find out what they are interested in outside work, suggest doing activities they enjoy, show an interest in their culture, ask them to pick the venue for the after-work drinks, involve them in conversations, and, finally, just be open to really learning about them.

"I see you" is a small phrase that sums up "the nod," given from one Black professional to another in white spaces. For those who are not familiar with "the nod," it goes something like this: you're walking down the corridor and as you look in the same direction you lock eyes with a stranger, and a nod takes place. The nod can either be the simple nodding of the head or in some cases just the lifting of the head. In both cases, they are symbols of respect, acknowledgment, and solidarity. This acknowledgment is often done between Black professionals who do not even know each other within the workplace.

When you're a Black professional, you are one of only a few, and it's very easy to pinpoint how many Black people there are in a company, even from the first week. You may not even speak to them, and it might not even be someone who you build a relationship with, but that nod is an appreciation that you are both in this space and are potentially experiencing the same struggles. When you're Black, having the skills to navigate white spaces is key to being successful, whether you're someone at the top level of your career or not; at some point, you may have felt the need to code switch, felt like an imposter, and experienced microaggressions. Being "Black, but not too Black" in certain spaces is a challenge that we have to endure, as is the sense that we must find ways to make those who are not Black feel comfortable. If you read this chapter and relate to any or all of the struggles discussed, my advice would be to reflect on the advice from some of the industry pioneers who we have spoken with to write this book. Just because navigating these spaces is difficult does not mean it is not achievable. Keep working hard, and remember: you deserve to be in these spaces. We see you and we believe in you.

CHARLENE WHITE ON BEING YOURSELF

Charlene is a well-respected news reporter in the UK. On April 9, 2014, White became the first Black woman to present *ITV News at Ten*. As well as being the lead presenter of ITV News London's primetime 6 p.m. program, she is also a cast member of ITV's popular magazine show *Loose Women*. On being yourself, Charlene says,

"A lot of people will feel that by being themselves, you become the other. You want to become like everybody else so you don't necessarily stand out, because you know you already stand out because you're Black. You wouldn't want to become the loudest person in the room, even if that's your character, because sometimes the assumption is that you're loud because you're Black. You then instinctively become a quieter version of yourself. With me, the more comfortable I became at work, the higher up I got because I was able to be my whole self."

NEXT STEPS AND REFLECTION

- What do you find hardest about navigating white spaces?

- What action can you take to overcome this?

- Do you suffer from imposter syndrome? What steps will you take to manage this?

- Whether you're an ally or Black professional, how can you challenge racial stereotypes in your workplace moving forward?

- If you're an ally, how can you make white spaces more inclusive for all?

GROWTH— DON'T LEAVE IT TO CHANCE

How to Track and Drive Your Development by *Opeyemi Sofoluke*

"MAKE PERSONAL GROWTH A DAILY PRIORITY."
–JOHN C. MAXWELL[1]

In the last couple of years, I have seen how effective it is to regularly assess how I keep track of my growth. This involves reviewing the quarterly goals I set myself; making sure I have accountability partners to keep me in check; revisiting my vision board on days I feel like giving up; and, most importantly, reviewing my mindset. While all the other factors I mentioned have an important role to play, I cannot emphasize enough how important it is to adopt, cultivate, and develop a healthy mindset that supports and promotes your growth. Ultimately, the way we think and process things plays a massive role in how we approach our goals—it lays the foundation for how we handle challenges and take on opportunities.

To grow on a personal or professional level is a journey that naturally comes with highs and lows. Similarly, the growth and development that occurs in an individual's career or business will include some degree of challenge. Challenges are universal and are experienced by people regardless of their race, but for the Black community, there is this extra layer of opposition we expect to face when it comes to advancing. Whether it's the fact that Black-owned firms are turned down for financing at a rate twice as high as white business owners,[2] or that more than 50 percent of Black Britons have expressed that their career development—in terms of hiring, training opportunities, and promotion—has been hampered as a result of racism,[3] we go out into the world knowing that our race influences our journey of growth and the rate at which we advance.

Therefore, part and parcel of the Black experience requires developing a resilient mindset. As much as we should not have to deal with this extra layer of challenge, I am often reminded that we cannot be naive about the nature of the world we live in and the structures that uphold the institutions we interact with on a daily basis. While we hope for a day where, to quote Martin Luther King Jr., "We will live in a nation where we will not be judged by the color of our skin, but by the content of their character;"[4] that day is not here yet. So being confident about who you are even when society tries to tell you otherwise is a very important part of being intentional about your growth in the midst of challenges.

Growth is something that should not be left to chance. In the same way a person may invest in their physical appearance by working out, maintaining a balanced diet, and so on, we ought to do the same when it comes to our professional growth. Ask yourself, "What steps am I actively taking to grow in my career or business?" Think about it for a minute. When was the last time you read a book or listened to a podcast to aid your professional growth? Have you completed any training in the last six months to support your business or your career? Do you remember what your New Year's resolutions were, and were they tied to your growth? If yes, then you actually deserve a pat on the back because not enough of us: a) invest in things that will develop our professional and business self; and b) remember what our New Year's resolutions are after the first week of January.

Granted, we all want to grow and eventually win at our goals, but in order to get to the next level, we must be mentally prepared to plan and work toward such achievements. Think about it like this: an individual wouldn't just show up to the gym without having a goal in mind. The most effective way to achieve your desired result is to have a target to push toward. Whether the goal is to lose weight or train to run 5k in 30 minutes, there is something to work toward. The same principle applies to your professional growth—you need to have a goal you are working toward and alongside that goal, a plan; and alongside that plan, a strong work ethic.

As Mathew Knowles explains, "It's great to have million-dollar dreams, but a lot of people will have a million-dollar dream with a minimum-wage work ethic." He is absolutely right; your work ethic needs to match your aspirations. Elevation is not a result of idle hands; it is, rather, the result of someone who has cultivated the right mindset, studied their craft, put in the work, and persevered through the hard times.

As you seek to develop in your business or career, consider the following strategies for growth. This list is not exhaustive but includes some ideas to consider along the way.

DON'T JUST WORK HARD, WORK SMART

I have always been the type of person to push myself and can identify with the words of St. Jerome: "Good, better, best / Never let it rest / Till your good is better / And your better best."[5] In fact, the first time I heard that quote, it was from my Aunty Jane. She had taught my sisters and I a song with the lyrics:

"Good, better, best. I will never rest,
Good, better, best. I will never rest,
Until my good is better and my better best."

As kids, we would have a party singing those lyrics, jumping around the living room, banging on the talking drum, and shaking the shekere on beat. In hindsight, Aunty Jane was instilling a truly powerful value in us all. A value that my parents also ingrained in me early on in life, which was, mediocrity is not the one. In order to advance, working hard is essential. However, when I think about the words in that song, one thing that stands out is the point of rest. Rest is actually a necessary part of working smart. While the sentiment of this song is something I can identify with, as an adult I see how those lyrics could potentially encourage burnout—something many of us have experienced on the journey of pursuing our goals. As a wife, mom, career woman, and founder, I am guilty of finding ways to keep going even when my body tells me it's time to rest. To avoid experiencing burnout, I have learned (and am still learning) to make a conscious effort to factor in rest.

I first learned about working smart during my time at college. I always thought that spending the entire day in the library meant that you were "killing it." If you looked like a hot mess and spent hours of your day behind your laptop writing up revision notes, then surely you were on top of your work—or at least that's what I thought. I recall a conversation that I had with my dad that changed my perspective on studying. I was in the library trying to pull a crazy shift like the one I have just described, but nothing was sticking. I could not concentrate, and the longer I spent trying to read, the more tired I felt. So I took a break and called my dad for a chat. I remember telling him about how many hours I had planned to stay in the library and, to my surprise, he didn't think that it would be the best use of my time, particularly if I was already tired. He made some kind of reference to the law of diminishing returns and encouraged me, saying, "It's not the amount of hours you spend in the library that matters. What matters is making sure you understand and are retaining what you have studied." He continued, "If that means you have three to four productive hours of study a day, that is better than sitting down in the library from morning to night and not being able to recall a thing."

He was absolutely right. What would be the point of putting in a crazy shift only to reap minimal returns? Learning that in my first year of college enabled me to be more aware of what worked best for me when it came to my work style. Of course, there were times where I would study for hours on end, but knowing when that was necessary was important. Working smart is "planning or mentally preparing, being confident in one's ability to alter behavior, and making situationally appropriate adjustments in behavior."[6] It's the ability to know how and when to flex your working style; it's about being agile and adaptable; it's about learning what needs your energy and what doesn't; it's about delivering results and knowing who to share your successes with. Knowing our *why* is important, but working smart requires us to keep the *how* at the forefront of our minds.

For a Black person in the working world, when it comes to career progression and taking on opportunities, it is important to be able to not just work hard, but to work smart. For many Black people, working hard is in many ways a part of our culture; however, it's the working smart part that we need to master. Let me help you understand exactly what it means in different contexts. For Glenda McNeal, working hard is something that had been instilled in her from an early age. Taking us through her childhood experiences, Glenda shares,

> "I grew up the last of eight kids—seven girls and one boy. So we had to do everything. A good work ethic was a huge part of the value system I had growing up. My mother believed that women can do what men do, and 'girls can do what boys do' was definitely my father's position. My father used to always say, 'You have to be better than the average, you have to be better than everybody else, you have to perform better.' There was an expectation I grew up with, that average is not good. There's no substitution for good performance. Now, the other part of that story, as I've learned over the years is yes, work is part of it, but there's a whole lot more that you have got to do in order to be successful."

As someone who has made history as the first-ever Black woman to sit on the Executive Committee of American Express, Glenda is clearly someone who knows what it means to work hard, but as she rightly points out, hard work is only part of the full picture.

For entrepreneur and executive coach David McQueen, working "twice as hard" was something that he was encouraged to do based on the experiences his parents had in the working world. David shares, "I remember my mum said to me that when I go into work, I need to 'work twice as hard to get half as much as white people.' I'm like, 'that doesn't make sense.' But what I realized was that it was said with the greatest intent for us to be able to succeed. Because, at the end of the day, both of my parents had to work hard. They had more than one job and did night school and all this kind of stuff to make life sustainable for us. What I realized was much of that intent existed because of the racism that they had to endure."

David continues, "You should work hard. I totally agree with that. I think you should work hard and you should put in the hours, have the expertise, and know your craft. But I also think you should work smart. Learn about better decision-making, learn about problem-solving, learn about understanding workplace politics. You should be able to read the room, understand behaviors, understand how people navigate certain spaces."

Pamela Hutchinson echoes this sentiment. Working hard was something she could identify with growing up. Pamela explains, "I was raised to work hard. My parents came from the Caribbean; it was hard for them to come to the UK, it was hard to build a life. They had to graft [work]; it was part and parcel of who they were, even back in the Caribbean. And so hard work was just part of my narrative. My parents never once said, 'You need to work twice as hard'; they said, 'You need to work harder than everybody else, Black or white.'"

Let's return to what St. Jerome said. We know that in the environments we work in, it is not enough to be good or even better than our counterparts. We need to be the best—or at least strive to be. Aiming to be the best doesn't mean that you will succeed; rather, it means that even in failure, you can look at your efforts with pride. Why? Because you tried your best, you worked hard, and you persevered. This is equally as important.

Touching on the impact of racism, Pamela points out that her approach to work is reflective of a resilient mindset. "I'm not glossing over racism, because of course it exists," Pamela says. "But you need to be the best—end of. And that's all I expect. That's what my parents expected from me. So I've never felt like, oh gosh, I'm in a room full of white people and I've got to work harder than them in order to progress. I think everyone, frankly, has to work hard in organizations. If our careers were just based on working hard, we'd all be successful. But it's not just that. There's a lot of other things that come into play that help you progress in organizations. And I think, as Black people, we haven't necessarily known what those protocols and those codes are, because we've never had anybody there to tell us what they are because we don't have enough Black people at the top of organizations to share that insight."

So how can we go beyond just hard work? Pamela provides a good starting point. "You can work damn hard, but you've also got to be well networked, you've also got to be visible, you've got to have a voice. You can sit in a room and be the hardest-working person in that team, but if you say nothing, if you don't contribute, who's going to notice you? Even if you are the only Black person in the room, you will become invisible," she says. "Recognize what else it takes to be successful in an organization."

For entrepreneurs, it is easy to overwork, which makes developing smart working habits even more important. Some of these simple steps can add value to the way you operate:

- **Understand when it is time to put in the hours and when it is time to take a break.** Running a business requires a different level of commitment to working for an organization. I am sure many of you find yourselves working weekends, as well as weekdays. In many ways, this level of commitment and dedication is a demonstration of your passion for what you are doing but, as I tell my husband on a regular basis, do not neglect rest. Working smart means avoiding burnout, so while you may be dedicating a lot of time to work, learn to build healthy work habits that work for you. Create a system that ensures you're able to take a break to recharge. Block out time in your calendar, grab a snack, go for a walk, watch a funny episode of your favorite show guilt-free—whatever it is, factor in time away from your screen. In addition to this, plan rest days to recharge. More recommendations on maintaining sound self-care while running a business can be found in Chapter 7.

- **Connect with people who are already on a similar path to you and learn from their journey.** Andy Davis, co-founder of 10x10, a preseed fund investing in exceptional Black founders in the UK, recommends, "Surround yourself with people who are smarter than you, who are doing work similar to you, and have been where you've been so you can see how they work, and use those methods or replicate them." Andy expresses his hope for the Black community, emphasizing, "I want us to just win and do well and to not have any obstacles or walls in the way or not take the hard road that others have walked before us ... I want Black people to cheat history," he says. "Cheating history simply means learning from the mistakes of others and taking a smarter route."

- **Utilize the relationships you have built to seek advice and guidance—don't allow fear or pride to hold you back.** As much as owning a business can be a rewarding experience, it can also be very humbling. On this journey, you experience peaks and troughs, and during the more challenging days, don't shy away from asking for advice or support. If that means contacting your mentor, phoning a friend who understands the work you do, or reaching out to your network, it is likely someone out there has gone through something similar and can offer relevant advice which you can benefit from—do it. Arlan Hamilton, investor and founder of Backstage Capital, tells us that one of the best pieces of advice she received was "from Therese Tucker, who is a pink-haired 50-something-year-old white woman and CEO of BlackLine, a billion-dollar accounting firm. I was interviewing her for a podcast three years ago,[7] and she was talking about her early days and payroll, and some of the challenges she faced. There was one instance where she had to ask a friend to help her bring money to the bank. And I was like, 'How did you do that?' She said, 'Well, pride is not an asset; what's pride going to do for me?' and now every time I think about picking up the phone to ask for help, I remind myself pride is not an asset, let's go!"

- **Find people you trust and distribute work to them in order to free yourself up to focus on other key areas of your business.** If you have the resources to do so, learn to delegate effectively. Byron Cole, CEO of The BLC Group, shares that as a visionary he has learned to be comfortable with delegating tasks. "The reality is, over time it may not be practical or sustainable for everything regarding your business to fall on your shoulders, so identify what you are good at and delegate the other tasks accordingly. It's important to recognize that you're not good at everything, so get people that have the expertise and skills to do their part for the success of the company," Byron says. We spoke with William Ray Norwood Jr.—famously known as entrepreneur, actor, and singer Ray J—who also offers advice on building a strong team: "Once the company revenue starts to go past a number that you feel makes it now possible for it to be a legitimate successful business in a long-term format, that's when you have to start thinking about bringing more people in; opening up some of that equity, even if it's small; and finding the right team members to really start growing your business. It could be about finding the right CEO, the right CFO, the right COO, or the right CMO, but you have to build the team. You have to let new experts come in and help you grow the company, especially if there's potential for it to be extremely successful." As you build your business, recognize that you cannot play every role. Delegating tasks is not always easy, particularly when you are personally attached to the business. It is natural to want to be in control of every aspect of it. Ray J's advice in this area is, "Breathe. I know it might be the project of your life, and it's your baby, but eventually, in order for it to be extremely successful, there have to be other partners, there have to be the right people sitting behind the desk doing things that they're good at so you can do what you're good at. If you're just the founder, fine, you're the founder. Don't play CEO just because you own the company when you don't know what that is or what it takes to really be successful in that position. Just be Phil Jackson[8] and put a hell of a team together."

Whether you're a business owner or employed, take time to figure out what working smart looks like for you in your space and organization. Understand what qualities, behaviors, or traits can contribute to your success and align them with your values and vision.

DON'T DESPISE BEING UNDERESTIMATED

The reason Black people are often required to work harder is directly connected to how we are perceived by others. Too often, we see Black employees take on roles that give them access but minimal decision-making power. Black employees find themselves in "important functions, but they are not the gut functions that make the business grow or bring in revenue. And they are not the jobs that prepare an executive to be a CEO."[9] Granted, this is not always the case, but for many it has and still is their reality. Being underestimated can be frustrating, and some colleagues may not even recognize that they are doing it. The same applies in business. Many Black founders and entrepreneurs are not given equal opportunities and are often underestimated, undervalued, and overlooked. Finding yourself in this position can be frustrating; however, understanding how to use it to your advantage is of greater gain.

As someone who is famously recognized for his career in entertainment and reality television, Ray J made a move into the tech world in 2015, launching the Scoot-E-Bike. In 2017, Ray J closed a multi-million-dollar partnership with Cowboy Wholesale, a leading distributor of consumer electronics, to form Raycon, where he now oversees marketing and global branding strategy.[10] Ray J shares with us how he handles being underestimated, despite establishing a hugely profitable global tech business. "I think you never want to show somebody that 'you underestimated me, so boom, here I am,' right? You want the success to do that. You want the success to shock them in the long run," he says. "I'm extremely underestimated, and that's the blessing. To be underestimated is the most powerful weapon I have. Because now, nobody's blocking me out of the room because I'm not seen as a threat. When you're humble and you're just selling, people can underestimate you all they want. It doesn't even matter because the numbers are there."

For Ray J, it's about focusing your energy on the quality of your output. You can say all you want to change someone's mind concerning you, but if they already have a negative perception of you, it is likely words will do very little. Action, on the other hand, is tangible, and people cannot deny results.

Adrian Grant, writer and producer, spoke to us about a time where he was underestimated and which exemplifies microaggression in the form of micro-insults:

"I remember having a chat with an older white guy. We were talking about business—he had done really well for himself and owned lots of bakeries around the country. In our conversation, I had shared that I worked in theater. After our chat, he came back to me 10 minutes later and asked, 'So what kind of theater do you do? Do you dance? Do you sing?' And I said, 'I produce shows.' And he goes, 'Alright, so what kind of shows? Amateur dramatics?' I said 'No, I have a show in the West End.' Then he continued, 'Okay, the West End?' I said 'Yeah.' Then he asked, 'What show's that?' I replied, Thriller Live. *Then he took a second and said, 'Okay. Alright. It's really surprising. For someone from your background, you've done really well.' Just the fact that he said someone from my background was really quite offensive, to be honest. And I could have asked him what he meant by my background, but I didn't because the fact is, I didn't need to say anything, you know, the show is there. The show is already successful."*

Something Raphael always talks about when it comes to business as Black entrepreneurs is the need to execute with excellence. When launching the UK Black Business Show, many people—both inside and outside of the Black community—underestimated him and questioned whether the show would be a success. But as Raphael has demonstrated, when you deliver, people's opinions will change, whether they want to or not.

Be careful not to allow your own insecurities to be a roadblock in your growth journey. The way you think about yourself is important. Mathew Knowles shares his ideas on mindsets: "Most people are boxed-in thinkers who have been conditioned since childhood. Who you are, who I am is really based on our upbringing. Growing up, we heard mixed messages from our parents, our teachers, and from society that influences the way we think today."

To illustrate his point, Mathew talks through a practical visualization exercise. "Imagine you are in a box," he says. "What are you experiencing? It would be walls. Most of us, unfortunately, are boxed-in thinkers. What's a boxed-in thinker? Well it goes back to what I said earlier; we've been conditioned. We may tell ourselves, 'Because I'm Black, I can't achieve that.' 'Because I'm a woman, I can't achieve that.' 'Because I'm poor, I can't achieve that.' Although we're older and have grown already, we still hear these messages from our childhood."

In order to grow, it is important to address your thinking pattern. In the words of the ancient Chinese proverb, "Watch your thoughts, they become your words; watch your words, they become your actions; watch your actions, they become your habits; watch your habits, they become your character; watch your character, it becomes your destiny."[11]

Everything starts in the mind. When you underestimate yourself because others underestimate you, you find that you lack the confidence and boldness to pursue your goals, so it is necessary that you challenge such thoughts. Mathew continues his analogy by emphasizing the importance of carefully considering the kinds of people you choose to connect with, particularly if you are someone who has the tendency to underestimate yourself. "If you are a boxed-in thinker, the type of people you invite into your box is usually someone just like you. So if you're a hater, guess who's in your box ... another damn hater," he says.

Surround yourself with people who think differently to you, but also people who encourage you to grow, to develop, to learn, to aspire for more. Really, the key is to change your way of thinking because as Mathew advises, "When you step outside of your box and walk around it, there's not one wall. All the constraints you see when you have that boxed-in way of thinking go away."

While it is good to be aware of how others perceive you, do not allow negative perceptions to hold you back or discourage you from achieving what you believe you are capable of. Don't despise being underestimated; instead, allow this to motivate you to be great. Be conscious of the type of mindset you are cultivating and challenge yourself to step outside of your comfort zone, as this often encourages growth.

SET A STANDARD FOR YOURSELF AND DON'T LOWER THE BAR

If you are being underestimated, you must not let your standards drop. Be sure to uphold a high standard when it comes to the quality of the work you produce and the goals you seek to attain. In instances where others expect less from you, you will exceed their expectations. Growth is about not lowering your standards, even when the world underestimates you. Despite making up the largest segment of women-owned businesses in 2019, Black women in the United States struggled to secure funding for new business ventures; the average amount of money they were able to raise is just $36,000 compared to $1.5 million for the average white male.[12] Such disparities are also seen in the UK, where just 0.24 percent of venture capital went to teams of Black entrepreneurs—38 businesses in total—between 2009 and 2019. Out of those, only one Black female founder raised Series A funding across the 10 year period. So it is no surprise that when Black women successfully raise over $1 million, it is widely celebrated in the community. In 2016, Asmau Ahmed was one of 12 Black women ever to accomplish this in the United States. Since then, this number has gone up, and in 2020, over 90 Black women had reached or surpassed this level. For Asmau, while she understands why such achievements are celebrated, she is passionate that, as a community, we continue to push for more. "I have people say things to me like, 'Oh you've achieved so much,' and 'You've gotten to where we want to get,' and I appreciate all of that, but I also feel like we should all be here, but we're just at the starting line," she says. No one would be celebrating a million dollars if I were a white man. So, for me, it's not amazing. Why do we set these really low standards for ourselves?"

Asmau continues, "It's not an accolade that I like at all. Maybe in a sense it is celebrated, because you know that I've been through the gauntlet to get there, but I don't want my daughter to grow up and what she's celebrating as my legacy is, 'Mommy raised a million dollars,' when other people are exiting with billions. What does that say to her about what she can reach for? I don't want that to be okay. We have to be uncomfortable with the lowered standards. We have to push for change."

Growth is also found by not lowering your standards when it comes to your personal values. Asmau shares,

"Being an entrepreneur is tough. But the toughest part of my Plum Perfect journey was when I realized that, fundamentally, I was just a higher-risk investment. When my investors realized that, they approached me and said, 'We needed somebody else that could come in and raise money,' and that person happened to be white. I knew they weren't going to explicitly say why, but I knew. They brought in another Black woman to kind of relay the story back to me and emphasize that, you know, it was 'just optics,' and everything would remain the same. I said 'no' to that. That person could have brought in an infusion of capital, but it was wrong on so many levels. I don't know how many Black entrepreneurs have succumbed to having this proxy of success in order to advance, but it's a real thing."

Being a Black entrepreneur or professional requires you to be bold and to be true to who you are because going against your personal values for professional gain will only leave you questioning yourself further along the line. Do not allow the opinions of others to make you drop your standards or lower your ambitions.

Munya Chawawa, comedian, presenter, and producer, is someone who is no stranger to working hard. He explains to us, "I was always driven to be academic because of my dad, who is Zimbabwean. The expectation of, you know, of your 'classic African parent,' is to be the best." Sharing how he developed his career as a creative, Munya tells us, "I was always very geared toward public speaking. My dad worked within the realm of law, and I think he wanted me to follow in his footsteps."

Not necessarily having any particular passion for law, Munya decided to follow a career that was more in line with his personal interests. "I liked making people laugh, so I was pursuing that dream in the form of presenting," he says.

"I thought it would be the most obvious way of being on screen and entertaining people. It's when I was approaching TV stations, I realized, it would be a very long road and that there were definitely some unseen barriers that my peers weren't facing. I was told, 'Look, you might not have enough of a profile to be a presenter now, but you can write so, you know, why not be a producer?' So I became a writer for presenters. It was there that I really cut my teeth. I learned to write jokes and punchlines, and about pacing and comedic timing. I could see my jokes were working on television for others and thought it would make sense for me to be delivering my own jokes. That's when I began to put my sketches out on Instagram—the third one went viral."

Munya's commitment to honing his skills while still pursuing his goals is an important lesson—timing is everything. During his years as a producer, Munya learned valuable skills that have contributed to his success today. Delay is not denial. Do not be discouraged if you are currently not where you want to be. Munya did not allow the barriers he faced to hold him back or cause him to give up on his dream. Instead, he changed his route, and his diligence and dedication brought him to his desired destination. Do not be afraid if you have to change your plans; growth is about being adaptable. Once you know where you are going and the standard you have set for yourself, be open to amending your plans to get to where you aim to be.

Munya ruminates over the concept of success: "It doesn't make sense for success to be limited to the white race in this context." He continues, "I think of it the same way as I think about land. Ultimately, nobody built this earth, and so it's a very bizarre concept for people to go, 'Okay, we get this bit and you get that bit, and you can't come into our bit.' Success was not invented by white people or by any other race."

We all experience varying degrees of imposter syndrome. Remind yourself on a regular basis that you deserve to succeed. Munya adds,

"When a Black person begins to succeed, they feel a sense of cognitive dissonance that is more of a reflection of what society has taught them than a true reflection of how they should feel. Success is a concept that is ubiquitous; it's everywhere, for everyone. So, I say, run with it. Success is up for grabs to everybody who works for it. Once you get it— providing you've got it through hard work—then there's nothing illegitimate about that gain. You've got to own it; you've got to relish it. Instead of saying, 'I want to be the best Black person in my class, in my field, or in my industry, or be the best Black entertainer, or comedian,' remember you can just be the best—full stop."

Set high standards for yourself and strive to be the best you can be.

IDENTIFY YOUR SUPPORTERS AND MANAGE YOUR RELATIONSHIPS

Building the right relationships is absolutely key to your growth. When it comes to advancing in your career, as much as your knowledge and skill-set is valuable, the old adage that "it's not what you know, it's who you know" holds a great amount of truth.

Promotion, advancement, or being selected for a new opportunity often comes down to who you know, and more importantly who knows you. Socializing and building genuine relationships across an organization can be an effective tool for career advancement and can strengthen your chances of progression. India Gary-Martin is someone who held several senior positions before setting up her own executive coaching and leadership business. According to India, you can never underestimate the power of building the right relationships and having the right support. India shares, "Relationships are huge, right? You cannot move up if you do not have the support; and to have the support, you have got to *build* the support, which means you have to get to know people and build relationships. Establishing genuine connections with those in decision-making roles can give impetus to the advancement, progression, and growth an individual is looking for."

Recalling a business relationship that advanced her career, India explains, "I had this amazing boss. He's actually the person responsible for me getting to the tables that I got to. He did everything to make sure that I was recognized for my talent and my skills. I mean, I was very good at what I did, there's no question about that. But he promoted me three years in a row, which never happens. He was like, 'I've gotta catch you up.'"

Many Black people in organizations tend to operate at levels below their ability. What do I mean by this? Well, if it isn't the fact that we are overlooked for opportunities that could advance our career or that we work in environments that make it difficult to be our best selves at work, fully capable Black people are often not given the access they deserve. We often hear white women talk about a "glass ceiling," but for Black women in particular, the struggle starts simply trying to get through the door, let alone being able to see the glass ceiling. Black women face the intersectional challenge of being both women and Black, so the barriers we face in terms of career progression are a lot more complex than those of Black men. When you understand the dynamic of discrimination we often come up against, you can appreciate what it meant for India to have a manager—an ally—who saw her value and took the necessary steps to put her in the position she deserved to be in. India's manager is what my mom would refer to as a "Godsend." He used his position of leadership and influence to catch her up.

So many Black women find themselves in similar situations but lack the support to progress as they ought to. As India observes, "He was not playing in terms of my trajectory. Those relationships are really important." Identifying supporters who will champion you can provide tangible positive outcomes, resulting in growth.

Having supporters at work can also be impactful. We all felt it when actress, screenwriter, and producer Issa Rae said, "I'm rooting for everybody Black."[13] So much power and pride came from that statement. It was bold. It was unapologetic. I personally could identify with it because for so long it has felt like no one has rooted for us to win, and even when we root for one another, we're careful to not come off as someone who shows partiality. It's okay for Black people to want to see other Black people win, and when people outside of the community are rooting for us, too, that's when we can see even greater progress.

The importance of having people in your circle that encourage you, lift you up, and root for you cannot be ignored. However, what do we do when we do not have the best relationship with senior stakeholders? India Gary-Martin shares a particularly challenging relationship that she managed to turn around.

"Relationships are really important. One of my manager's peers could not stand me, and made it clear. I mean, every time I was with him, he was snarky to me and just nasty. I decided to see what I could do about it because I know that I need those people because they are the ones who are going to have something to say about whether or not I get promoted. Your boss might put you up for promotion, but the more senior you become, there are a whole bunch of folks who get engaged in that conversation about whether or not you make it. Anyway, I set up a meeting in the man's diary and I said, 'There are some things that you do really well. I'm wondering if I could come and see you from time to time to pick your brain on those things so that I can learn.' After that, his whole perspective changed. He was a completely different person because I stroked his ego a little bit. I was okay with that compromise, because I wasn't gonna do anything I didn't believe, by any stretch. But it's about being able to navigate and build those relationships and get what you need from them."

Building relationships is not always easy, but it is necessary. If you create those relationships, people will be advocates for you in all different kinds of places. But if you don't, then it's a hard road because you won't have the navigational tools to be able to move through it. That is done by relationships at a certain level.

When we discuss networking or building work relationships, we often focus on building relationships with people who are most likely to already be in our corner, but understanding how to approach relationships that are more strained is just as vital for career growth and progression. While the outcome for India was positive, you may find yourself in a situation where it is slightly more difficult to get a senior leader on your side. If this does happen, that's when your hard work and credibility provide a cushion to fall back on. Continue to work at strengthening these relationships, and if you are faced with a challenging work relationship, try not to allow the negative behavior of others dim your light.

A key part of managing relationships is learning how to effectively communicate to a group or an audience that may not always understand you. Using his experience as a playwright, Inua Ellams explains the importance of cultural translation when looking for ways to overcome some of the barriers Black people face when it comes to progression. He shares that when the National Theatre took on his play *Barber Shop Chronicles*, it was in many ways considered a risk. Inua says, "They had never seen a play like that, and that many Black men on stage could be alienating to a predominantly white audience." However, as Inua rightly points out, "Black barbershop culture is just men talking and having fun, and the joy of that is universal. So they had to see the play to understand this aspect of our culture can be found in theirs. Maybe they have that in pubs or in saunas, but we have it in barbershops. It's the same human transaction, and they had to see the play to get it. I think that is the main barrier for Black people in my industry—trying to convince a white audience or, you know, the 'powers that be' that, despite your skin color or those of your characters, your play is universally human."

Something I took away from this conversation is that we as Black people often find ourselves having to adapt our style and approach to "fit" within the framework of mainstream white culture. It rarely is the other way around. Part of navigating our way through the world of work is figuring out how to cultivate professional relationships based on common understanding. As Inua emphasizes, "Really, the big barrier is cultural translation. It's because they don't understand us, and they don't see *how* they can understand us. And this is where working 'twice as hard' comes into play—we have to go that extra length to translate ourselves before they let us do what we want to do."

VISIBILITY IS VITAL

If you are seeking growth, advancement, and progression, the idea of just keeping your head down and working hard simply does not cut it. There is certainly not a scarcity of high-performing Black talent, so the fact that very few Black people make it to senior positions or the c-suite in the corporate community reinforces two things. First, many of the environments that Black people work in are inequitable and are set up to only support a select group of people. And second, the onus is therefore on us to find ways to be seen and valued in order to advance.

Bianca Miller-Cole adds to this, "It isn't enough to do your work really well but be in the shadows, particularly when you're Black. You can't just be working away diligently thinking that someone is going to notice it. You have to do some legwork to raise your reputation and visibility while also aligning with the culture."

Shedding light on a time where she enacted this message, Bianca explains,

"I remember starting at a company when I was new to the corporate world. I was fresh out of college, but I had to be clear about what my plan was. I didn't know I was doing this at the time, but I strategically put myself in a position where I would get the best visibility to build my reputation. Even though my role was as an HR advisor, I also said to myself, 'Let me go on the HR committee, because I know the people who are there include the Senior HR Director and the Head of the Graduate Community.' I needed to make sure they knew who I was."

Bianca built relationships outside of her role and took on additional responsibility to be seen by the key figures in her organization. "From a corporate perspective, it's not just about knowing everyone on your level, because we already know our peers really well," Bianca continues. "You might know your manager, because you have to have a meeting every now and again, but actually, do the decision-makers know who you are? I think it's so important when you're building your personal brand to work out who is on your dream stakeholder list."

Bianca encourages you to ask yourself regularly, "Who should know who I am and the value that I add? How do I get the right visibility, so they are aware of who I am?" She advises, "Whether that's having a virtual coffee, reaching out to them by email, or making sure you're in a company newsletter, let's make sure we do that because I think we're not doing it enough as a community."

Is it fair that we have to take on more responsibility and bear the mental and emotional strain of constantly pushing ourselves so that we are seen? Of course not. But this is the reality we face. In order to be viewed as competent, Black people experience a very real pressure to find ways to highlight their achievements in ways that their peers do not. Even when we are visible, we still have to prove our credibility. The 2019 study by the Korn Ferry Institute in Partnership with the Executive Leadership Council found that Black professionals face significant challenges in getting on the radar of common consciousness at their organizations. The study concludes that 57 percent of the Black leaders they interviewed reported needing to work twice as hard to be seen at the same level as their counterparts, and of this group, more than three-quarters talked about having to prove themselves to show their worth to senior leadership, who often underestimated their skills.[14]

Even when we are visible, we are not always granted the benefit of the doubt. Nearly 60 percent of the Black Executives from Fortune 500 companies expressed that despite their achievements and exceeding expectations, they had to repeatedly perform well in tough assignments before they could climb the corporate ladder. Many of their co-workers, on the other hand, seemed to be judged on potential and given opportunities based on that perceived potential.[15] While growth and advancement is possible, it is still necessary for Black professionals to be recognized by the right people before we can progress. "Be visible," they say, but even that doesn't always feel like enough. Managers can certainly do better and do more to position Black talent to lead on projects and assignments that increase their visibility. It is important that organizations are intentional about providing growth opportunities that will set up Black talent in organizations for success. Management and employees alike have a role to play.

For business owners, while developing a high-quality product or service is necessary, your target audience needs to know you exist. It is paramount that you understand your audience—how best to engage with them and how to remain relevant. Without clients or customers, your business will not grow. Think about how to attract your audience and how to build a relationship with them. This is your growth accelerator.

If there is anyone who knows how to build and grow a visible business, it's Angelica Nwandu. Her company's audience of over 22 million active followers on Instagram generates over 6 billion impressions a month and was ranked as the second most engaging platform on Instagram in 2019.[16] The Shade Room has mastered the art of connecting with its audience. For Angelica, regularly communicating with her audience early on in the business proved to be an effective way of remaining visible to her ever-growing "Roommates." After launching the platform in 2014, within 10 days, the page had 10,000 followers. Speaking on how quickly the Instagram page built traction, Angelica says,

"I knew that it was going to be something big because of how quickly it was building an audience. I would also spend a lot of time in the DMs communicating with them. And they would tell me, 'This is gonna be big,' 'It's gonna blow.' I'm telling you, they will be the ones that would pump me up. One of the Roommates came into my DMs and said, 'You should name us the Roommates. This is the Shade Room and we live in the Shade Room.' I said, 'Oh, that's true. That's a good idea.' That taught me that when you talk to your audience in a personal way, you could discover that they will have the best ideas for you to help you grow. Because they want to see you grow, they'll be loyal to you."

Having regular interaction with and listening to your audience, giving them a sense of ownership and building a direct relationship with them, is essential if you want to stand out and make your business more visible.

Jenny Francis, DJ and presenter, established her career in an era where social media did not exist, yet she is widely recognized as the "Lady of Soul." Jenny tells us that as you build your audience, you should consider ways of connecting with people beyond social media platforms. "I think a lot of youngsters nowadays don't know what it's like to build themselves without the use of social media. Of course, we have to move with the times, but I didn't have that during my time. It was about building your audience based on what you had to offer. There were no social media platforms with X amount of followers for you to have that 'credibility,'" she says. "I think most people have forgotten about the old way of doing things, but combining the old school with the new school can be very effective." Arlan Hamilton offers ways to do this: "When you speak to your audience, do you send any newsletters? Or do you produce a podcast? Think about the other ways you can connect beyond the main social media platforms."

KNOW WHEN IT IS TIME TO MOVE ON, TO MOVE UP

I often look at work the same way I would a platonic or romantic relationship. If one of my friends were in a relationship where they were constantly undervalued, overlooked, unappreciated, or ignored, I would not have to think twice before telling them that it is time to move on. Very often, people remain in situations that are not conducive to their growth because they would rather stay in a situation that feels familiar or comfortable regardless of how detrimental it may be. Similarly, in a work context, I have spoken to so many of my Black peers who at one point in their career have felt like they were in a bad relationship. While some people choose to move on and look for new opportunities (in another team or a completely new company), others endure working in unhealthy work environments hoping that something will change. But being in a toxic work environment can eventually have the adverse effect of fueling low self-esteem and a lack of confidence.

If you believe that you are not being considered for opportunities, even though you are performing well and are delivering results, there are three approaches you can try.

The first is to evaluate yourself. Is there anything you may be doing that is contributing to a lack of development? Is your work under par? Do you have a poor relationship with your manager? Have you been slacking in any areas? Herman Bulls tells us that, "We should start by looking internally. We have to take a self-portrait to ask ourselves, 'Are we doing everything we could possibly do to pursue excellence?'"

Herman encourages that you ask yourself, "Did I take the extra steps that makes it possible for me to do my job better? Did I volunteer to take on the extra responsibility? What are my interpersonal skills like? Was I able to connect and expand the business's network?" He continues, "Remember, a promotion is not that you have the potential to do the next job at the next level; the promotion shows you've already demonstrated the ability to do the job at the next level, and that's what people sometimes get mixed up. So it's not, 'I'm going to get good after you promote me.' You've got to get good now, and then you get promoted. My advice is to pursue excellence. Get valid and timely feedback. And if your skills are still not being appropriately recognized and appreciated, then I would encourage you to find an organization that does."

After reflecting on yourself and assessing your performance, if you are confident in the quality of the work you are producing, then as Herman points out, the next step is to seek "valid and timely feedback." I am a big believer in seeking constructive feedback. Whenever working with people outside of your direct team or with a manager that is not in your reporting line, ask for feedback. Obviously, don't overdo it, but if it is an important piece of work or project that you have led or played an important role in directing or supporting, gather feedback from co-workers and managers. If you do not have a supportive manager who genuinely cares about your progression, then having others outside of your team providing meaningful feedback is valuable.

Keeping a record of the positive experience people have through working with you and their appraisal on the quality of work you deliver will prove to be helpful in the long run. When you have the receipts, it's a different kind of conversation—you can directly pinpoint examples where you have delivered; you are able to demonstrate clearly that you are doing something right, and it becomes easier to highlight that the problem doesn't lie with you. Honest and direct feedback is so valuable, and Pamela Hutchinson points to the need to ask for feedback from multiple people as a means to identify possible trends in your performance. "I would say this of everyone, not just Black people—if you're constantly being overlooked, get some real feedback," Pamela says.

"It could be race, but it also equally could be any number of things. I think one of the things that I have learned is that minorities and women don't always get true feedback. Because of a fear of offending or being thought of as being racist, or sexist, or whatever the reason managers aren't always truthful in the feedback that they give individuals. As a result, a lot of people go around making assumptions as to why they're overlooked. If you've got lots of different feedback and it's showing that actually there is a gap, then you know that is probably the reason you're not getting a role. Equally, if you get lots of feedback, and it is completely different to what your manager is saying, you've got evidence that there may be an issue here.

As a leader, my team gives me feedback all the time. I think that's really, really important, as you can't just rely on one person's feedback. Your manager may have another agenda; you might be so good that they don't want you to go anywhere else. It could be a whole host of reasons as to why you're being overlooked. And so relying just on one person's perspective is naive, actually. I think you should go out and get as much feedback as possible."

Third, always think about how you are communicating your efforts to those who need to know about them. Make sure your manager is aware of the work you are doing. Glenda McNeal shares an anecdote on the need to keep your manager well informed of your performance.

"I was going into a midlevel vice president's role, and it was a new job for me. I was very focused on performance. It was my first client management role in American Express and I had a couple of very difficult clients where I felt like I had to over prepare. There was one client in particular for whom I did a tremendous amount of work before every conversation and I made sure I spoke to him at least once a week or once every two weeks. This was an industry that I really hadn't managed, so in those weekly calls, I would give an update and share any idea I had.

One day, my boss called me to his office and said, 'You didn't tell me about the work that you're doing with Bob.' And I ask, 'Okay, what work?' He said, 'Bob gave me a call and just spoke very highly of you. I shouldn't hear from Bob about the work that you're doing; I should be hearing from you.'"

Glenda explains that, growing up, she was taught to just do the hard work. "I was told 'Don't brag about it, don't break your arm patting yourself on the back. If you do good work, people will notice.'" But this mentality meant that Glenda's hard work could have gone unnoticed had Bob not shared such positive feedback with her manager. That experience taught Glenda the value of clearly highlighting the impact she was making across the business. "I learned how to let people know the work that I was doing and how to highlight the things that I thought were most impactful in my work," she says. "I began to leverage my updates very differently with my boss, as opposed to just giving him a checklist of all the things I'm working on."

Glenda explains how she would talk her manager through the contracts that had been negotiated, the challenges that may have cropped up, and how she resolved them. Glenda's one-to-ones with her manager became an opportunity to demonstrate how she was thoughtful about processes, that she was strategic, that she was a critical thinker, she had good problem-solving skills, her ability to form good relationships with clients was strong, and so on. Because she took him through the work she was doing, she never had to say, "I'm making an impact"; he could just see it. Glenda advises, "What you don't want to do is build your case for promotion when the job is there; you want to build your case for promotion every day. If you feel you're being overlooked, I am a true believer, today, more than ever, you have to advocate for yourself. Personal advocacy is a thing."

KNOW YOUR WORTH

Realizing your greatness and potential is a key factor in your growth journey. A Bible verse I hold dear reads, "Do not conform to the pattern of this world, but be transformed by the renewing of your mind."[17] For decades, the pattern of this world has tried to chip away at our self-worth as a Black community. The pattern has said you can go, but only so far. It has made us question our God-given talent and continues to be a massive stumbling block in the lives of so many.

My faith has played a massive role in helping me to shake off the shackles of a negative mindset, a mindset that from an early age was influenced by—the quiet yet crippling effects of racism and discrimination. As a young child, I was told by a fellow child, "I don't want to play with you because you are Black." I have experienced working in environments where it felt that despite what I brought to the table, I was not deserving of recognition. I know what it feels like to be in a place where you constantly question your ability. Racism has been sewn into the fabric of this nation; it has been so delicately stitched into the structure of the Western world that there exists a pattern of discrimination toward the Black community everywhere you go. So recognizing our greatness and transforming ourselves by renewing our mindsets is imperative for our growth—we must know our worth.

For Inua Ellams, growing up in Nigeria where he was not in the racial minority had a profound impact on the way he viewed life. In the early formative years of his life, Inua had not come up against the barriers of racism in the same way his peers in the UK had, and this gave him a privilege that Black people who grow up in the United States or the UK typically do not experience. This privilege meant he grew up with a confidence to be ambitious. Inua says,

"When I was a kid, I wanted to be a town planner. It was the first thing that I created. I just sketched out a loose plan for

*a city when we were in Jos in Nigeria, and my father liked
the drawing and put it in his briefcase, which was God's
hand luggage as far as I was concerned. He took it to work to
show all his mates, and I remember looking at my hands
and thinking, 'Look what I created!' And to a certain extent,
I think all I've wanted to do ever since, is to humble adults
with my hands. That fascination of trying to create
wondrous things with my fingers hasn't quite left me."*

Inua's dream of becoming a city planner was born in an environment where race was not an obstacle. He was brought up in a culture that had an appreciation for education. Inua explains,

*"My father really championed reading when we were in
Nigeria. I was nine years old, reading Charles Dickens'*
Oliver Twist *and* A Tale of Two Cities, *and just really
enjoying the language. When we came over here in the UK,
I was reading novels by Jeffrey Archer and Terry
Pratchett. I really, really loved reading and had an ability
that was far beyond my years. My English teacher told me
I was good at English and good at writing. But this was in
the mid-90s, a different world; I just thought my teacher
was trying to gas me up or something, just to make the kid
from Nigeria with the thick accent feel better.*

*I had an awareness of my own privileges. One day in
school, the Black British kids were making fun of me; they
were saying "stop acting white." I would ask, "What do you
mean? I just came from Nigeria, I'm the darkest-skinned
person here, my accent is so thick, it's like a forest." I didn't
understand what they meant until I moved to Ireland.*

When I arrived in Dublin, I was the only Black boy in the entire school. Ireland was in its infancy regarding race relations; they were racist in ways that they couldn't even articulate to themselves. They didn't know it was wrong to begin to try to right it."

Being in such an environment does not promote growth of any kind. In such an environment, it is easy to question who you are.

"After the first year of facing that, I realized that something was happening to me. I'd go into conversations expecting to be insulted, expecting to be belittled, and expecting to be ridiculed. Because of that, I was becoming aggressive. I would go out with my shield up and a frown on my face. When I realized this was happening to me, I thought, 'Hold on a second; this isn't who you are.' I had grown up in a country where people didn't expect little of me. In Nigeria, people didn't taunt me because of my skin; people didn't think I'd be dumber than them. I lived in an environment that showed I could achieve anything. Retrospectively, I realized Black kids in London had grown up in hyperracist societies, surrounded by people who expected less of them, so when telling me to stop acting white, they were telling me to stop acting as if the world would bend over backward and all the doors would open."

We have all heard stories of children at school being told to limit their aspirations. The actual words "because you're Black" may not have been said to you, but it certainly could have been implied. Danielle Prescod, Co-Founder of 2BG Consulting, a consulting agency that aims to guide brands

Know your worth.
Do not allow
the negative
perceptions of
others cause you
to doubt yourself.

toward becoming more equitable and inclusive, explains how racism can impact self-worth. "The toll of white supremacy starts to affect your self-esteem," she says. "When it comes to negotiating a salary, if you don't have a sense of self-worth that is going to demand that people pay you what you're worth, you're just going to keep accepting pennies and peanuts. That is probably where the more damaging effects of white supremacy starts to creep in."

Know your worth. Do not allow the negative perceptions of others cause you to doubt yourself. As David McQueen says, make sure "you have a support network around you that reminds you of your worth and what you bring to the table." Keep going and keep growing.

NEXT STEPS AND REFLECTION

- What are three things you could do differently at work or in your business to work smarter?

- How will you aim to implement these things to be more efficient in your line of work?

- When was the last time you actively sought out feedback about your business or your work? Gather feedback from at least two trusted colleagues or partners to identify ways you can continue to deliver excellence in your respective field.

- Do you factor time to rest or take a break? If you have had an intense week at work, make a list of at least three things you will do differently next week.

MONEY, MONEY, MONEY

Learn to Earn

by *Raphael Sofoluke*

"MONEY, LIKE EMOTIONS, IS SOMETHING YOU MUST CONTROL TO KEEP YOUR LIFE ON THE RIGHT TRACK."
−NATASHA MUNSON[1]

Money is a tool that enables us to have more control over our lives. When you accumulate money, you are able to choose your own paths. When there is a lack of money, your choices in life will be limited by comparison to those with substantial amounts. Being able to handle and manage money enables you to navigate a world that is heavily reliant on this commodity to survive. This chapter considers exactly how Black professionals and entrepreneurs can better manage money, make money, and also build a legacy. We will go through a number of barriers that affect Black working people and discuss solutions to help you excel when it comes to your finances.

As well as a lack of Black senior leadership in organizations, it is suggested that Black workers still earn less than their white counterparts. This claim is backed up by Jackson Gruver, a data analyst at compensation data and software firm PayScale, who conducted some very interesting research on the matter. In discussing his findings, he says, "We find equal pay for equal work is still not a reality, and even as Black or African American men climb the corporate ladder, they still make less than equally qualified white men. They are the only racial or ethnic group that does not achieve pay parity with white men at some level."[2]

As a Black entrepreneur, money is key to helping your company grow, especially when you are getting started. Just as we have discussed some of the biases in the workplace, there are institutional biases throughout society that require change. When I think of the barriers of access to finance for Black entrepreneurs, I relate it to creating a piece of art. When creating a piece of art, the artist starts off with a blank canvas like all entrepreneurs. Unfortunately, not all entrepreneurs have the same strength of brush; many Black entrepreneurs are given brushes with weaker bristles, which have a direct impact on the art "or business" they create. White entrepreneurs are given the stronger resources to succeed. They have better access to finance, and so it is not surprising that Black entrepreneurs struggle to create viable businesses and the completed "art form" because white entrepreneurs tend to look like a better prospect and therefore become more profitable.[3]

We spoke with entrepreneur Demi Ariyo, who decided to position his business within the market to focus specifically on those entrepreneurs who found they were marginalized by High Street banks. Demi says, "Any small business that comes from specific communities that in the past have been overlooked, underserved, and for some reason received a high-level rejection, we cater for them." With many Black entrepreneurs struggling to raise capital, Lendoe has positioned itself as one of the go-to companies for Black entrepreneurs in the UK seeking to gain access to capital to start or grow their business.

Demi gained a passion for financial markets at 17 years old during the 2008 recession and then, at 23, got involved in corporate debt within the retail bond market. During his time in the bond market, he frequently had people approaching him from his own community asking him for capital. After refusing to give out loans due to the fact that personal loans were regulated, he finally caved when someone approached him with a business—a hair salon, which soon became Lendoe's first official customer.

Previously, Demi's family and friends were asking for money to buy cars and other things, but this particular client was asking for money to set up a new salon. They already had one salon generating revenue, making them the ideal client for Demi to issue his first loan to.

In a *Forbes* interview, Arlan Hamilton said, "My whole life I've been underestimated. I've been counted out. I wasn't listened to when I had the right answer."[4] Arlan, who specializes in giving investment to founders from underrepresented backgrounds through her company Backstage Capital, tells us,

"We talk about being underestimated at Backstage Capital; that's the biggest part of it. When someone immediately gives you a boundary or a limitation based on how you look or how they perceive you to no fault of your own, this can be a handicap. Our job is to break through all that. And I think it's important to talk about what we face. The start-up world is a microcosm of the real world—we face the same indecencies, the goalpost is moved several times over, the standards are different, and the insult to injury is how we are neglected and sort of left to our own devices to figure it all out."

As you can see, the distribution of money for Black business owners is a problem that needs to be addressed. Being able to discuss money, use money, and make more money will be imperative in not only your career development, but in your family's long-term stability.

MANAGING MONEY FOR PROFESSIONALS WITH SALARIES

Former Prime Minister Theresa May launched a consultation in 2018, with the sole purpose of finding out whether mandatory reporting of pay gaps by ethnicity could improve conditions for those from ethnic minority backgrounds.[5] She said, "Minorities often feel like they are hitting a brick wall at work." In the UK between 2012 to 2018, regardless of gender, employees from Black African, Caribbean, or Black British backgrounds earned on average 5 to 10 percent less than their white British counterparts.

These issues still seem to hold true today, so it begs the question, why is it that Black professionals are paid less than their white counterparts? Are we seen as cheaper labor? Historically, Black people were sold in slavery for pennies, and it makes you think, has this same mentality been carried forward in today's workforce? Are Black professionals seen as a valuable commodity that employers can get on the cheap?

The Confederation of British Industry (CBI) says a "failure to tackle the ethnicity pay gap is costing the British economy as much as £24 billion [$33 billion] a year and those organizations with the most ethnically and culturally diverse executive teams are 33 percent more likely to outperform their peers on profitability."[6] With such staggering evidence, you would think organizations would pay more attention to how they treat their employees from diverse backgrounds. Despite the growing awareness of how diverse companies perform better, many companies still lack the structure to be able to hire and keep their Black employees.

I often speak to organizations about how to make their companies more diverse and inclusive and how to recruit Black talent, but even when a company is able to attract and hire Black talent, the issue has always been retention. Undervaluation and demotivation run as an undercurrent to the retention issue of Black professionals. Many people feel that companies don't invest in them as an individual in terms of value and discover that a number of their white peers are earning more, which results in a lack of motivation. It is one reason why rather than fight for the salary they truly deserve, many Black professionals would rather move on to a new job that is paying them in recognition of their worth.

In the United States, the National Women's Law Center suggests Black women who work full time earn just $0.61 for every dollar made by white men, and the Economic Policy Institute in Washington says that regardless of age, gender, education, and religion, Black workers are paid 14.9 percent less than white workers.[7] Disparities like this are shocking but all too common and, like Theresa May said, sometimes it may feel like we are hitting a brick wall as pay issues between races continue to be a huge problem with a long history.

Get Your Money Up—How to Get a Pay Raise

With so many Black professionals being underpaid, let's address the big question: How do you get what you deserve at work? What are the steps you can take to ensure that you are not overlooked when it comes to increasing your salary? How do you ensure that you are being paid on par with your peers? Pay and pay raises are generally things that people don't talk about in the workplace, and because employees are encouraged not to speak with each other about it, it's easy for organizations to underpay their staff and not be held accountable.

David McQueen sums this up nicely: "Discussions around pay are very subtle, you know? Someone gets a pay rise and everybody's told, 'We don't talk about salary.' So because we don't talk about it, you don't know that the person at the other side of the office has got a bigger bonus than you until you overhear that 'Brian is buying a brand new Jeep or a Range Rover,' and you're thinking, 'How? We're on the same salary?' But then you find out that they are on more than you and it makes sense."

Emmanuel Asuquo, a qualified financial advisor with over 15 years' experience reiterates David's point. Emmanuel featured as one of four experts on the popular Channel 4 finance show *Save Well, Spend Better,* and in June 2020 he featured as an expert for the BBC One show *Your Money and Your Life,* helping a family save just under £10,000 ($14,000) on their annual household bills. Emmanuel discusses how he used to go about getting pay raises. "The way I always went about getting a pay rise was understanding what the pay structures were. I think one of the big struggles is that we don't actually know how much people around us get paid because they don't talk about their salaries. I would go online and look at what the next level up from my current position was and use the description as a guide of what I had to do if I wanted to get a pay rise," Emmanuel explains. "So if the descriptions stated that they wanted someone who's worked on certain projects, I'd get myself onto that type of project. If they needed someone with a specific type of experience, I'd go and get it. When they say it's 'not essential, but desirable' to have a certain type of qualification, I would go and get the qualification. So, when I did apply for a pay rise, I'd already put myself in a great position because I used their template," he says.

Emmanuel cleverly used job descriptions as a way to ensure he measured up and often, in fact, he was overqualified by ensuring he had skills that were considered nonessential. In my opinion, this is a good technique to use as a case for a pay raise.

Jamelia Donaldson offers a new viewpoint when she told us, "I just wish I had someone that could share the rules of the game with me. To be like, this is how you navigate pay and this is how you ask for promotions. The fact that you can even ask to be promoted or ask for a pay rise I didn't know until I left the corporate world."

Many of us are likely to be earning less than we should. If a company can get away with saving money, they will. This leaves it up to you to ensure that you are being paid appropriately to your worth. Knowing how to ask for a pay raise when the time is right is another key point in the successful management of your career.

We spoke to leading senior Black professionals who told us exactly how to go about asking for a pay raise. Pamela Hutchinson shares her insight on how to get a pay raise alongside some of the struggles Black professionals have with seeking one. She says,

"Generally, women and minorities tend to be more uncomfortable to ask for pay rises. I think very often, as

Black people, we get very upset. We feel that we're not paid fairly compared to our white counterparts and that may well be true in many cases, but I also think we have to ask for what we want, too. We're not good at asking for that pay increase; we're not good at asking for a promotion. But I've always believed that if you're a great performer, and you delivered what you should have, and you've gone over and above what was expected of you, then you should feel comfortable to go in and ask for a pay rise. Don't go in and ask for a pay rise if you have only just met your objective. Be skillful. Plan for the conversation first and be clear about what it is you're asking for. Be very clear about what you have done and exactly why you think you deserve it. Leave it there and hope that your manager agrees with you. But you've got to be able to go in with something concrete, something spectacular.

I remember many years ago, somebody saying something that had a profound effect on me. They said, 'Pamela, the reason that you're angry is because you think you still believe the world is fair,' and it was true. I believed the world should be fair and the reality is, it isn't. They continued, 'The moment you realize the world is not fair, and you accept that, you can leverage your skills in order to move yourself forward—you'll move much faster.'

I realized then that the world is not fair for many groups of people. There are LGBTQ people who struggle to progress; there are disabled people who struggle to progress. So my focus has been on leveraging where I am amazing and bringing that to the attention of the organization. Because I'm Black and because of the way I was raised, no one else *can offer my perspective. So stop worrying about looking like someone else, or acting like someone else, or not getting a role. Utilize what is special about you."*

Pamela Hutchinson raises some fantastic points about asking for a pay raise. One that stuck out for me was that when you ask for a pay raise, you should be asking because you have gone over and above your job description and not just met your objectives—meeting your objectives is just what you are there to do. Secondly, instead of being upset about pay disparity, make sure you can prove your worth to the organization to show why what you bring to the organization cannot be replicated by anyone else. Finally, the fear of asking for a promotion or pay raise is something I can resonate with and that the many Black professionals I have spoken to do also. We spoke about imposter syndrome in Chapter 4, and feeling like you're not worthy of being in the space may contribute to that fear of asking for what you truly deserve.

Rondette Amoy Smith also gave some powerful advice about asking for a pay raise. "If you walk into a meeting with your manager at the end of the year and you're hearing consistent feedback, like 'you're doing a great job and your performance is stellar,' but you've done your research and learn that the salary for your role should be $80–100k, for example, but you're getting $60,000 or even $70,000, that's not good enough," Rondette says. "Find a way to articulate that you have done research. Say with confidence: 'I think I'm outside the range of where my peers are sitting. Can you help me understand if that's the case? And if so, I'd like to talk to you about what you need to see from me to ensure that I'm exceeding this threshold.' It's how you position it.

If you come in, articulate yourself well, and show that you've done your research, you can ensure that you're getting what you deserve."

It's about preparation and ensuring that when you are going into that meeting with your manager, you can prove that you are delivering in your role. Make sure that you have researched the market and you know exactly what an organization should be paying for someone who is doing your role. Use sites like Glassdoor to find out your market value. Rondette was also very intentional about her wording—it's important to control your emotions and choose your words wisely; you do not want your manager to feel like you are attacking them. You must articulate and prove your point professionally.

Further, Rondette went on to say that if you are not successful when you ask for a deserved pay raise, then don't feel afraid to leave. Knowing when it's time to move on is an important part of professional growth, as explored by Opeyemi in chapter 5. Unfortunately, not all companies are willing to pay employees more or value them enough, so don't be afraid to consider your options if you feel you have tried everything else.

When we spoke with Shellye Archambeau, we asked her if she had any personal experience of asking for a pay raise as specifically as someone who has worked with a number of Fortune 500 companies.

"It goes back to asking for what you want; it starts from day one and should always continue. When a previous company first hired me, they hired me as a newbie and I'm sure they've got a standard that they pay a new person coming out of college. They made me an offer and I said, 'Thank you so much, I so appreciate this, this is the

company that I absolutely want to work for; however, I built my budget and I've looked at what it's going to cost me to live and what I have to pay for my student loans.' I then went through all my expenses and told him how much more I needed. It wasn't a lot more, but I always believe you can ask for 10% more.

The guy was shocked I was asking for more money, but I did it in a way in which I was asking for his 'help' because I wanted to take the job, but I was having trouble making the numbers work for me. I said that I'd really appreciate it if the salary could be increased by $3,000. So I ended up getting it and, in fact, I got a little more than that because I hadn't realized they work in round numbers. So I already started ahead of everyone else because when I get my 6 percent raise or my 3 percent raise, it's all based upon what I earned to begin with. So I always tell people to always ask for more. The worst they can say is 'no.'"

Shellye adds her view on being underpaid: "If you feel like you're being underpaid, then you have to talk about it, but not just at pay time. During pay cycle time, a lot of people are asking for a pay rise, so you need to make sure that you're asking for it off cycle, and then reinforcing it during cycle." Shellye says, "It's really easy these days to know what jobs pay. So find out, and go to your boss and say, 'I've invested a lot in my career, and I really want to stay here, but I want to make sure I'm being paid what I deserve.' Now you have a conversation going that gets them emotionally tied to wanting to help you."

In both of these scenarios—making sure she asked for more money before accepting the job and asking for a raise—Shellye made sure that she spoke to her employer in a way that made them felt obliged to help her.

MANAGING MONEY FOR ENTREPRENEURS AND PAYING YOURSELF

So you've started your business and you've started to earn a bit of money. I'm a firm believer in working hard but also enjoying the rewards of what you've worked hard for. Psalm 128 is a Bible verse that resonates for me—it says, "You shall eat the fruit of the labor of your hands; you shall be blessed, and it shall be well with you."[8] In essence, this verse is a reminder that the labor and hard work you put in should be rewarded and is there to be enjoyed. Now, when you run a business and have staff, overheads, or things to pay for that will enable growth, it is important that you get the balance right of how much you should pay yourself with how much you reinvest and pay others. Paying yourself should not be at the detriment of the business's future. It's important you think of ways in which you can reward yourself and still keep the business in great shape.

Demi Ariyo offers some fantastic advice about how entrepreneurs should pay themselves. "I've always seen businesses like babies and the question is, when your newborn baby is relatively young, how much are you expecting that baby to do for you? Or how much are you expecting them to look after you? When you're about to have a baby, you always have to make sure you're financially stable enough to look after that baby for the first few years. So what you should be thinking more about is, do I have enough capital right now to be able to look after this business in the case that it can't pay me anything?" he says. "Ask yourself: 'Do I have enough capital to invest in this business so that at the earliest stages where I'm not taking anything from this business, the later stages will pay me in heaps and bounds from dividends?' At the earliest stages of the business, I didn't pay myself anything. Now I have a structure where I receive remuneration, but I'm very mindful that this business is still a baby and the more I invest in it and the more I look after it, then in the future, it will pay me dividends."

As a father of two myself, I found Demi's example of a newborn baby to be extremely insightful, and it's advice that I feel all entrepreneurs should take on board. Ultimately, Demi alluded to the fact that depending on the age of your business and how mature it is will depend on how much you pay yourself. Using the analogy of a newborn baby was very helpful, as we often treat our businesses like our babies—we are so protective over them. This analogy makes complete sense in evaluating how to decide what salary you are paying yourself and potentially your staff.

In determining how much a business owner should pay themselves, Emmanuel Asuquo uses his "Needs vs Wants" analysis. He says, "Ask yourself, 'What is my basic standard of living? How much is my rent or food? How much does that cost? Can my company pay that directly?' Consider if the amount you're getting is not even enough for that so you still need to be working on something else to cover your needs. As your business progresses, you can then start to add in some 'wants,' but the basis of what you should and can pay yourself should be about your needs."

Emmanuel's approach is calculated and a very good model to use. Clearly define your wants and needs because it is critical in deciding how much you should initially pay yourself, how much you should save, and how much you should reinvest in your business.

Christina Okorocha shares how she and her team first paid each other when they started making money. "We split the money into five. There are three co-founders, then we had a savings account and a cost account. We didn't take salaries at the time, so essentially we were freelancers. And that's what we had to do at the beginning before we could earn from salaries through the company."

In a very similar fashion to Demi, Christina and her team looked closely at the age of the business and paid themselves accordingly, relative to what the business was earning. What I like about Christina's method is the forward thinking she had by creating another account for savings and costs. This ensured that when things needed to be paid for, they had an account to go into, as well as a savings account for rainy days.

SAVING FOR PROFESSIONALS

Indian households have (similar to US cents per dollar) 90-95 pence for every £1 of white British wealth, Pakistani households have around 50 pence, Black Caribbean around 20 pence, and Black African and Bangladeshi approximately 10 pence, according to the Runnymede report released in April 2020.[9]

Saving the money you earn is almost as important as accumulating it. Without a strategy in place to save money, you will be unable to reach your financial milestones and have enough money for the things you desire. Saving is part of money management, and being able to handle your money so you aren't living from paycheck to paycheck will alleviate stress. Working professionals on a monthly salary are paid 12 times each year, so how can you ensure that each time you are paid you are able to pay for your essentials, enjoy the things you love, and also save for your future?

Emmanuel Asuquo spoke to us about the need to retune our minds to accept delayed gratification. "We live in a world of instant gratification. We want something? We buy it now. That fear of missing out is causing us to just react, and so wherever we have the savings, we'll take that money and use it for things we don't really need, and that's how people end up in debt, using overdrafts, accumulating credit cards, and so on," he says. "For me, it's about understanding the importance of delayed gratification. Ask yourself: 'Am I prepared to delay right now in order to give me the resources to save?'"

There are a number of steps you can take to save money from your salary. The first thing is to create a budget—decide how much you want to spend on certain things based on what money you are earning each month. There are a number of budget templates online that you can use to help you create a fixed budget for how you spend your salary. Next, I suggest you do an audit of your spending habits. Find out what you are potentially wasting your money on and what's essential, like your rent or mortgage, food shopping, and bills. Once you have done that, look at the "nice to haves." Are they essential? Are you actually using them? When I reviewed my own "nice to haves," I realized that my Cineworld membership card had to go. Yes, it allowed me to go to the movies as many times as I wanted throughout the month, but I hadn't been going for six or seven months, and when I thought about it in isolation, it was actually just a waste of my money. Confronting your spending habits and auditing yourself is key to saving and making change. When you can step back to recognize some of these bad habits, you can start to eradicate them. Maybe it's that coffee you get in the mornings every day. Can you make it at home instead? Start finding viable alternatives that cost less or no money.

After auditing your spending, you will be able to understand how much you can put aside each month. It would be wise for you to save money right after you receive your paycheck and put it into a separate savings account. Adjust how you set your bills up to come out of your account at the same time and set an amount that goes directly into your savings. Once you have created a standing order, it means you don't have to constantly remember to transfer money for saving, which makes it 100 percent more likely to happen.

Clearing your debts is next on the agenda. Now that you've gotten rid of some of your bad spending habits, you can reuse some of the money you are saving to pay off any debts and loans you have. Paying off debts and loans allows you to keep more of your salary, meaning you can pay for more things, save more, and put the money toward something more useful. If you are paying interest on a loan, getting rid of this type of agreement will allow you to have more capital.

If you are in a position where you can get bonuses or salary increases, use your bonuses or commission to help you reach some of your saving goals sooner than you planned. Instead of going wild and spending the extra on things that don't matter, by adding it to your savings, you are able to reach your financial milestones quicker.

Finally, give yourself money to spend each week and be accountable for it. You can do this by using money management apps that you can download on your phone. I use Monzo—it's easy to use and almost holds you accountable after every single transaction with its notification alerts.

Confronting your spending habits and auditing yourself is key to saving and making change.

SAVING FOR ENTREPRENEURS

As an entrepreneur, saving money may look a bit different to a working professional. As a working professional, you have a lot more financial stability, as you are getting paid every month and know exactly how much you can expect in every paycheck—down to the last penny. As an entrepreneur, especially for those at the start of their business journey, money may come in bursts, and sometimes not at all.

Demi Ariyo has some great advice on how entrepreneurs should save:

"There's nothing wrong with being an entrepreneur; however, if you're not working other jobs at the time or in work and doing your business on the side, you have to be able to understand that your salary could fluctuate based on the environment.

When you're not in an establishment, you're not protected by other professionals or other stakeholders. When you're running a business, it's like being on a roller coaster—you actually feel the full ride of things. So you need to make sure that first, you've got a 'life survival budget.' In that life survival budget, there's a certain amount that goes consistently into savings, and it's not saving for a car or something fancy—it's saving for a rainy day, because in entrepreneurship, they are going to come. When things are really good, save a lot more. When things are rough, go to the stash that you created for when things are bad."

Financial wellness coach Bola Sol also shared her tips as an entrepreneur and some of the ways she saves money. Bola is the creator of a platform called Refined Currency, which provides information on debt, budgeting, saving, and making money. She is also the author of the essential money guide *How To Save It* and founder of Rich Girl Chronicles, a money accountability group for women looking to be empowered by their finances.[10]

Bola says, "Know when it's the time to spend and when it's the time to save. Twice a year, I go shopping and I set a limit in my head. Once I'm done, I'm done. On the shopping trips, I spend a percentage of my income, as opposed to a number. Think about why you actually want to save, because there have been times where I have saved for like a year and scraped through."

Bola raises a great point about knowing and having that awareness of when you should spend or save, and it is key to improving your saving habits, and also being intentional about when you spend.

While discussing saving, Arlan Hamilton also touches on the importance of having a great accountant for your business.

"Whether you agree that this is fair or not, every Black-owned company is representing other Black people. If someone is found out to be siphoning capital for themselves and spending money willy-nilly the way that they're not supposed to be, it will not be a good reflection. So it's important to have good professional people around you who can read every single document and keep your business in check. If your signature is going to be on something, take the time to read it. Even if you have a legal team or an accounting team, know what's going on around you because you don't want to be caught off guard."

Having a good accountant is a step toward saving, too. Investing in a good accountant can mean the difference between finding you are fined for late payments or overpaying on taxes, essentially losing money that could be saved, or making money and saving it in a way that can in fact earn you more.

BARRIERS TO ENTRY AND SERVING THE BLACK COMMUNITY

In a *Financial Times* interview, Eric Collins the Head of Venture Capital firm Impact X called for the immediate financing for Black-owned businesses, who receive proportionately less than their white-owned counterparts, instead of reparations for past profit from slavery.[11] Eric highlights the need for finance to be provided to Black business owners, as he sees the advantage that other races have had when they are able to access finance.

When speaking about the barriers for entry when it comes to financial backing or funding, Emmanuel Asuquo puts it bluntly: "The fact that there's a barrier to entry for Black people goes back to what we say about trust. The people that we tend to be asking for money are white, and they tend to have a natural level of trust, understanding, and belief in people that look like them and a distrust of people who don't."

So what are the barriers for Black entrepreneurs when it comes to accessing finance?

Demi Ariyo says,

"The operators in the current market don't always have the level of understanding that is needed to be able to navigate

through what the entrepreneur is trying to accomplish and get a clear idea of how it can work. If you're an entrepreneur from China and you're specifically solving a problem in China, but you're only going to investors or lenders from the US and the UK, yes, they may be able to understand the financial numbers of what you're trying to achieve, but it might not sit well with them because they haven't experienced that particular problem.

Now, if an investor is from the same community or background and has experienced those problems which this entrepreneur is trying to solve, they can relate on a much deeper level, and also add value by offering suggestions for the business. As a Black entrepreneur, it's likely you will receive financial backing when the investors understand your problem."

Warren Buffet says, "Risk comes from not knowing what you're doing." As a credit or equity investor, you need to understand the industry you're investing in, as well as understand the entrepreneur you're investing in—what makes them tick, why they started their business, and what problem they're solving. This diminishes the level of risk significantly.

Demi delves deeper:

"Sometimes investors don't understand how to communicate with Black entrepreneurs. For example, Black entrepreneurs in the UK are two to four times less likely to be accepted for finance when they apply for it in comparison to their white counterparts, and sometimes that's because these banks don't understand what the

entrepreneur is trying to accomplish. The banks don't understand how to communicate with them to build the necessary trust to even encourage them to apply with any confidence. Not only are they more likely to be rejected, but Caribbean entrepreneurs in the UK, in particular, are 35 percent and African entrepreneurs 44 percent less likely to try to apply for credit from a bank because they simply don't believe the banks are going to accept them. The first entrepreneur who we supported (the one who wanted to buy the second hair salon) had a perfect credit score, the perfect profile for investment, but they felt like the bank didn't treat them how they should be treated.

As a lender or investor, when there is no communication, it becomes a risk, but understanding the entrepreneur lowers the level of risk that someone is taking because they understand what they're getting into."

Demi raised an important point that because investors who are not Black may not understand the market that a Black founder is trying to reach, it's very likely that they will be hesitant to invest. For me, this makes it even more important for Black investors to invest in Black founders, as they are people who may understand the product better than anyone else and can offer more than just their money. Andy Davis, co-founder of 10x10 and Investor in Residence at Google for Startups, was really clear on the importance of investing in Black founders.

"I get asked all the time why aren't white investors investing in Black founders. There are investors out there who think that it's a mistake for businesses to focus on Black

consumers, as Black people are the minority in the country. That's interesting because I'm not thinking that Black people are going to be the 'minority' in 20 years' time. If we have 25 percent Black and mixed people in the UK in 20 years' time, 25 percent is not a minority. If you go back to 1975, when Bill Gates started Microsoft, and he said, 'I'm going to put a computer in every home,' people said it was just for the rich. But eventually people started putting them in their homes, universities, and corporations, and now almost everyone has one. So I look at Microsoft and ask someone if you could go back in time, would you have invested into the company? The answer is 'yes.' So why wouldn't you focus on Black businesses or Black customers, which is potentially going to be one of the fastest-growing markets and populations in the world? Is it still your mentality and excuse that the Black market is a niche one, and you don't understand? Are you investing for today's return or for 10 years' time?"

Arlan Hamilton adds that many people do not see the potential in investing in Black founders and their ideas. "Everybody sort of skips the part where Bill Gates was just a punk kid in his garage to begin with, and everybody skips the part where Mark Zuckerberg was just thinking about finding cute girls online and rating them before it turned into Facebook. Everybody forgets about Y Combinator, who, when they started 15 years ago, would give people $15,000 or $12,000 and a home-cooked chili dinner on Tuesdays, and then match them with all of the mentorship they could handle. Today they've helped companies like AirBnB, Dropbox, and more," she says.

Arlan continues, "Everybody has to start somewhere. So it is incredibly frustrating for people to look at the majority of Black founders, especially in the early stages, and not just see our potential. Look at what we've done so far with the little we have. Not only do we have limited resources, but every time we get them, they are plucked from us. Imagine what we'll look like 10 years from now? If you are fortunate enough to be on the cusp of that wave, where you can invest in Black founders, you should cap yourself fortunate. That's how I look at it."

Many Black entrepreneurs are frustrated by being written off right away—the potential that is granted to other races is clearly not being given to Black entrepreneurs. The problems are greater than just not seeing Black founders as an asset, nor seeing only the potential hindrances to opportunity for many Black founders.

Entrepreneurs Bianca Miller-Cole and Byron Cole are doing a number of things to push Black business owners forward. Bianca explains, "Black businesses are not invested in, and banks are more likely to turn them down compared to businesses created by white owners, so if they can't get traditional investment, I try to help as much as I can." Byron adds, "We have a Black Business School Scholarship Fund, which will help Black businesses go through our mentoring program, which is funded by a number of corporations and crowdfunding."

MAKING YOURSELF AN ASSET—WHAT INVESTORS ARE LOOKING FOR

So how do you make yourself an "asset"? When I think of the term asset, I think of being valuable. The definition of valuable is "having considerable monetary worth; costing or bringing a high price." As an entrepreneur, you need to start thinking about how you portray your monetary worth to an investor. When you go shopping and you are looking at buying designer clothes, ultimately it is down to you, the buyer, to decide if this product is valuable enough for you to spend the high price that has been set by the brand. Now think about your thought process and purchasing decisions when buying. What are you looking for in that product? Is it good quality? Is it unique? What are people saying about this product? How much does it cost? These are all questions we think about when making buying decisions. Now think about the investor; regardless of the price you set for your brand or the value you place on yourself, if you cannot portray this to the buyer, then they will not be willing to part with their cash to invest in you.

We've discussed some of the barriers for Black entrepreneurs in raising finance, but it's also important to share some advice on what you can do to ensure that, despite some of these hindrances, you are positioned in the best way possible to try to gain capital. We asked the contributors we interviewed who invest themselves to share some advice on what Black entrepreneurs could do better to get access to finance.

Demi Ariyo says,

"The first thing you really want to do is build trust. You have to figure out a way to separate yourself from the crowd, and you do that through building trust. Do you have stability? Can I trust you with my capital? Can I trust that your business has the capacity to make the repayments needed over time to repay the full principle that I'm giving you? And does your story give me that belief that at the end of this journey, I'm going to be able to make a return?

In regard to equity, we always talk about the three Ts: team, traction, and tech. Who's in your team? Do I get a feeling that I can trust this team to deliver on this project? Based on what you've done to date, is there traction? Because equity investors are looking for growth and stability. Is your idea geared toward tech? Or how is tech involved in how you scale? Because that's something that's usually more sought after.

Can I see that, after all of your expenses, you can make the payments and, from a margin perspective, how much you have after all of those expenses? Can I see that what you're projecting to do with the money I'm giving you makes sense? Assets are also important. You need to show the assets your business currently has, and, if they're not yet tangible, what are you willing to put on the line? This allows lenders to know that you're sticking with this business or idea for the long term."

Demi emphasizes that the key to getting people on board is trust. In the finance world, trust is built through your credit score and not your word, so ensuring that you can handle your own money is essential before other people can trust you to handle theirs. Ensure that you have your numbers in place and that everything adds up so that lenders can see that you will be able to pay back their money.

Byron Cole shares his feeling that the importance of the first conversation or first meeting between entrepreneur and investor is significant.

"I've met enough people now to be able to know within 30 seconds whether or not I'm going to be able to work

with them, or if I like their idea. I want to know if it's worthwhile or sustainable. I also ask a lot of questions; for example, I may say to you, 'Okay, so this is a really high-risk business for me, do you think so?' If the person says, 'No,' I'll say, 'If you think that it's not going to be a risk, would you be willing for me to loan you the money personally, and if it doesn't work within a certain time frame, will you pay me back that money on an agreed schedule? I just want to see your intentions, and if you are honorable. Because if we're gonna lose, we're gonna lose together and, if we win, we win together."

When I'm looking at investing in people, honesty is imperative.

If you don't know an answer, just say that you don't know. Sometimes bluffing and blinding doesn't get you results, especially with someone who's experienced in the investing game."

Like many investors and those who grant loans, Byron is very keen on sussing out the character of a person. He wants to ensure that whoever he gets into business with has good moral traits, so ensuring that you are trustworthy, honest, and you know your business is a major component in getting the investment that you need.

Another piece of advice Byron shares is about giving away parts of your business for investment. It's something that worries many entrepreneurs, but sometimes it may be the best thing for your growth. "Do not be afraid to give away a portion of your business, if that means you can start that business tomorrow," Byron says. "Take the money, push the business forward, make it successful, sell it, and start again by yourself. Sometimes it's just good to take on board that additional help to propel your business forward fast."

Andy Davis discusses the characteristics of a business he looks for when investing. "I invest in businesses, but I certainly invest in the founders, too. I'm looking for obsession," he says. "You have to be obsessed with your business. Obsessed people have insight that no one else has; you've seen something that is missing and you know you can solve the problem. You have to want to do this for the next 10 years of your life. It's a long road."

As someone who runs a business, I can agree that obsession is essential. Are you passionate about what you do? I am extremely passionate and obsessed with the UK Black Business Show, and it's that sort of obsession that drives you to do and achieve things that others can't.

GENERATIONAL WEALTH AND BUILDING A LEGACY

Generational wealth is often pushed to the back of our minds. The term "generational wealth" represents assets passed down from one generation to another. If you have the ability to pass down a significant inheritance to your descendants, this is deemed as generational wealth. Assets passed down can include: real estate, stock market investments, a business, or anything else which has monetary value. In the United States, there are staggering racial disparities within wealth. In 2016, it was reported that at $171,000, the net worth of a typical white family, is nearly 10 times greater than that of a Black family at $17,150.[12] These gaps in the United States wealth systems convey the effect of inequality and discrimination over time. So why is this important? Inheritance makes up a great deal of the current wealth in the US; it was projected in 2020 that Americans would inherit about $765 billion in gifts. Inheritances account for roughly 4 percent of annual household income, much of which goes untaxed by the US government.[13]

A report released in April 2020 called the "Color of Money," by Runnymede, the UK's leading independent race equality think tank, revealed that Black African and Bangladeshi households have 10 times less wealth than White British people.[14] This report highlighted a number of attributes that contributed to racial inequality, which impacts the generational wealth of Black people in the UK.

The report continues that 5 percent of Black African workers are paid below the national minimum wage, compared to 3 percent of white workers. While BAME (Black, Asian, and minority ethnic) people are more likely to have a college degree, the monetary value of that qualification is worth less in the labor market, with nearly 40 percent of Black African graduates in nongraduate jobs (nearly double the white British rate of 20 percent)[15], and Black and minority ethnic men have much higher unemployment rates than white British men.[16]

These statistics highlight that systematic racism is one of the contributing factors in the generational wealth problem within the Black community, and it must be tackled through policy reform, as well as social change. Although it may seem like we are fighting a losing battle, there are a few things we can do to create generational wealth. If we all make a conscious effort to think about this and how it affects our future children, we can make a difference.

Emmanuel Asuquo explains how he feels in regard to some of the problems facing Black people when it comes to generational wealth. "We don't own enough profitable businesses, and also we don't own our business premises," he says. "When we own our properties, when we own stocks and shares and investments, then all of a sudden we're no longer just consumers. One of the biggest problems is that we are targeted as consumers, and Black consumers have been amazing for so many businesses. Black consumers and what we like and wear sets a lot of trends. We've helped so many businesses that don't even like us, and may even be upset that we buy their clothes, yet we have made them billionaires."

So what are the ways you can create generational wealth? One way is investing in stocks. Stocks are considered one of the best ways to build long-term wealth. Investing in index funds that carry low costs could be a great way to start. There are bank accounts and whole industries dedicated to helping you do this—research investment ISAs in the UK or other types of investment-based savings accounts. Also take a look at apps that can make these processes easier for you. Moneybox is a user-friendly app that is perfect for those who are new to the world of investing—it allows you to round up your loose change and add it to a stocks and shares ISA, which quietly builds up behind the scenes. When you are receiving wealth from multiple sources, it's important that you put money aside and in bank accounts that allow your money to continually grow.[17] This goes back to Mark Maciver's point on networking and trying to find "perfect places" where "you feel like your seeds are going to grow." The more ways you invest your money, the more likely it is that something positive will happen.

Andy Davis suggested that we need to start building and owning things for long periods of time, as ownership is important. He also said we need to do more to redistribute capital to aspiring entrepreneurs. "Would you rather build a £200 million [$277 million] business which just fails? Or sell 50 percent of that business in order to help it grow and then redistribute £40 million [$55 million] of that back into potentially thousands of Black founders who can create thousands of multi-million-pound [dollar] businesses? We need to understand capital better. Generational wealth starts with education and exposure." Building a profitable business to pass down to your children is another great way to keep wealth in your family for a number of years, even after you have passed on. In North America, the Census Bureau states that 90 percent of all business enterprises are family firms.[18] One thing to remember is that if you do pass it down to a family member, they need to be knowledgeable about the business and know how to run it so the business doesn't fail in their hands.

Finally, the last way to build generational wealth is building your succession plan. When I say this, I mean making sure that you have an up-to-date will or even perhaps a will at all. According to Black Enterprise, nearly 70 percent of African Americans have no will or estate plan in place.[19] A study by Caring.com said that, "Lack of estate planning is one of several factors that lead to the loss of land in the African American community. In the absence of a will, the land becomes vulnerable to partition and sale. When this happens, families lose property and wealth built by previous generations."[20] Having a will ensures that all the hard work you have put into acquiring wealth, land, businesses, and property does not go to waste. Other succession plans to keep hold of wealth within your family include taking out life insurance, creating an estate plan, and naming beneficiaries for your financial accounts.

Demi Ariyo gave some more insight into the importance of generational wealth and building a legacy: "I think generational wealth and building legacy kind of go together, and I say that because the definition of 'legacy' itself is really about what you would leave behind when you're gone. Generational wealth is about what you leave for the generations after you. This could mean investing in a whole bunch of things, not just businesses, starting businesses, and leaving businesses behind—but also relationships. Relationships could also be assets, and we need to invest in them. In business, your name is super-critical. If I have a good business relationship with you, for instance, and I happen to pass away and my son says to you, 'I'm trying to start something, can you support me,' that legacy which I've left behind allows him to start to build his own wealth on the basis of my generational wealth."

Bianca Miller-Cole adds that "Multiple streams of income are important. Just having a salary may not be enough. Think about other ways you can invest your time, money, and energy. It doesn't have to be having a side hustle. It might be investments in property. A second way to have generational wealth that I'm really upset the Black community doesn't have good enough education about is legacy planning such as life insurance [and] long-term sickness insurance. The reason why some people have generational wealth is because they've understood how to protect their wealth and pass it to the next generation without exorbitant tax."

ALTERNATIVE FINANCE

Alternative finance refers to financial channels, processes, and instruments that fall outside the traditional finance system, such as regulated banks and capital banks. With so many issues surrounding Black entrepreneurs accessing finance, alternative finance products could be a better solution than going through the traditional banks. Alternative finance products can include loans, asset finance, stock finance, supply-chain financing, pension-backed financing, and crowdfunding. Finance expert Demi Ariyo also adds to this.

"Peer-to-peer lending tends to be cheaper for the borrower because effectively they don't have to pay the bank fees, and the investor gets a higher return. Peer-to-peer lending is also cheaper for the borrower due to the fact that they cut out intermediaries, such as banks. For a Black entrepreneur who may not be used to having an institution that understands them, they can all of a sudden promote their investment to a wide community of other Black entrepreneurs, who can now access that investment because they don't have to have millions of pounds [dollars] to be able to influence the bank to invest in it. It democratizes finance.

Revenue share is also a great financing model because, again, there's a lot of minority entrepreneurs that start businesses, which may not be scalable on a global level very quickly. Businesses want to retain their ownership, and they want to make sure they can leave these businesses for their kids, but because they're not scalable on a global level at an extremely fast pace, venture capitalists are not willing to give them the money. With revenue-sharing models, you can now get the same level of flexibility that equity gives you through a debt product and not have to give up your ownership."

When talking about alternative finance, Arlan Hamilton says that bootstrapping is her favorite way of raising money. "Bootstrapping" is the idea of building a company from the ground up with just your personal savings and using the cash from your sales to maintain the business. "I have an online course about raising capital, but the punchline is that it is really about bootstrapping with the customer and making your customers be your best investor," she says.

I started the UK Black Business Show through bootstrapping. It can be a good way to make a good business grow naturally and create a solid customer base who love your product because they are actually invested in it.

Arlan continues,

"There is also crowdfunding and crowd-equity funding. It takes time, and you have to kind of have a system for it, but it can pay off in a really wonderful way.

It would be remiss not to mention pitch competitions, too. I've seen a couple of companies recently building an entire first round of funding based on winning pitch competitions. It could feel scrappy, but if you can be innovative and inventive, and if you are good at articulating and presenting your company—especially if your company has substance— that's a good way of raising funds at the idea stage."

Through reading this chapter, please reflect on the parts that speak to you most and really try to implement them into your life. These gems will not only put you in a good position, but also your family, and future generations to come.

NEXT STEPS AND REFLECTION

- Consider this: How can I better manage my salary?

- Do you feel as though you deserve a pay raise? If so, why? How can you articulate this best?

- How are you saving money? Can you improve on this, and what steps will you take to do this?

- What ways can I help build a legacy or generational wealth for my family or my business?

HEALTH IS WEALTH

How to Stay Mentally and
Physically Strong at Work
by *Raphael Sofoluke*

*"IT IS HEALTH THAT IS THE REAL WEALTH AND NOT
PIECES OF GOLD AND SILVER."*
–MAHATMA GANDHI[1]

Money is viewed as the most valuable and precious asset to keep us alive, yet the term "health is wealth" is a saying that has been used to emphasize that the value we place on money needs to be reciprocated in the value we put on our health. Are you paying the same attention to your mental and physical health as you do to your finances? In this chapter we focus on a number of sensitive topics which may trigger a traumatic experience or event you have been through. If at any point you feel like this chapter is too heavy for you, I urge you to take a break and turn to the Resources on page 336, where you can find further advice.

Throughout my career, I've experienced a number of the health issues we will discuss in this chapter, and I'm still working on implementing some of the amazing advice you will read into my own personal life.

As you read on, you will realize that the health issues we discuss are very common and are nothing to be ashamed of.

When thinking about our careers, we often think about the exciting parts like branding, networking, and promotion. But we tend to avoid the parts that really force us to address our lifestyle, mental state, and the things which others cannot see or monitor. When I think of how important our health is, I often relate it to the function of a smartphone. It has so many amazing tools, such as WhatsApp, Instagram, Facebook, Twitter, LinkedIn, email, photos, and many more, but if we fail to charge our phone and keep our battery at a good level, it fails to be useful. The same goes for our mental health.

Shellye Archambeau discusses the importance of taking care of your mental health and making it a priority. "In life, you have to figure out what you need first before helping others," she says. "When you're on a plane and they're giving you instructions of what to do during an emergency, they tell you to put your oxygen mask on first and then you can help the person next to you."

It's an easy analogy—our ability to keep ourselves in optimum health should be our first priority, and doing this will only place us in a better position to help others.

According to HSE (Health and Safety Executive), "One in four people in the UK will have a mental health problem at some point and while mental health problems are common, most are mild, tend to be short term, and are normally successfully treated, with medication, by a GP [primary care physician]."[2] Anxiety and depression are still the most common mental health concerns and are generally related to a difficult life experience or bereavement, but these types of issues can also be caused by work-related issues.[3] Prolonged work stress can often lead to physical and psychological damage, causing mental issues such as anxiety and depression. Preexisting health conditions can also be aggravated by issues that take place in the working and professional world.

Thinking back to my experience at a previous job (the one I discussed in Chapter 4 where I spoke out against the discriminatory actions of my manager), it's only now I realize the level of toxicity I was subjected to in that environment. The job was sold to me as an incredible role, but within my first week, I noticed things were a bit off. During the interview process, I was told, "The office is a mess at the moment, as we are in the process of moving." Little did I know this was the story they had been telling all the new hires. The office space was extremely dark, some lights were broken, and there was no flooring. This was the backdrop to a horrible office culture where I encountered aggressive, racist management who treated staff with zero respect. The dread of going into work each day manifested in constant headaches, as a direct result of the constant stress, aggression, and pressure my management would place on all of the employees and particularly on me.

Law requires that employers are obligated to help employees with mental health and measure the potential risks of work-related mental health issues within their staff. When these risks are identified, the employer must take the steps to remove it or reduce the cause as far as reasonably possible. Employers also have legal requirements to make reasonable adjustments for preexisting physical or mental health conditions under the Equalities Legislation Act.[4] It's important to know your rights as an employee. Clearly, the company I worked for had contributed to my headaches because of its poor environment. Had I known that taking care of staff mental health was a legal requirement, maybe I would have spoken up and raised this with my manager and HR.

Are there any potential risks at your workplace that are causing you stress? Be sure to raise it with HR as soon as possible to ensure other staff members are not affected. Many workplaces now have onsite gyms to cater to employees' physical health needs, but there is still taboo around the discussion of employees' mental state in the workplace.

The stigma attached to mental health disorders often leaves employees reluctant to seek treatment or speak out, mainly due to fear that they will be risking their roles in doing so. When I have felt stressed at work, I have never spoken to anyone about it apart from my wife. I always felt that if I spoke to anyone at work, it would seem like I was not capable of dealing with the everyday pressures of the job. Former professional footballer (soccer player) Marvin Sordell is all too familiar with this type of situation.

Marvin played for a number of well-known Premier League soccer clubs and represented England at national level. He and retired at the early age of 28. He is now one of the leading ambassadors for mental health within the soccer industry in the UK.

Upon retiring, Marvin was quoted in the *Guardian* saying, "I will be a happier man," revealing that soccer is "a beautiful game with an ugly persona" and that his professional career as a player had detrimentally affected his mental health.[5] Speaking with us about his journey to better mental health, Marvin says, "The highs and lows in football [soccer] happen very rapidly. They peak and trough to the extreme, within moments of each other. Now that's fine if that's just in the context of your career and how you're performing. But if that's what's happening with your emotions, it is extremely unhealthy."

At the height of his career, Marvin was at the deepest point of his depression. Becoming stronger and more resilient following this episode made him want to share his experience to help others deal with situations like he had experienced—before it is too late. Marvin makes a really powerful point in regard to mental health: "You can't quantify mental health issues; there is no description for what it is. It doesn't look like anything; it just exists."

Knowing that people will not always be able to explain the state of their mental health is paramount. Mental illness is often described as the invisible killer. Considering the issue of not being able to speak up about mental health due to the impact it may have on your career, Marvin reveals his experience in the football (soccer) industry. "One of the reasons why poor mental health is rife within the football industry is because people talk about it when they retire from the professional level, not when they are standing in that environment because they are not sure what will happen," he says. "I'm one of only a few players who spoke about my mental health during my time playing, and it affected my career. I was dropped from games because managers thought different things. I even had a friend who said a club didn't want to sign him because they heard he was 'crazy.'"

Marvin also spoke about how the lack of players seeking help means they turn to other things to cope, such as substances and other addictions. This may feel like a solution, but in fact, it makes dealing with whatever stress or illness even harder. Co-occurring disorder or dual diagnosis is when you have both "a substance abuse problem and a mental health issue such as depression, bipolar disorder, or anxiety."[6] According to reports published in the *Journal of the American Medical Association*, around 50 percent of individuals with severe mental disorders are affected by substance abuse; 37 percent of alcohol abusers and 53 percent of drug abusers also have at least one serious mental illness; and of all people diagnosed as mentally ill, 29 percent abuse alcohol or drugs. The correlation between the two is very clear, and an article in the help guide says, "Alcohol and drugs are often used to self-medicate the symptoms of mental health problems."[7] Many people are using alcohol and drugs to ease symptoms of undiagnosed mental disorders, as this often acts as a coping mechanism to deal with their emotions or temporarily change their mood. It's important to realize that you cannot self-medicate with drugs and alcohol and that it generally leads to side effects and worsening of the symptoms you are trying to suppress. It's common to sometimes have a drink when you're feeling stressed, but there is a clear difference between doing this and abusing alcohol to cover up things by drinking it excessively.

He also addresses how toxic masculinity is rife in the industry: "Toxic masculinity is one of the biggest barriers. Being strong and tough means 'nothing hurts you.' But showing affection is to be tough, to be real, to be honest, to be vulnerable," Marvin says. "In the industry, to be 'tough,' you have to be the person that is the alpha male, [with] nothing to fix, and they never cry, and they never get upset, and they never get sad. But these people hide their issues with different things. So drinking, sex, and gambling are coping mechanisms for pain, and often in the football industry, these things are celebrated, but they shouldn't be. We sit in a changing room in a circle, but every single person in that circle is wearing a mask. Every person behind that mask is feeling something and has something going on in their life, as we all do. But nobody wants to be the first person to take that mask off, because they're the one that's different."

With experiences like this, it is not surprising that many professionals feel they cannot speak openly about their health issues. Being labeled "crazy" for your mental health issues should not be tolerated in any profession.

Marvin speaks openly and publicly on the biggest issues facing players who speak out about mental health. "The biggest areas for concern would be: how it's going to affect your career—in terms of clubs signing you, whether you'll be picked to play, but also, how fans are going to react? Finally, what will be the reactions of your friends, your club and opposition clubs?"

In Marvin's case, he talks about feeling worried about his employability (getting signed), his performance in front of his peers (the fans' reactions), the impact on his personal relationships, and how his work would stand up to his competitors (other clubs and their fans). It's a very neat explanation of an extremely unfair situation where one person, player, or employee's mental health is not prioritized within their environment, club, or business. This has to change, and it is clear to me (and to all who choose to see it) that people in senior positions in every business need to be more accountable in helping people seek help and feel comfortable about expressing their concerns.

Marvin adds that within the sports industry, toxic masculinity creates a hostile environment. He explains that people with different sexual orientations and mental illnesses are readily met with bad attitudes, bullying, and homophobia, which further contributes to the reasons why so many players cover up their issues.

RACE AND MENTAL HEALTH

Different communities have different experiences with mental health. Black men and white men experience similar levels of common mental health problems,[8] but Black women experience substantially higher rates of mental health disorders compared to their white counterparts. Racism is extremely damaging to mental health, and according to MHFA (Mental Health First Aid), in England, millions of Black and ethnic minority workers feel they can't be their "real" selves at work and need more support for their mental health.[9] In the United States, according to the Health and Human Services Office of Minority Health, Black Americans are 20 percent more likely to experience serious mental health problems than the general population,[10] with many Black Americans having trouble recognizing the signs and symptoms of mental health conditions such as anxiety and depression, which leads to them underestimating the effects on their mental health.[11]

ANXIETY, STRESS, AND DEPRESSION

Anxiety is one of the most common concerns in mental health. Feeling stressed at work is also common, but it is when this is prolonged and persistent that it starts to affect your mental and physical state. In relation to race, anxiety for Black professionals can be caused by a number of factors, including microaggressions, code switching, and imposter syndrome—all of which we will explore shortly. Stress at work is often related to pressure. Stress is not an illness in itself; it's a state of mind. Like anxiety, the longer this state continues, the higher the likelihood that a person's mental and physical health will be affected, which can result in illness.

Pressure and stress are completely different things, and it's important to make a clear distinction between the two. It's even more important to recognize when an employee is under pressure or under stress. Some degree of pressure is essential in every job, as it helps you achieve goals, meet deadlines, and reach targets. But add to this the pressure placed on Black professionals both from the individual and senior management because of the color of their skin, and you risk creating stress that can cause a number of mental and sometimes physical health problems.

Asmau Ahmed spoke about how she deals with stress and told us some of the practical measures she takes to protect her health at work. "I just remove myself from any kind of toxic environment, and just doing that alone gives me so much more peace of mind," she says. "I like my alone time. I live by a riverside park, so I run at least 6 to 8 miles a day, and just for that hour of running, I am focused on running and nothing else. I just focus on taking one step to the next."

It may be easier in some cases than others for you to leave a toxic work environment. Recognizing when to leave a space is as important as recognizing the triggers in your life that are detrimental to your mental health. Jay-Ann Lopez speaks about studying your triggers: "I think it's knowing your patterns, knowing how you react to things, knowing how you process things, so that you can counteract it," she says. "I've been through time periods of anxiety and depression when I have lost my hair as a result, and now I know when I have to stop."

The American Institute of Stress also discusses the impact of stress on physical health. New York dermatologist Doris Day says that, "When we get super stressed, our body takes a major hit. It responds by releasing hormones that increase breathing and heart rates, and our muscles get tighter and ready to respond to the perceived danger."[12] Stress hormones are actually designed to help us survive life-threatening situations, and during stress the body is on high alert, which allows us to think more clearly, which enhances our learning memory. However, during these times when that stress is piled on, our physiological response doesn't turn off and stress levels stay elevated longer than necessary. It's during these bouts that these physical symptoms begin to manifest from the inside and out."[13] This is a good reminder that not looking after our mental health can have an effect on our physical health, too.

According to Workplace Mental Health Org, "Depression costs employers an estimated $44 billion each year in lost productivity. About half of employees with depression are untreated."[14] Depression is not just about having a "bad day." It can affect the way a person feels, thinks, and acts, decreasing their ability to function well at home and at work. Depression is serious, and employers need to recognize the signs in their employees. Workers also need to recognize the signs themselves and seek appropriate help. Monitoring mental health for employees is not only the right thing to do, but also, if spotted earlier, it can save organizations a lot of money in relation to productivity.

Leaving depression untreated can have serious implications on work performance. Depression contributes to presenteeism (working while sick), employees not being engaged, and absenteeism (intentional or habitual absence from work). Like most other health conditions, early detection and effective treatment lessen the severity and impact of this condition.

MICROAGGRESSIONS

When we look at some of the challenges we discussed in Chapter 4, such as code switching, imposter syndrome, challenging stereotypes, and microaggressions, it is not surprising that Black and minority ethnic professionals encounter mental health trauma.

Black professionals' experience of daily microaggressions combined with the pressures of constant code switching (plus the actual work) can be extremely draining on mental strength. Employers should not underestimate the impact of these stressors, and how a build-up of a lifetime of microaggressions can be absolutely devastating to a Black person's health.

According to research, racism and discrimination contribute to poor health among those from the Black communities, which increases rates of depression, prolonged stress, trauma, anxiety, heart disease, and also type-2 diabetes. Dr. Joy Bradford, a licensed psychologist and speaker who examined the racial climate and microaggressions at college campuses in the United States, found that African American students experienced more depression, self-doubt, frustration, and isolation that impacted their education as a result.[15]

She explains, "The experience of having to question whether something happened to you because of your race, or constantly being on edge because your environment is hostile, can often leave people feeling invisible, silenced, angry, and resentful." Because some microaggressions are

Black professionals' experience of daily microaggressions combined with the pressures of constant code switching (plus the actual work) can be extremely draining on mental strength.

covert and subtle, it can lead to constant personal questioning and doubt. Racial gaslighting can be seen as a form of emotional abuse and is often used to manipulate a person into doubting themselves. Very similar to microinvalidations, which we discussed in Chapter 5, this undermines a person's experience through methods of denial and can have serious long-term effects.

Dr. Bradford also acknowledges that, "Increased stress related to things like microaggressions in the workplace and experiences with discrimination can lead to physical concerns like headaches, high blood pressure, and difficulties with sleep."[16] Stress headaches are very common, and it is something which I dealt with when a previous manager of mine would exhibit numerous racist behaviors. At first, these instances made me think, "Perhaps I'm in the wrong?" But it was when two or three white colleagues raised concerns with me and said that he was treating me differently that I actually felt more encouraged to speak out about it. On this occasion, I was lucky to have people who were fighting in my corner, but for the Black professionals who are going through this alone, it can be an even more traumatic experience.

So what can you do if microaggressions are currently hindering you at work and affecting your mental health? Well, first, you need to seek help. Find a safe space to talk about your worries, whether that's with colleagues, therapists, family, friends, or the senior management within your workplace. Second, remember that you are not the issue. The reason you are feeling vulnerable is not your fault. Do not change yourself or your behavior to be accepted in hostile environments. And finally, as already mentioned, if an environment is simply too toxic—know when it's time to leave.

CODE SWITCHING

We discussed code switching in Chapter 4, but we did not go into the many negative implications it can have on a Black professionals' mental health.

Myles Durkee, PhD, an assistant professor of psychology at the University of Michigan who studies code switching's mental and physiological effects, explains that, "When we force individuals to code switch, when it doesn't come natural to them, it's now a stressor." Code switching is not easy. It's stressful and, as mentioned previously, any sort of stress that occurs over prolonged periods can cause mental health issues.

Inua Ellams reiterates this point. He says, "The mental health issues faced by Black people come from the need to perform to a white audience." Playing a role every day that you have been conditioned to play is problematic. Code switching can cause mental and emotional stress for people who feel like they need to constantly modify their behavior or limit parts of their personality to succeed.

So what can you do to avoid code switching and how it affects your or your colleagues' mental health?

- **Find your tribe.** Identify people who help you feel comfortable. Many organizations now have networks for Black employees to connect and discuss issues of concern openly in a way that helps you to bring parts of yourself to work.

- **Be conscious of ways to be more inclusive.** Black colleagues often feel the need to change their behavior in order to fit in. Do your part to learn more about the cultural differences of the people you work with. Take time to understand any biases you may have and challenge them. You may not be in a position to change the entire company culture, but you can be proactive in your team to create an environment where the Black employees you work with feel more comfortable to be themselves.

- **Focus on creating a culture of belonging.** There is no point recruiting diverse talent into an organization where they feel they do not belong. Communicate the actions you intend to take to tackle under-representation across all levels of the organization. Companies should assess their culture and look to develop one of inclusion and belonging where Black employees are not under pressure to reinvent themselves to feel accepted.

IMPOSTER SYNDROME

We also considered the effects of imposter syndrome in Chapter 4—the experience of "individuals who doubt their achievements, intellect, and fear that others will expose them as fraudulent."[17]

Research shows that Black women experience imposter syndrome more than others.[18] Verbal and nonverbal messages conveyed to them that they aren't good enough, they don't belong, and they will never be as successful as their male counterparts or women of other races are messages that are portrayed to them constantly within the professional world.

For both men and women, feeling like an imposter can cause a number of stress-related issues, feelings of isolation, and lack of advancement in your career because of the fear that you don't deserve to take up that space. Anxiety in meetings with senior leaders or other team members can affect your ability to be able to lead and deliver projects.

So what can you do if you are going through this right now? Here are two things you can try to start with.

- **Change your mindset about your abilities.** Realize that you have earned your position and that you have all the skills required to succeed in this role. If you are an employer and you know someone who is struggling with this, you can support them by acknowledging their contributions, expertise, milestones, and accomplishments.

- **Avoid making comparisons to others.** "Comparison is the biggest thief of joy"[17]; focus on measuring your own success and achievements rather than comparing yourself to your peers. Success and failure are a part of life, but don't let imposter syndrome hinder you from taking new opportunities.

Marvyn Harrison, founder of Dope Black Dads, a platform designed to change the narrative around being a Black father, shares some great advice in dealing with imposter syndrome. "I had to tackle it in a very particular way, based on the things that I was finding challenging," Marvyn says. "It's not a one-size-fits-all piece of advice. But what I will say is that if you're not bringing your full self to work, you're not even in the game. Nobody's going to create an environment for you to excel in. It just doesn't happen. If you don't make it work for you, you will always be too much in your head, and you will rob the world of who you really are. So my advice is to work on being an authentic person, so that you can actually find a home for your gift."

Marvyn raises a great point. The workplace is a space that you deserve to be in, so you need to realize that you have all the skills it takes to succeed there. Allowing the effects of imposter syndrome to take over will only lead to you missing out on great opportunities.

MENTAL RESILIENCE AND BECOMING A "CORPORATE ATHLETE"

The word "athlete" is a name for someone who is proficient in sports; "corporate" describes it as related to a business or group. When we talk about being a "corporate athlete," we describe a person who is proficient in all forms of activity in the corporate world, who is able to handle any situation that arises because they are mentally healthy and therefore equipped to deal with competitive situations. When you consider some of the key traits of an athlete, it's not surprising that they are transferable to the skills required to succeed at work. When I think of an athlete, I picture someone who is dedicated, shows perseverance, can work in a team, has discipline, has leadership skills, and is resilient. When I think of leading athletes of the past and present, they all embody these characteristics.

The term "corporate athlete" was coined by Jim Loehr and Tony Schwartz in the *Harvard Business Review* in 2001.[19] In this piece, the pair explain how executives can better manage their energy to achieve sustained performance. Using lessons from the physical training regimes of top athletes, they identify why the expectation we have of employees for continuous high-level performance is counterproductive and works in opposition to the outcomes business leaders desire.[20]

Considering the consistency of good performance, Jim and Tony explain that to consistently perform well in high-stress environments, executives must focus on more than the skills they need specific to their field, but more broadly on living a life that fulfills them physically, emotionally, mentally, and spiritually. Creating balance in all areas of your life must be achieved before you can create excellence in work.

As a corporate athlete, success is heavily reliant on good mental health—it requires focus, resilience, and the capacity to think broadly. However, the corporate athlete must pay attention to all aspects of their body—they cannot keep up their high-level performance without ensuring they are physically well.

Corporate professionals who neglect their bodies risk burning out. Pay attention to diet, exercise, sleep, and a program of physical well-being cannot be ignored when excellence is the objective. Shellye Archambeau is intentional about her diet and wellness and ensures she looks after her body. She says, "I need to exercise, and I need to eat three healthy meals a day. I bring my own lunch to work because I want to make sure I eat something healthy. If I haven't brought my lunch, then I might be tempted to go grab something not so healthy," she says. "I eat breakfast, and I make sure I eat dinner. I eat well, and that's important to how I feel. So, as long as I'm getting exercise and I'm eating right, that's the right foundation for me. The third thing I need is to get my energy from people. So I have to build in activities that involve others." Shellye understands the importance of exercise, healthy eating, and spending time in good company. These things are crucial for her to be able to have a productive day.

Trevor Nelson also pays attention to his physical health and limits his alcohol intake, as well as acknowledging the toll overworking can have on our physical appearance. "I'm not a massive drinker or anything like that," he says. "I'm conscious of my health because at some point 20 years ago, I was working so hard that I was killing myself, to be honest."

Working hard and not resting can have extremely damaging long-term effects on an individual. Rest is a key component for the corporate athlete, and Trevor acknowledges that to maintain a successful career in the music industry, he could not keep up the momentum of work without proper rest.

The corporate athlete must be emotionally aware and pay attention to their emotional state. The person who allows emotions such as anger or frustration to overcome them could land themselves in trouble. Let's use another example. When a soccer player is visibly frustrated during a game, it's a manager's job to substitute them to keep them from getting a penalty card, but it is also the player's job to calm down on the field if they want to avoid being substituted by their boss or sent off by the referee.

As a corporate athlete, knowing how to control your emotions is imperative for success. If you truly want to be excellent, this ability cannot be taken for granted.

Being able to control our attention helps us stay focused on what matters, and also is key in helping us recover from stress or trauma. Athletes who are at the top of their game are also able to use their mental stress to turn their attention away from negative and destructive thoughts and, in some extremes, away from physical pain to be able to continue performing to the highest level when it matters most.

Sometimes there are things that won't go your way at work or in business. It's deciding to let go and separating your emotions that will allow you to put in a great performance. When you are able to do that, your performance will go from good to great.

"The football [soccer] world is an oppressive environment where you as a person almost don't exist," Marvin Sordell says about dealing with emotions and separating yourself from negative thoughts. "You are not a person with feelings, but a financial figure that fits into a group of larger numbers—that's how football players are predominantly seen. When you look at how fans interact with players, they are mainly focused on performance of the team. They don't care about anything else, or that a player has their own life, their own things going on, their own issues, or own families."

When players go home from work, they are not allowed to break away from that life like most people. Other people are able to leave the physical space of work, and they can just break away from it at that moment. The soccer industry is very different from the professional world in the sense that, even after the game, you have to deal with the results. If it's a good result for your team, you can go home and be happy, but if it's a bad result, then you're taking this home with you and have to deal with the media and social media commenting about your performance. In an industry where the world knows when you are not performing well, it can be extremely difficult to detach from work, but it is vital even for the professional soccer player to be able to control their emotions and switch off so they can recover from the stress or disappointment of a previous game. The same goes for us, too.

Journalist Charlene White tells us about how she finds ways to separate her emotions from the serious issues she reports. She speaks about how she took responsibility for her own self-care, but also that of her viewers, during the tragic killing of George Floyd in 2020. "At the height of the Black Lives Matter protests following George Floyd's murder, I was on maternity leave, but when I returned to work, the story was still in the headlines. It was hard. Because of my position at ITV news, I had a responsibility to get other people to understand how impactful that story was," she says.

"It was about getting people to understand that using that footage gratuitously over and over again has an impact on the viewers. There needed to be an understanding that this footage was real, his a human life, that we were witnessing someone be lynched in public. This footage can be really upsetting for people. So my role within the media was always to get the viewers to understand someone else's perspective, and doing that isn't an easy task at all.

The nature of the job means that I'm exposed to so many upsetting stories. Covering the earthquakes in Haiti was a really difficult news story for me to report, because my parents are from the Caribbean, and seeing so many Black people in so much distress and just so much death was hard. I had to be able to navigate that reaction as a journalist and still be able to tell the story. As a reporter, I see being able to control my emotions as a key ingredient to being able to work in this industry."

Charlene continues, "People say that journalists have to be a little bit cold-hearted, because we wouldn't be able to do our jobs on a daily basis and tell so many emotional stories otherwise." Charlene's ability to separate her emotions from her job has helped her become one of the best-established news reporters in the UK and shows she is using a key attribute of the corporate athlete.

On a spiritual level, the corporate athlete must discover meaning in their life—why they are doing what they are doing, what is important to them, and the values that they present in their work. It may seem strange to have this as a key characteristic, but it is your sense of purpose and what people call your "why" that is key to helping you avoid burnout and giving you a sense of drive and determination when you feel you can't continue. When I think about some of the late nights I spent working on the UK Black Business Show, I know it's my drive and determination that helped me continue when I felt like giving up. I'm also a man of faith and often reflect on the verse from Joshua 1:9, which says, "Be strong and courageous; do not be frightened and do not be dismayed, for the Lord your God is with you wherever you go."

Angelica Nwandu shares how a relationship with God helps her on a spiritual level to be able to relax. She says,

"One thing I will say is I don't overwork myself. I'm very close to God and there is a scripture in Proverbs 10:22 that says, 'The blessing of the Lord brings wealth without the painful toil for you.'[21] The way that I've always interpreted that statement was that God could provide wealth without you having to stress every day about how you're going to get it. There are some people who literally stress over strategizing their whole life to become a billionaire. I sometimes feel that we don't know how God is using us. I know how God is using me. It's not the obvious way, but I know what he has shown me and how the end will be. In life, you have to work hard, try and rely on Him."

It is Angelica's faith in God that gives her a sense of

purpose. It keeps her motivated when she does not have strength. As a professional, it's important to take some time to think about what it is that motivates you, and what helps you to keep going.

You must nourish all areas of your life so you can maintain high-level performance in your career. Consider how you can take care of your physical, mental, emotional, and spiritual health as a means to improve your success at work.

AVOIDING BURNOUT

Burnout is something that many working people are aware of and often unable to prevent. "Burnout is described as a state of emotional, physical, and mental exhaustion caused by excessive and prolonged stress. It occurs when you feel overwhelmed, emotionally drained, and unable to meet constant demands."[22]

David McQueen shares how he manages his energy to avoid burnout but maintain good form. "Working smart includes mental health as well. I don't work on Saturdays. Discipline for me is to be able to just shut down my work. Nothing is that important," he says. "While I'm here, I've got to be able to look after myself and ensure I have a support network around me that champions me to make sure that I look after myself." It's about your work environment and relationships—are there things you can change to improve your ability to simply step away from work, like David?

He continues,

"The one thing that made a massive difference for me was focus. As an entrepreneur, focusing on that one thing that's

going to make the difference and that's going to bring in the money is important. I have around 17 different business ideas running through my head. My wife says, 'unless you can show me how you're gonna make half a million, then you need to put it in the bin.'

The second thing for me, which made a massive difference, was systems. What do I mean by systems? One of the beautiful things about technology now is how much stuff you can automate. Whether you're putting out content or you're dealing with invoices, if you build a system properly, you won't need to work all hours of the night. A lot of the mental well-being we talked about is because we don't switch off, or our phone always has alerts popping up. The last part of that system is your support network. Those people who will champion you are not afraid to pull you up and say, 'Listen, why are you working this late?'"

David raises some great points about how focusing on what really matters is key to avoiding burnout. So many businesspeople try to juggle too many things at one time, and this can in fact make you less productive.

Jay-Ann Lopez also discusses burnout. "I feel like as a creative it's hard to stop, because everyone's always going in," she says. "There's always new content, there's always a new trend, there's always something new. But sometimes you just have to understand that you are not a machine. Sometimes you just have to pull away. So once I shut off, I shut off. I grew up thinking it was a bad thing, but actually, it's not. It's good to be able to just let go and then come back on Monday, ready to get into the game."

As someone who is in charge of a community of gamers,

Jay also explains how she takes a break, knowing they rely on her for content. "I just tell them in advance that I'm taking a break. When Trina and I go away for Curlture work, I tell them I'm not logging on unless it's something urgent," she says. "Have a structure in place to delegate tasks also."

Angelica Nwandu says that just before she gets to the point of burnout, she takes action and shuts down. "I'll go off the map, go get a massage, or go to therapy," she says. "I'll still communicate with my staff, but I won't do anything like answer any emails or anything. Sometimes it's necessary to shut down and take some space to ensure that you can recover from overstimulation properly."

WORK-LIFE BALANCE

Finding a work-life balance seems to be a struggle for everyone. The term seems to have grown in use more than ever in the last few years. It appeals to millennials in the workplace who, according to reports, are set to take up 75 percent of the workforce by 2025.[23]

Dr. Wayne Frederick, who balances the life of a surgeon with being President of a university, explains what he believes a work-life balance is:

"You have to be organized and you have to prioritize. On a day-to-day, week-to-week, month-to-month, and year-to-year basis, you have to know what is most important to you and stay focused on achieving those goals. Productivity is not about doing everything with the same level of passion—it is about doing some things and not others, as well as allotting only the energy that each task deserves. You also have to make sure that your

journey is never complete, that you're constantly refilling your well with new passions and projects that inspire you to keep moving toward new targets."

Companies that are able to incorporate balance into their structure will see huge benefits for staff productivity. Having a work-life balance allows you to reduce stress and avoid burnout.

We spoke with Marvyn Harrison, and he described in depth how he relaxes, but also how he manages his time so that he can spend time with his family and have personal time for himself.

"One day, when I was really tired and feeling stressed out, I was like, 'You know what? I'm gonna have a bath.' I just wanted to sit somewhere and not be disturbed listening to my Erykah Badu playlist uninterrupted. At the end of it, I actually cried. I was like, 'Who knew that this was so amazing?' I also order myself cookies and shortbread, and it's sheer gratuitous nonsense, but it's important. I am super intentional about my recharge."

It's great to hear how passionate Marvyn is about his rest time. In addition, Marvyn also ensures that he can spend quality time with his wife and children, and like his personal time, he is very intentional about doing this.

"Monday and Friday mornings, I make sure I stay at home and take my son to school. I spend an hour or two with my 3-year-old daughter. I sit with her and just listen.

Friday, Saturday, Sunday, and Monday, I'll be with the

kids, then Tuesday, Wednesday, and Thursday, I probably work 12- to 15-hour days and I try to put as much into that space as humanly possible, and that works for me. My wife and I have intentional time; we have like an hour and a half in the evenings and we ringfence it to protect the time. Ringfencing time means that I'm not sitting there feeling like a bad father or a bad husband, and it also just means that everyone knows when it's time for Marvyn."

Pamela Hutchinson also shares how she uses family time to be able to relax and switch off from the corporate world:

"Family is really important to me, and family's really important to a lot of Black people. I think that's just at the heart, the heart of everything, family, eating, and coming together.

Food is central to who we are, and for me, keeping my sanity means going back to my roots—it's going back to the food, it's sitting with people I know and feeling comfortable. It's, you know, slipping into my dialect at home when I need to, and that's what keeps me grounded and reminds me of who I am. In the world that we work in, it's so easy to get sucked in and absorbed by it and suddenly not recognize and forget who you are, who you really are."

Being an entrepreneur has its own unique stress, and it is important that you know how to manage yourself and be aware of the signs and signals of when your body is telling you to stop.

When we spoke with India Gary-Martin, she rejected

the phrase "work-life balance" and believes that you cannot have a balance, as ultimately one will suffer. "I don't know about this work-life balance thing," she says. "Work-life balance is elusive because it doesn't exist. I think that it's work-work, or life-life, and not very often do the two meet in between. Something's going to suffer regardless. So if you're working, your life is going to suffer, and if you're living, work suffers—that's just the reality. You can't be in two places at one time doing both; it does not work."

India raises an important question: Is a work-life balance unachievable? Does one have to suffer? Or can you actually create a balance between two hectic schedules?

Continuing, India says, "The question is, what are you going to sacrifice in this moment? Because frankly, that's what it boils down to. Now you can make some decisions about what you're not going to do at work—for example, saying, 'I'm not going to work past this time.' You can put some boundaries around it if you want to if you have that level of control, but the balancing is a myth."

June Angelidis talks about how she ensures she finds balance by also setting her own boundaries and not working past certain times of day. She also finds time to do things that she enjoys while recognizing that she can't say "yes" to every opportunity. "I think the key has been delegating 100 percent where I can, so on the days I'm working, I am conscious to sleep early," June says.

"I'm very, very, very firm on not working past 5 p.m., because when the kids get back from school, I want to spend time with them. I want to be home so I can make dinner. Cooking is part of my self-care, and having that creative time to make what I want and then hanging out

with the kids playing games.

I also enjoy sitting down and watching something on Netflix or just having a call with my friends. When I'm being disciplined, I will practice yoga, which I think is really important. I love baking and gardening, and I'm just very intentional to not overstretch myself or say 'yes' to too many things. I've gotten comfortable with saying 'no.' I need to leave time for me and my family, because when you get pulled in too many directions, you're not helping anyone when you break down."

Whether you opt to balance or juggle work and life, it is helpful to find separation between the two to make time for you.

DEALING WITH SUCCESS

There is a lot of discussion about how you deal with failure, but how do you deal with success?

Trevor Nelson speaks about dealing with success. He says,

"You know, there's an illusion that you've 'got the life' when you 'make it,' when in reality, maybe you haven't yet. It is really important that a Black person who's successful knows it's very, very lonely when you get to certain stages. When you've got your real best friends is when you have nothing. You're sharing the tango, getting the night bus, excited about getting into a club, but the moment one of you steps out and becomes successful, everyone's on your coattails to begin with, but that can easily change. When you trailblaze, there's a problem with that; no one understands how you're

doing it, no one understands what you're doing or the time
you may need to sacrifice with friends to achieve this."

A phrase my father-in-law always says that sticks with me is, "Twenty children cannot play together for twenty years." As we progress in our careers, we may develop new hobbies, our way of thinking may change, we may develop a more intense schedule, meaning that we are unable to spend our time as we did before. In some cases, you may notice that you have less in common with your friends and with others the relationships may remain the same.

Acknowledge that friendship dynamics may change but that drifting apart doesn't make you a bad person or the other people bad people. Moving on is a part of life, and it happens in all areas of our lives.

SEEKING HELP

So you recognize you need help—you've noticed the symptoms and all the signs of anxiety, depression, burnout, or other potential mental health struggles. So what do you do next? Asking for help is not easy, but it is vital for maintaining good mental health or recovering from and managing mental-ill health. Getting help is brave and is not a weak thing to do.[24]

For anyone who is struggling mentally, The Mental Health Foundation says that talking to people is the right step in getting help.

It all starts with talking; when you talk about your feelings, this is the first step to taking charge of your mental health. No one can help you if you are not speaking about your concerns; you have a number of options, whether that's family and friends, someone close to you, community groups, therapy, peer support, and online communities—reach out to them.

Mental health advocate Marvin Sordell leaves us with some vital words: "Showing affection is to be tough, is to be real, to be honest, to be vulnerable." Speaking out and getting help about your issues is the bravest thing you can do; hiding your problems benefits no one. I urge you, if you are going through any of the issues raised in the chapter, to speak to the relevant person and get help.

For information on mental health services you can access, please refer to the Glossary starting on page 336.

NEXT STEPS AND REFLECTION

- Do you think you may be suffering from anxiety, stress, or depression?

- Is it time for you to seek expert help?

- What steps can you take to overcome imposter syndrome? Write down 10 things about yourself and your personality that makes you great at what you do.

- How can you become a corporate athlete? Write down one thing that you value about each of the four types of health: physical, mental, emotional, and spiritual.

- What can you do to relax when you are not working? How can you start to build healthy work-life habits?

"ALLY"—IT'S A DOING WORD

What It Really Means to Support the Black Community by *Opeyemi Sofoluke*

"ANY REAL CHANGE IMPLIES THE BREAKUP OF THE WORLD AS ONE HAS ALWAYS KNOWN IT, THE LOSS OF ALL THAT GAVE ONE AN IDENTITY, THE END OF SAFETY. YET, IT IS ONLY WHEN A MAN IS ABLE, WITHOUT BITTERNESS OR SELF-PITY, TO SURRENDER A DREAM HE HAS LONG POSSESSED THAT HE IS SET FREE—HE HAS SET HIMSELF FREE—FOR HIGHER DREAMS, FOR GREATER PRIVILEGES."
—JAMES BALDWIN[1]

A few years ago, I was traveling with a colleague and we got into a conversation about race. This led us to other topics, including the Civil Rights Movement, and eventually we landed on slavery. As a passing comment, I said, "There are some eras I am so thankful I was not born into. I really don't know how I would survive that kind of life." After I made this remark, my colleague paused, then he sighed. With a look of remorse, he said, "Wow, that thought has never crossed my mind." As a white male in his forties, he had never wondered what life would have been like if he had been born in the 17th century and sold as a slave. In that moment, I realized that even the most well-meaning allies do not and cannot truly understand our struggle. Many white and non-Black people cannot comprehend what it is like to live in our world. They have not had to put themselves in our shoes. Our history is not their history, our pain is not their pain, our struggles are certainly not their struggles, but their privilege is often at our expense. White people have been born with an exterior layer of protection, which grants them societal advantages that safeguard them against the negative effects of systemic and institutional racism. That conversation with my colleague not only highlighted to me that we really are from different worlds, it reinforced that his world is a world laced with white privilege.

What is privilege? I am sure you could spot it in its most obvious forms, like male privilege over women who did not have the same voting rights as men in the United Kingdom until 1928, or able-bodied privilege, where you do not have to constantly consider disability access as you plan your journey around busy cities like London or New York. By definition, privilege is described as a special advantage, immunity, permission, right, or benefit granted to or enjoyed by an individual, class, or caste. Such an advantage, immunity, or right is exercised to the exclusion of others.[2] The James Baldwin quote at the beginning of this chapter addresses the outcome and impact of change, but not just any kind of change—the type of change that results in the surrendering of unearned privilege and power. It's a type of change that can be uncomfortable for those who have been enjoying the benefits of marginalization, because ultimately if a group of people are being marginalized, then surely another group somewhere is reaping the benefits and it's those people, the beneficiaries, that can make a change.

Introducing allyship. At its core, allyship is about recognizing that you experience privilege of some kind and making a conscious decision to use your privilege as a strategic mechanism to create opportunities, challenge injustice, and encourage equality. To be an effective ally, it is absolutely necessary to understand and unpack what your privilege offers you and how you can use this to be an agent of change. Before we consider ways in which people can be better allies, it is important to establish that while the focus of our particular discussion is based on race, allyship as a concept is by no means limited to conversations around race. As Angeliki Fanouria Giannaki asserts in her article, "The Role of 'Privileged' Allies in the Struggle for Social Justice," there are multiple factors that can make a person an ally: "Allyship cannot be defined merely on the basis of binaries such as Black and White, oppressed and oppressor, less and more privileged. For privilege itself cannot be determined only through the variables of race and class. Rather, it is multidimensional, shaped by intersectionalities, that is, by the combination of each individual's multiple identities and lived experiences." An ally, therefore, is a person who by virtue of their privilege (whatever that privilege is) refuses to accept the "that's just the way it is" narrative of society and is willing to stand up against systemic issues such as we saw take place in 2020.

The year 2020 was one like no other. For many, it was a heavy year that brought about a drastic shift in the way we now "do" life. The abrupt and devastating effects of the COVID-19 pandemic threw us a curveball we never expected. Not only were we all forced to accept a restricted version of life, with limits placed on how and when we moved around and socialized, we were told that this way of life would be the "new normal." In the midst of this chaos, news reports on the impact of the pandemic began to highlight and exacerbate existing disparities in the socioeconomic conditions between Black and white communities, Black and minority ethnic people were at greater risk of catching and dying from the virus.[3] Sadly, this reality was consistent across the United States and UK. COVID-19 impacted Black communities in a disproportionate way. As the racial implications of the pandemic were being uncovered, tensions heightened as footage of police brutality was broadcast across our social media feeds. I specifically recall sitting in my living room a few days after the murder of George Floyd, scrolling through my Twitter feed and just crying. It was tiring and traumatic. Post after post was a story of some kind of violence against Black people rooted in racism. Old events resurfaced, and more recent incidents were reshared.

It became apparent that not only were we in the middle of fighting the pandemic, there was another virus we needed to deal with—racism. A virus that institutions have perpetuated for centuries in order to uphold and maintain the interests of the majority. In the posts I saw, white civilians and police alike exercised a blatant and unapologetic disregard for Black lives. I felt triggered. How could all of this still be happening in the 21st century? How was it okay for a white man to shoot a Black man on his morning run because he "looked suspicious"? How was it okay for police to barge into a couple's home unannounced in the middle of the night and kill an innocent woman by firing eight shots toward her room as she lay in her bed? How was it okay for a white woman to be so bold as to use her whiteness as a weapon by calling the police on an innocent Black man and mentioning his race, knowing full well the implications of her actions? How was it okay to read news reports with the headline: "Police have killed at least one Black man or woman every week in 2020 in the United States"?[4] How was any of this okay?

As I sat down watching horrific videos of Black people suffering at the hands of mainly white people, I cried. I cried because I felt helpless. I cried because I was angry. And I cried because despite the fight for equality that had been ongoing for decades, despite the passing of legislation to address explicit forms of systemic racism and discrimination, such as the Civil Rights Act of 1964—and in the UK, the Race Relations Act of 1965—I could see no change. I was not alone in my observation. Ciara LeRoy, a professional artist and founder of Pretty Strange Design, agrees:

"In 2020, we saw a lot of virtue signaling. People wanted to be a part of the conversation and didn't want to appear like they weren't woke or didn't care. So they were putting something out there, even though it may not have been super well thought out. After the moment had passed on social media, they moved on and didn't do anything in their daily lives as privileged people to break down and dismantle oppression. And this is the work that needs to be done. It is the hard work that remains after the vast share of people have moved on. That's why these systems persist."

For Herman Bulls, allyship is important and should not be confused with performative allyship: "What I've been talking about in my speeches is the concept of 'optical allyship.' Such people, in their mind, probably truly, truly think that they are an ally, but as a result of their unconscious bias and their tendency to enact microaggressions, they aren't," he says.

The proliferation of social media as a news source has contributed to the rise of such allies—people who believe that just "resharing a post" is enough. While it is good to have an active online presence, if that does not translate offline into measurable action or tangible results, then does it matter?

Herman shares how he approaches topics on race when giving speeches: "In my speeches, what I'll do is, I'll say, 'Hey, who here feels that they have unconscious bias?'" Herman notes that the response of his audience is usually along the lines of, "Yeah, yeah, I've got it." People are open to acknowledging bias when it is considered to be unconscious. Herman usually follows up this question with a direct and challenging response: "Okay, who in here is racist?" This question is often answered with an awkward silence. Herman then explains that at this point, he continues his speech in such a way that will cause his audience to reflect on their bias. Herman's response is typically along the lines of, "Here's the question: is it possible that your unconscious bias could be perceived by the recipient of it as racist?" Herman continues, "And I've had people come to me saying, 'I just never thought of that.' In their mind, they are thinking, 'I am the least racist person I've ever seen in my life. I don't see color. I don't see color; I just see ability.' You know, and that's when my antennae go up." Herman explains that it's that sense of self-adulation and self-promotion, of constantly wanting to be perceived as a "good person," that can get in the way of being a true ally.

Acknowledging the challenge and struggles that the Black community experience requires you to see color—it requires you to be attentive to the differences in experiences people face because of their color, and so to not see color is to be dismissive of the challenges Black people face because of their appearance.

There are so many people that are experts in "talking the talk," or, in some cases "posting the post," but not as many people are genuinely making the effort to *walk the talk*. Some of you may have gone on marches and, don't get me wrong, such demonstrations are important. But after the march, after holding up posters, after all the hashtags—what's next? Well, it's the actions you take in your day-to-day lives that can have a real impact on Black lives. No matter how small or big, it is action that creates results.

So where do we go from here? There are a number of ways to become an active ally, and I will share my recommendations along with the valuable insights from some of our contributors. Again, while this list is not exhaustive, it provides a starting point. My hope is that, as you read this, you will be able to reflect and consider how you can take action to make a difference.

UNDERSTAND YOUR PRIVILEGE

For anyone with the desire to be an ally, it is incumbent that you, as a white or non-Black person, are able to recognize and understand how your race can afford you certain types of privilege. This is not to say that you do not face challenges or have not encountered struggles; rather, it is about recognizing how in some circumstances, your race has not been the reason for those challenges. In taking the time to reflect on this, you may be able to spot scenarios in your life where you have been at an advantage because of your race. We spoke to ally Oliver Holmes, Head of Diversity and

To not see color is to be dismissive of the challenges Black people face because of their appearance.

Inclusion at Browne Jacobson LLP, who shared how and when he began to recognize his privilege as a white man:

"I grew up with a very diverse set of friends. Where I was living at the time as a child, we had a big Ghanaian and Nigerian community. And so I grew up surrounded by diversity, thinking that was the norm. That was my life. My friends were all very different to each other, so it wasn't until I was a teenager that I thought not only about white privilege, but privilege in general. When I got into my twenties and entered the working world, I realized that these environments did not reflect the community I grew up in. It makes you think, 'Something is not right here.' I just thought, 'Wow, how lucky am I to have so many friends from very different places with different experiences who have just enriched my life for the better.'"

Oliver's experience of realizing that the working world did not reflect the community he grew up in may be familiar to the experiences of many Black people.

Oliver continues, "There had been times where my Black friends and I would go out to the shop, and they would get followed around by security guards, and I wouldn't. We were the same age, we were from the same place, we spoke the same language, we would dress very similarly—there was absolutely no difference to us, except the color of our skin," he says. "This was when we were like 16 or 17, and it was only when we talked about it that I realized it was just the reality for them when they went shopping. I remember, I was just astounded that that could happen for no reason. So that's when I really became aware of race and ethnicity and the biases that people have."

Comparing this to the way racial bias exhibits itself in the workplace, Oliver shares, "Going into the corporate world, you then start to really unpick the more subtle behaviors. It could be anything from not inviting people to lunch, or giving some people certain types of work and other people other kinds of work, or not putting people on a platform," he says.

> "That's when I really became aware of it at a more corporate and more sinister level because it wasn't outward exclusion—it's very subtle, but it was very, very obvious to me. So I can only imagine what it was like for my Black friends and colleagues at the time. That's when I really started finding my voice in speaking up for other people. The burden of that shouldn't fall on them. It should be for anyone in the room who witnesses anything like that to say, 'This is not right.' In terms of finding your voice and realizing your privilege, I think I knew mine quite early on. But there's no point in realizing it if you're not going to do anything about it."

As you recognize your privilege, begin to identify ways to use it for good. Giving up your privilege may feel like "the breakup of the world as one has always known it" or "the end of safety," but as research shows, time and time again, a more diverse and inclusive world opens us all up to greater benefits.

DO YOUR HOMEWORK

You cannot expect to become an ally by taking no ownership when it comes to learning about the Black community. Self-educate; be ready and willing to take the time to learn and familiarize yourself with the challenges faced by the Black community. As Arlan Hamilton puts it, "It's up to you to be educated. It's up to you to learn what you need to learn and not put it on us to teach you everything, and then applaud you for everything."

If you want to develop a new skill, you have to make a conscious effort to research, study, and learn about whatever skill it is you are trying to build. Similarly, if you are really passionate about being an ally, be ready to do the work. When I started my career, I remember a good piece of advice from my first manager. He said, "If you don't understand something, don't just come and ask me for the answer. Be proactive and try to figure it out yourself first. If you try a number of things and still feel like you have not found the answer you're looking for, then come and find me, and when I ask you what you have already tried, you will be able to demonstrate that you have made an effort to figure it out."

The key word here is "effort." Effort cannot be achieved without action. Effort requires that you do something. That is the essence of allyship—doing something, taking actions to make a positive difference, and that can start by simply doing your research. Take time to develop an understanding of how our experiences differ to the "AME" in BAME (Black, Asian, and minority ethnic). Look into why the term BAME can be problematic when exploring the challenges of the Black community. Whether you prefer to read books and articles, listen to podcasts, or watch films and documentaries, there are a plethora of resources available that can provide a great starting point in your journey of understanding race and racism as it pertains to the Black community.

Rondette Amoy-Smith provides a great analogy on this:

"The way I look at being an ally is this: imagine you visit a country like Mexico, Jamaica, Peru, China, Thailand, Italy, wherever. And you love the cuisine that you're getting there. When you get back, you're not gonna run up on a Mexican person and say, 'Hey! Teach me how to make tacos; in fact, make it for me.' You're not going to do that. After you get back from your vacation, you'll look for a recipe or a cookbook, and figure out how to do it. You're going to go to the supermarket, pick up your ingredients, and you're going to do the work."

Rondette explains that after buying all the ingredients, the next step would be to go to your kitchen and attempt to make the dish. Of course, as a rookie chef, you may make some errors along the way, but the important thing is you are trying.

She continues, "After you've tried it and you realize you've made a complete blunder, and it's not perfect because it's not native to you, you're going to call your Mexican co-worker or friend and say, 'Can you help me understand where I might have gone wrong? Did I miss an ingredient out?' That's when they'll be able to say, 'Well, actually, you probably put too much oregano, or you should have probably put a bit more tomato, and here's how you do it.'"

For Rondette, this kind of approach allows for a greater dialogue, as an individual demonstrates genuine interest and passion. "You've got to demonstrate that you have tried, you've attempted to do it, you looked up all the ingredients, you bought the ingredients, you used the ingredients," Rondette says. "So now we can have a dialogue. I can stand there side-by-side with you in the kitchen and we can do it together. That's how I view allyship."

Rondette's analogy is spot on. While it is easier to simply ask a Black person to tell you how to better support the Black community or how to be a better ally, you will learn more by taking the proactive step of educating yourself before asking those questions. Once you have taken this step, you can further enhance your knowledge and understanding by listening to the experiences of those who are willing to share.

LISTEN WITH UNDERSTANDING

While it should not be the responsibility of Black people to constantly play the role of an educator, we recognize the power of telling our stories. When asked whether it should be the role of Black employees to teach their colleagues about racism, India Gary-Martin emphasizes that, "It is not the role of Black employees by any stretch of the imagination. We cannot solve something we did not create. However, as painful as it may be, we have to participate—if we can."

Our participation, particularly in a work or business environment, provides a level of insight that only we can bring. As an ally, it is important that when you have those very important conversations, you listen with a teachable mindset.

Following the murder of George Floyd in 2020, many organizations began to engage in conversations on racism.[5] Glenda McNeal shares her experience of breaking down to a white colleague how it feels to be a Black working mother in this climate. "As a Black woman who is performing at a high level, who has achieved success, who seemingly has a life that's 'similar' to that of a high-achieving white person, you think of me in that way, but you don't think of me as a

Black mother. A Black mother who had to sit my preschool age child down to have 'that conversation,'" Glenda says.

"Now, we all have the conversation about the 'birds and the bees,' but there are two other conversations we have to have. One when our kids are young, to talk about how someone may call you a name, someone may not let you play with them, someone might judge you because of the color of your skin or the kind of hair you have. These kinds of conversations take away from the magic of that child's childhood at a very, very young age. And you, as a white person, you don't have to have that conversation.

The other conversation is when it's time for my Black son to drive a car or to be out at night. And I have to say, 'If you're stopped by police, this is what you're supposed to do, and this is how you're supposed to act.' Real conversations like this give allies an idea of the kind of world we live in.

Allyship is about having those uncomfortable conversations to understand my experience so that you can share in it and then you can empathize and be a voice for me. It is less about just saying 'I'm an ally'; it's really about the action that goes behind those words. As an ally, allowing yourself to be uncomfortable in the conversation so you learn more is so important, because when you have understanding, you can shut down bad conversations and you are able to speak from a more informed position. It's really hard for you to empathize with me if you don't understand my situation."

For some people, however, talking about their personal experiences of racism can be extremely difficult and upsetting.

I remember watching a Sky News interview where journalist Mark Austin interviewed former West Indies cricketer Michael Holding on racism in the UK. It was moving to see the emotion Michael was overcome with as he shared with the viewers his experiences and his hope for change. As pain-filled tears left his eyes, Michael expressed that he recognized change would be a slow process but urged us all to keep going, "Even if it's a baby step at a time, even if its snail's pace, I am hoping it will continue in the right direction."[6]

In your conversations with Black people, be aware of how topics around race and racism can open up old and, in some cases, fresh wounds. Be conscious of this and avoid telling people how to feel. Though well-intentioned, comments like, "Try not to let it bother you" or "Just ignore their ignorance" can invalidate how a Black person feels. So listen and be thoughtful in your response. Many Black people have experienced racial gaslighting when sharing their experiences; we've been told that we're overthinking, overreacting, or "playing the race card." Such remarks undermine our very real and lived experiences.

Omar Wasow explains,

"One of the simplest things you can do is just listen. I think a lot of times having privilege means that you feel like you know the answer or you understand somebody's problem. To really sit and listen with empathy takes a certain kind of intention and work, a quieting of your own ego. It's not just listening, but listening with empathy and really trying to hear what it is somebody is feeling. Sometimes something can seem quite trivial to you as somebody who might have privilege or power, but for that person who has experienced something 50 times before, it is a raw spot where they are

mistreated in a particular way again, and again, and again. Let's take something simple, like a mispronunciation of a name. It may be easy to say 'That's not a big deal, right?' But if it's part of a way in which people repeatedly disregard your humanity, or maybe it's done intentionally, it's going to sting a little more. I think being able to hear with empathy is important; it's not just about the specific facts, but about the history that somebody might bring to a moment."

Recognize that the stories you hear are coming from people who have had to find ways to deal with the emotions related to those situations. So listen with the willingness to learn.

For any Black person reading or listening to this that has been asked to tell your story, India has some advice: "If it's too traumatic, it's okay to say, 'I'm not in a space to do/discuss that.' That's okay. There are plenty of Black people who are prepared to have those conversations. I'm one of them for sure." India jokes, "I'm like, 'Listen, what y'all need to do is this ...' And so, I think that there are enough of us who are prepared to have the conversation and we can be the barrier for those that aren't, and there's no shame in that. Because, frankly, the trauma and grief that people have experienced and are continuing to experience because of being Black in Western societies means that, for some of us, having this conversation is all too draining."

Pamela Hutchinson shares her recommendations for Black people who are tired of talking. "I was having a conversation the other day with somebody who said, 'You know what, Pamela? I'm tired of talking about race to white people ... Why do I have to educate them? I've learned to navigate in their world. Why can't they just learn to navigate in mine?' And I said, 'Look, you know what, it's frustrating and it's tiring, and I hate doing it, too. But the reality is, they didn't wake up in our world, and they have not walked in our shoes, and they do not know our experiences, and the only way they'll know is through us sharing in order to raise people's level of awareness and engagement.'"

So as you listen to our experiences, show an appreciation of what it has taken for us to share our stories. Be thoughtful; be kind.

GET COMFORTABLE WITH BEING UNCOMFORTABLE

As an ally, you may find yourself in conversations that are awkward or uncomfortable—in fact, that should be expected. To tackle workplace racism, it is necessary that you create spaces for honest conversations to take place, regardless of how these discussions make you feel. It is important to be able to get past the awkwardness of difficult dialogue. If Black people sharing their experiences makes you uncomfortable to the point that you choose not to read, watch, or hear our stories, then you are not ready to be an ally. Such behavior demonstrates that you are either unable to come to terms with the reality of your privilege, or you want to hold onto your privilege. Either way, it says to a Black person, "Your pain makes me feel uneasy, so I'd rather not hear about it. I'd rather remain in my bubble of ignorance." This is not the attitude to have. It is not about you and how you feel, it's about taking the steps to change the spheres you find yourself in.

If you really want to support the cause and develop as a true ally, you must learn to stop focusing on your feelings and start focusing on the bigger picture. Don't be afraid to make mistakes; the fear of getting it wrong or causing offense often causes many to shy away from being allies, but understand that this will be part of the process. Remember Rondette's analogy about making a particular cuisine? Again, you might make a mistake, but the fact that you have made an effort is what matters. Take time to learn, be patient, and exercise a level of grace as you develop on this journey. Keep the goal in mind, build resilience, and continue to push for change. If you really want to be committed for the long haul, stop focusing on your feelings and take action.

USE YOUR VOICE

I don't know what it is about the phrase "use your voice," but whenever I hear it, a particular scene from *Sister Act 2: Back in the Habit* comes to my mind. Sister Mary Clarence, who is played by Whoopi Goldberg, has been training her class of mischievous yet musically talented high school students to sing as a choir. After much practice, the group of students prepare for their first performance in front of the school. As they start singing, "Oh Happy Day," the nerves and timidity of the newly formed choir would have you thinking that they were singing a more somber chorus. But with some encouragement from Sister Mary Clarence, the lead singer Ahmal, played by Ryan Toby, steps out and gradually grows in confidence. As his voice increases in volume, the power of his melody ushers his nerves away. As he becomes more comfortable on stage, so does the rest of the choir, and eventually, with arms outstretched, he belts out the impressive and legendary high note we all remember him for.

Having the confidence to use your voice may not come naturally, but it starts by simply speaking up. The more you do it, the bolder you will be about standing up for what is right. Like Ahmal, you may require a gentle nudge, but ultimately, it's down to you to use your voice. You must realize that the power of your privilege can spark change. Whether you realize it or not, being part of the majority group means the power of balance is often in your favor, so the more you call out injustice, challenge microaggressions, and speak up for those who are being unfairly treated, the more of an impact you can have as an ally. Ciara LeRoy adds to this, explaining that when it comes to allyship, sometimes:

> "The sentiment is, 'I'm only one person. What can I do? I don't have a lot of resources,' but you have your time, you have your influence. You don't have to be some kind of social media influencer or blogger. You have your family, your friends, you have your professional circle; look around and think about how you can influence them. That's how you can use your privilege every day. It's about actively thinking about how you can make the world more equitable. Because it's frustrating that it's left to the oppressed group to commonly break down the oppressive systems. That's so not fair. I wish that more people in privileged positions would take that moment to break down the systems that they have benefited from."

Additionally, speaking up requires you to be attentive to your work environment and surroundings. Be observant; take the time to understand the office culture; and, if you see behavior that excludes or discriminates against anyone, be prepared to correct such behavior. When it comes to intervening and shutting down racist behavior, Omar Wasow shares his advice on how to identify and approach this. "So there are often situations where this weird analogy applies." He begins by explaining how he and his wife used to raise chickens: "One of the things that was amazing about raising chickens was that they engage in these contests. You know, I didn't realize that 'the pecking order' isn't just some phrase in the English language; these chickens would literally peck each other in order to establish rank. And, as we were raising these chickens, I would watch the games they would play to establish a pecking order."

Omar explains how, through watching the chickens, he noticed similar "pecking order" traits that could be observed among humans. "It began to be something I started to see in social dynamics with people, where it's like, oh, that person isn't just making a joke at somebody's expense, they're pulling rank on that person. They're saying, 'I am higher rank than you.' And there are all of these small kinds of ways we engage with one another in asserting rank, asserting status, and denying other people rank and status."

Omar advises that when you become aware of such dynamics, you should find ways to intervene. "If you become attuned to that, you might observe that somebody is cutting somebody else down. And you as a third party can intervene in a way that might say, 'That's out of bounds,' or 'I'm uncomfortable with how you are not hearing that person,' or 'You are being disrespectful.' Be a person who can make the dynamics visible or, if that's too confrontational, at least intervene on behalf of the person who is being undercut in a way that tries to equalize things," he says. "I think that's a really important part of it being dynamic. It's not just watching from the sidelines, but figuring out how you can intervene in a way that helps."

Omar highlights the importance of being self-aware when it comes to your approach. As you speak up, think about your delivery and how what you're saying is being received. Of course, if someone is ignorant, they will most likely find fault in how you provide feedback, but always be conscious of your delivery.

In regard to the workplace, Omar emphasizes, "Within an organization, there are lots of ways to support. Ask yourself, 'Is this person being given opportunities?' But also, 'Does this person have an area they need to improve in?' And, you know, 'Can I help them?' It is about giving constructive feedback, right? And so, I think that's another important part of allyship—figuring out, 'How can I help someone be the best version of themselves to thrive in this organization?'"

Speaking up can come in the form of mentorship and sponsorship—it is about using your expertise to support the advancement of Black talent.

Using your voice as an ally also means doing so with the right intentions, and not because it makes you look good or because it forms part of your yearly review. Allyship should be genuine, Oliver Holmes expresses:

"A lot of it comes down to integrity. The way I've always thought about it is, if I get excluded, or if I don't get something because I'm speaking up for others, they can keep it. I don't need it. Speaking up doesn't always have to be a big thing. It can be really subtle. It can literally be giving somebody some feedback after a session, such as taking a manager aside and just saying, 'Did you realize you mispronounced their name three times, or you mentioned everybody else's name in the team except theirs?' I think that as long as your intentions are clear, and there's integrity behind what you're doing, everyone should feel empowered."

LOOK OUT FOR OPPORTUNITIES TO SUPPORT BLACK TALENT

As you use your voice, follow it up with action. In an environment where white people, specifically white men, make up the majority of boards, are in decision-making positions, and have the opportunity to drive significant change, having allies at the most senior levels who can influence organizational shifts is important. Saying this, it is equally as important to recognize that impact can be made through an individual regardless of their level.

Organizations should actively look for ways to recruit diverse talent. We often hear excuses like, "We can't find Black talent," which is simply a lazy response. The talent is out there. So, whether it's hiring from Historically Black Colleges and Universities like Howard University; sponsoring and recruiting from Black events organized to spotlight and celebrate Black talent, such as the UK Black Business Show or Black Women Talk Tech; or by encouraging and promoting referral programs, there are so many ways to hire Black talent. The question you need to ask yourself is, "Do I care enough to put in the effort to find Black talent?"

We spoke to Scarlett Allen-Horton, 2019 BBC *Apprentice* Finalist and Director of Harper Fox Search Partners, a recruitment company that specializes in placing leadership and executive-level talent across engineering and manufacturing industries with a focus on senior ethnic minority and female talent. As an ally, Scarlett shared how growing up in a diverse community meant that she became aware of race and racism at a relatively early age. "I was brought up in the inner city of Birmingham, so it was very, very diverse. I'm half Pakistani and white, so at a very young age, probably 6 or 7, I realized that people could treat you differently because of your race," she says. "I would hear racist slurs around me all the time, and most of the time, people didn't realize that I was half Pakistani, but we've got quite a lot of ethnic diversity in my family."

Scarlett explains that when it comes to recruiting talent, hiring managers are often influenced by affinity bias—which she regularly challenges. For Scarlett, managers need to acknowledge and address their bias and be held accountable.

"Sometimes when you're working with a client, and they've employed 'Dave' for the last 30 years, they naturally will look to reemploy and replace 'Dave' with another 'Dave.' And it's the same cycle. A lot of the work that we do is to question, 'Could we consider someone else apart from "Dave"? And for what reason, are we considering him or her?' I often encourage my clients to focus on the skill set they are after.

Such behaviors are not always internally challenged, especially in smaller businesses. A lot of the bigger corporate businesses have an agenda for Equality, Diversity, and Inclusion (EDI) which, as a first step, is really positive to see. But we need to ensure that EDI is something that is not just talked about."

Action from allies is essential, as Charlene White asserts: "Nothing changes without allies ... And unless they really make a point of changing things, of shaking things up, making things a lot more even, a lot more representative, giving everybody an equal chance to sit at the table— without those people wanting to do it—nothing changes. So we can all fight 'til the cows come home to try to instigate change, but if the gatekeepers who really affect that change aren't on board, then nothing happens." Radio DJ, presenter, and producer Jenny Francis further supports this and explains, "There's no point in having a conversation as Black people if we're not going to include white people in the conversation. On our own, we can't be the solution, because we're not oppressing ourselves."

A report released by Korn Ferry and the Korn Ferry Institute found that Black executives and talent at lower-level organizations have to contend with unconscious bias and unfair treatment that create undue barriers to career progress.[7] Jenny shares an experience she witnessed, one that I am sure many of us have seen in our own industries. "At a radio station I worked at, an opportunity came up for a program controller and, while there were capable candidates who were Black, the position was offered to a white tech op, someone who was essentially the runner," Jenny says. "He knew nothing about the music, nothing about R&B, but he was given that role."

Jenny explains that because the role was offered to someone who lacked the knowledge and skill set to execute in the position, it became the responsibility of those who had the knowledge to teach him.

"So in that role, Black people who were now considered junior to him, as well as the presenters, were actually teaching him how to do his role. Now, if he was a Black man or woman, do you think they would send somebody in to teach them to do the role they should already know how to do? And that's what needs to change. There needs to be more opportunities open to talented and capable Black people who have the ability but aren't being given the chances."

In organizations where managers and decision-makers display bias, many capable Black people miss out on opportunities. If such behaviors go unchecked, no one will be held accountable. Therefore, as an ally, do your part to address and call out bias. Recommend books and resources to colleagues who display bias. If your organization offers any kind of inclusion training or anti-racism training, push for your team to take the course.

As the director of a recruitment company that focuses on an industry that is known for its lack of diversity, Scarlett Allen-Horton shares that when she is working with clients, understanding how they approach diversity and inclusion is a key component in her discussions with them. At organizational level, it is important to assess whether the culture of your company makes it difficult for people to bring their best selves to work: "If we were to bring a Black professional into this environment, would that professional feel comfortable? Would they feel safe? Would they be able to thrive in the environment that you've got at the moment? If so, amazing. If not, then what do you need to do as an organization to address those points straight away and make changes?"

It is necessary for leaders to look at ways to reduce bias in their organizations. Action needs to be intentional and measurable. Companies and organizations should be able to effectively track and report on initiatives and programs that have been set up to support the Black community. Having the data to work with is key—you need to be able to know your current status and use that to guide where you want to go. Data powers progress, and without it you cannot measure how impactful a program is. Data enables you to tell a story, and as emphasized by Oliver Holmes, "It's that storytelling that is valuable, we've got to make sure that this is a movement and not a moment." Organizations ought to set out strategic action plans to improve representation of Black employees. Oliver adds,

> "I think for organizations, especially at scale, it's good to have an ambition in place that you can measure against; having a framework that uses data is a really good starting point for organizations wanting to make change. You can then branch that out into lots of other organizational functions to really promote diversity and inclusion. So, for example, let's take procurement. You can review how many Black-owned businesses your organization is working with. Who are your suppliers? Or for recruiting, how many African Caribbean societies at universities are you really engaging with? It shouldn't just be during Black History Month, then that's it. We should be looking at absolutely everything, and using the data helps. It gives you a good starting point and somewhere to head toward."

As you consider measurable steps you can take to be an active ally at work, be sure to continue sharing your progress. People are interested in the difference you are making, and keeping a record of it can prove to be beneficial in attracting more diverse talent because where inclusion leads, diversity follows.

SUPPORT BLACK BUSINESSES

Following the protests against racial injustice that took place in the summer of 2020, many people were looking for ways to better support Black-owned businesses. According to Google Trends data, searches for "How to find Black-owned businesses in your area" saw a 300 percent spike from June 1 to June 2 in the United States,[8] while searches for

"Black-owned restaurants near me" tripled.[9] In the UK, the first Black Pound Day took place on June 27, and consumers were encouraged to spend money with local and online UK Black-owned businesses.[10] Since its launch, Black people and allies are encouraged to spend with a Black-owned business every first Saturday of the month. A similar initiative was launched in the United States on July 7—Blackout Day, an economic protest encouraging Black Americans to cease spending for the day or to only spend with a Black-owned business, if necessary.[11] Both campaigns received popular support, and allies were beginning to demonstrate a recognition of the way they could also use their financial resources to advance and support Black-owned business.

As consumers, we have a lot more control, influence, and power than we give ourselves credit for. Therefore, being more thoughtful about how and with whom you shop with can have a lasting and positive impact on the Black economy.

Continue to push for the change you want to see, and never forget that "ally" is a doing word.

NEXT STEPS AND REFLECTION

- What privileges and biases do you have?

- What parts of Black experiences, cultures, and communities do you need to educate yourself on?

- List three actions you will take to learn more.

- What steps will you take from learning to action?

PEARLS OF WISDOM

Words of Advice from the
Twice As Hard Contributors

"BE CONFIDENT WHEREVER YOU FIND YOURSELF. YOU HAVE SOMETHING TO OFFER, SO ALWAYS STRIVE TO DELIVER YOUR BEST. FOCUS ON GROWTH, BE IT PROFESSIONAL, PERSONAL, OR SPIRITUAL. BE INTENTIONAL ABOUT NURTURING GROWTH. ON YOUR JOURNEY OF GROWTH, DON'T BE AFRAID OF CHALLENGES. CHALLENGES ARE TO BE EXPECTED, SO LOOK FOR THE LESSON IN EVERY CHALLENGE. AND FINALLY, MANAGE YOUR FEARS, AND DON'T LET YOUR FEARS MANAGE YOU. YOU'VE GOT WHAT IT TAKES!"
–OPEYEMI SOFOLUKE

"HAVE YOUR END GOAL IN MIND AND STRATEGICALLY PLAN YOUR WAY TO GET THERE. PATIENCE IS KEY, AND THE MORE LESSONS YOU LEARN, THE BIGGER THE WINS GET. GREAT EXECUTION, EXCELLENCE, AND LONGEVITY WILL ALWAYS BRING SUCCESS."
–RAPHAEL SOFOLUKE

As part of our research for writing this book, we asked the successful Black businesspeople interviewed this question: "What words of advice do you have for Black entrepreneurs and professionals on this journey?" This is what they said.

ADRIAN GRANT

"Know what you want, and don't think that there are any barriers in your way. Anything is possible, and having self-belief is very important. We all need to have belief in ourselves; nobody else is going to do this for you. We need great people around us. We need great teams and mentors around us, but the key person to achieving anything is you. So believe in yourself."

ANDY DAVIS

"Find out what the criteria for 'great' is where you are and do the work to be great."

ANGELICA NWANDU

"Never go into business purely for the purpose of making money. That's the wrong way to approach entrepreneurship. The best way to approach entrepreneurship is to figure out what skill, talent, or offering you can expertly give that will provide a solution to many people for a problem they have.

The second piece of advice I would give is to build a healthy business. I think that in this new era, where investment money is much easier to get, people forget to build healthy businesses—that should be the focus before raising a ton of money. And so, I would say, believe in yourself, that you can build first and only accept investment money when you have to.

Lastly, be honest with yourself, figure out what your weaknesses are, and don't be afraid to partner with or hire people that can fill in the blanks."

ARLAN HAMILTON

"Let your work speak for itself. Be consistent. Go above and beyond what is asked or expected until your work starts to stand out, and don't shrink yourself. When you do something great, be your biggest advocate within these power structures."

ASMAU AHMED

"I think we all need to acknowledge that we can't do this alone. Everybody needs a helping hand. So as you build relationships in your career, be willing to connect with somebody else as a human being. Be open, be willing to learn, and be willing to give. See it as a two-way relationship."

BIANCA MILLER-COLE

"Whether it's career or business, identify a problem and a solution that people are willing to engage with or purchase. Being the person that is solutions oriented will make you stand out from the crowd. If you can be that person in an organization, you become indispensable. And so I think it's important to find great problems and even better solutions."

BOLA SOL

"Speak up, and stand your ground. There's no job in the world that should make you forget your integrity."

BYRON COLE

"People have got big dreams but no clarity. Have absolutely crystal-clear clarity that is measurable so anyone can tell you whether or not you've achieved that task or goal."

CHARLENE WHITE

"Know your worth. Despite the obstacles that are in your way, if you know your worth, you'll always be able to get ahead. If you know your worth and you are good at what you do, you will succeed. When you make a decision to become a game changer, it's not easy. The easy decision is to not be a game changer. But once you decide to be a game changer, you realize just how much change you can affect. And hopefully, how much easier it could be for our children."

CHRISTINA OKOROCHA

"Be your authentic self. People will remember you for being you. If you try and be like everyone else, you will just blend in and people will forget you. You want to be remembered for something that you've done, something that you've said, something that you've accomplished. Also try to be excellent at things that you do. If you can be the best at what you do and don't skip corners—that's very important."

CIARA LEROY

"Don't be afraid to advocate for yourself and create your own opportunities. Opportunities aren't always going to be presented to you, so there will be certain tables where you just have to pull up your own chair. Don't be afraid to take up space with who you are and don't be tempted to shrink or contort yourself to fit into the expectations of other people. Finally, don't crumble under the weight of low expectations that other people may have for you, as a Black person."

DANIELLE PRESCOD

"Rest. Make sure that is a priority of yours, because rest is just as important as working hard and you deserve it. If you're sick, it's okay to take a day off and just be sick and get better. The world will keep turning; sometimes it feels like it won't, but it'll be fine. Notice the things that make you feel good and the things that make you feel not so good so that you can use that knowledge to improve your environment."

DAVID MCQUEEN

"There are incredible networks and individuals around you that you can learn from, whether you are going on your own entrepreneurially or pursuing a career in industry. Do the groundwork to find out exactly who and where they are. Talk; have a lot of conversations; connect with individuals who have gone before you; and, when you get to a certain point in your career, ask yourself 'Who can I help in return?'

Ultimately, I would say be authentic, understand what your values are, learn from people who have been successful, be resilient enough to know that there are going to be knock-backs—but figure out how to navigate them and keep going."

DEMI ARIYO

"Persistence and commitment always yield results. Be persistent and committed to whatever it is you desire to achieve. You're not born with persistence and commitment—it comes through experience.

Be laser-focused on what you're trying to do. At certain times, vision is the only thing that can keep you going, so have a clear focus on what the end goal is. In being focused, write your destination with a pen but your plans with a pencil. It's okay to be flexible with your plans, and sometimes you may have to understand that's life."

EMMANUEL ASUQUO

"The biggest thing that helped me has been understanding that I can't always be motivated, so I have to be disciplined. It can be hard, being the only Black person in an environment and feeling like you have to represent all Black people. That pressure is on us, so it can grind you down and you won't always feel motivated. It's not always happy days, but you have to be disciplined, and you have to be consistent, and you have to keep going—trusting that, by doing that, you will achieve what you're trying to do."

GLENDA MCNEAL

"Don't be afraid to be who you are unapologetically. Stand up for what you believe intentionally. Love and be loved freely. Forgive yourself frequently. And live life boldly. Be fearless; you'll be okay."

HERMAN BULLS

"Be authentically yourself. You are a Black person; you will always be a Black person. So that is not going to change. I would go back to these six traits: interpersonal skills, communication, analytical skills, leadership, risk-taking, and passion. Monitor them. Get your personal board of directors. These aren't people that are going to tell you what you want to hear; these are people that are going to give you their perception of how they see you. Lastly, pursue excellence in everything you do—become a symbol of excellence."

INDIA GARY-MARTIN

"Our journeys are so valuable, and they're individual. Trust the journey."

INUA ELLAMS

"Make sure your life outside your work is rich, and bring that to your work. Don't just park it outside; you have to be a whole human being in all spaces."

JAMELIA DONALDSON

"Be humble. Read. Listen. Then ask questions. There are many different words and names that people can give 'it,' but you have to listen to God, the voice, your intuition, because it will genuinely guide you.

You have to build a sustainable network and, beyond the network, you need to build a sustainable and robust business. So the sooner you get to grips with that, the better. The beauty and the strength of a business is in the unglamorous parts that get overshadowed by the glitz and glam. So I would say 'forget about the glitz and glam'; it will come."

JAY-ANN LOPEZ

"Try to know what you don't know; try to know what you're not good at so you can find people to fill that gap for you. Be open to change as a person, because business does change you. Be prepared. Being an entrepreneur is not the opposite of a nine-to-five job; in fact, it's even more hours. If you really want to do it, you'll make it happen."

JENNY FRANCIS

"If there's something you really want to achieve, go for it. With anything in life, there will be obstacles on the way, but don't let that stop you from reaching your end goal. Be ready to adapt. Think outside the box. Don't just give up."

JUNE ANGELIDIS

"Stay focused, do the things that actually move your business forward, and be very intentional about how you build your teams. Make sure you have the culture at the back of your mind with each hire; that's so critical. But also just be conscious of the biases that we all have. Regardless of what we look like, we all have biases, so we always need to be conscious of that."

KENNETH GIBBS

"Don't forget that you're Black, regardless of the heights of success that you may achieve. You've come a long way to be here, but you have a long way to go. Always remember, you deserve to enjoy the fruits of your labor and every step in your journey as much as anyone else does."

MATHEW KNOWLES

"If you are going to be an entrepreneur, it's more than just saying you are going to open a business. It's about knowing the who, the what, and the why. Who is my customer, what is my product, and why should they buy it? 'The who, the what, and the why' are three fundamental elements of being an entrepreneur, and if you don't know those elements, you're probably doomed for failure. So it's all of the above, and that's why nothing is easy when aiming to get to the top. Thinking that you can microwave success is absolutely foolish. Successful people didn't get there by a microwave. Learn from failure; failure is the opportunity to grow, not the reason to quit. Most people quit because of failure when there's an opportunity, so embrace failure. Embrace it."

MARVIN SORDELL

"Try to stay true to your 'why,' as in your mission, the reason why you embarked on the journey, regardless of how many twists and turns that takes you on. Explore different horizons. You don't have to be one thing—you don't have to stay in one place—follow your passions in different areas, too."

MARVYN HARRISON

"We all should have a very intense self-care practice list. And I think, if you are in Britain, as a Black person, and you are not proactively loving yourself, you won't make it. And I don't mean in terms of life and death; I mean you're not going to make it to the place you think you're going to go. So identify the work—the space between where you are now and where you're trying to get to emotionally. The sooner you do it, the better."

MIKE LITTLE

"Have the confidence to be your authentic self, to put yourself forward. Be yourself and don't try to emulate others. Get involved in networking, it's important, too, but the heart of it for me is absolutely about being your authentic self."

MUNYA CHAWAWA

"Success, regardless of who you are or where you are, is a journey. You get to the endpoint by being persistent and being open-minded enough to try different ways of getting there."

OMAR WASOW

"Part of the core skill to being successful in this modern economy is to be deeply curious. Keep learning and build your body of skills and knowledge so that you are well adapted for whatever should come along. That means often investing years in something where there's not an obvious payoff, until there is. A lot of what is going to allow somebody to thrive either as an entrepreneur or as an employee is being that person who's really up to speed on what is current, but really at the heart of that is: just have a passion for learning.

So it's about investing in yourself, investing in your skills, investing in your love of learning, so that you're in a position to be very adaptable and, when opportunities arise, to be prepared."

PAMELA HUTCHINSON

"I would say, 'don't leave it as long as I did to be your authentic self.' I would say, start your career being authentically who you are, but get advice on how you can do that in a way that is skillful, that is not going to harm your career. And the reason I say that is because whether organizations know it or not, actually the one thing that we can bring that no one else can bring is diversity; we can bring that, and we can bring it hard. Start off deciding who you're going to be and work with people to help you do that in a skillful way. That might mean leveraging mentors or leveraging people like me that you see speak on a panel or read a blog they've written or whatever. But figure out how you can make your diversity work for you and for your organization. Don't wait until you're 40 to do it."

RAY J

"Listen to your heart. If the opportunity is in front of your face, take it. But success comes when opportunity meets preparation. So if you're at home preparing and training for these moments that are going to happen in your life, when they arrive, you're prepared.

You've got to work hard; you've got to stay humble. The bigger and more successful you get, the more humble and the more understanding you should become. The more time you should make for people, the more you should find ways to give back. So stay humble and work hard."

RONDETTE AMOY SMITH

"Embrace who you are; embrace and showcase who you are. Start your board of directors early. Always demonstrate a level of gratitude, write that thank-you note and do that follow-up, express gratitude to people even for the smallest things, because that's how you build trust and that's how you build camaraderie—that's how you maintain your network and your circle. Work hard for your organization, but also have your passion outside of work, because that's what's going to keep you going."

RONKE LAWAL

"Find safe-space mechanisms. When I say 'safe-space mechanisms,' I mean make sure you build a tribe around you outside of work or business and also inside of work and business. You need that mechanism to lean on, to advocate on your behalf when you find you're struggling to advocate for yourself. Going back to that word of advocacy, learn how to use your voice. Don't let the world or society silence you; use your voice as a businessperson—speak up."

SHELLYE ARCHAMBEAU

"Make sure people know what you are doing. People start their job, they put their heads down, and they go to work, and especially when you're at lower levels, you work typically with a small group, where only the small group knows what you do. Make sure other people know what you do."

TOMMY WILLIAMS

"To a professional, I would say, first of all, don't feel intimidated by the environment; feel as though you belong there. Don't be afraid to ask awkward questions and put yourself out there. In terms of being an entrepreneur, before you embark on building a business, you need to understand what lifestyle you're building it for. Think about the journey you will have to take building the business, because you need to enjoy the journey; otherwise, you're not gonna get to the destination."

TREVOR NELSON

"Today's generation loves the term 'greatness,' and I think it's empowering. I understand it, and there is a need to be focused on delivering it. People need to recognize that we have a place. We are as talented—there are strings to our bow—and we've got so much going for us."

TRINA CHARLES

"Think about what it is that you're offering or what it is that you are trying to solve with your business—be really clear on that. Also, positioning is important: how are you going to position yourself in the market?"

DR. WAYNE FREDERICK

"You are not on this journey alone, and you should not be in it only for yourself. Your journey has been bolstered by the generations of Black entrepreneurs and professionals who came before you to blaze a trail and open doors so that your journey is less arduous. Black businesspeople have a responsibility of service to today's Black community and the next generation of African American children who are relying on them to bring our vision of a more equitable society closer and closer to reality."

REFERENCES

Let's Get to Work

1 The phrase "The issue of race is an issue we are forced to deal with, it is not our option" first appears in "Trial by Media: 41 Shots," NETFLIX, 2020.

2 Obama, Michelle, "Remarks by the First Lady at Tuskegee University Commencement Address," Tuskegee University, The Whitehouse President Barack Obama Archives, 2015.

3 Sippitt, Amy, "Job applicants with ethnic minority sounding names are less likely to be called for interview," Full Fact, 2015.

4 Siddique, Haroon, "Minority ethnic Britons face 'shocking' job discrimination," Guardian, 2019.

5 Morgan Roberts, Laura, & Mayo, Anthony J., "Toward a Racially Just Workplace," Harvard Business Review, 2019.

6 Koulopoulos, Thomas, "Harvard, Stanford, and MIT Researchers Study 1 Million Inventors to Find Secret to Success, And It's Not Talent," Inc., 2018.

7 Winfrey, Oprah, 2015.

Chapter 1

1 Makortoff, Kalyeena, "UK black professional representation 'has barely budged since 2014,'" Guardian, 2020.

2 Chritton, S., Define Your Audience for Your Personal Brand—For Dummies, John Wiley & Sons Inc., 2015.

3 White, Gillian B., "Black Workers Really Do Need to Be Twice As Good," The Atlantic, 2015.

4 Gaertner, S., & McLaughlin, J., "Racial Stereotypes: Associations and Ascriptions of Positive and Negative Characteristics," Social Psychology Quarterly, American Sociological Association, 1983.

5 Arie, India, "I Am Not My Hair," Testimony: Vol. 1, Life & Relationship, Motown Records, 2005.

6 James, H. R., "If you are attractive and you know it, please apply: appearance based discrimination and employer discretion," Valparaiso University Law Review, 2008.

7 Discover more about The Halo Collective here: www.halocollective.co.uk.

8 Phillips, Katherine W., Dumas, Tracy L., & Rothbard, Nancy P., "Minorities hesitate to share information about themselves at work. That's a problem for everyone," Harvard Business Review, 2018.

9 McPherson, M., Smith-Lovin, L., & Cook, J., "Birds of a Feather: Homophily in Social Networks," Annual Review of Sociology, 27, 2001.

10 Willis, Janine, & Todorov, Alexander, "First Impressions: Making Up Your Mind After a 100-Ms Exposure to a Face," Psychological Science, SAGE, 2006.

11 Mlodinow, Leonard, "How We Are Judged by Our Appearance," Psychology Today, 2012.

12 Kendi, Ibram X., "100 Women of the Year. 1971: Angela Davis," TIME, 2020.

13 Davis, A., "Afro Images: Politics, Fashion, and Nostalgia," Critical Inquiry, 21, The University of Chicago Press, 1994.

14 Freeman-Powell, Shamaan, "Why 56 black men are posing in hoodies," BBC News, 2019.

15 Discover more about the 56 Black Men Campaign here: www.56blackmen.com.

16 Lammy, David, "David Lammy on why there's nothing scary about a black man in a hoodie," Guardian, 2019.

17 "Media Representations and Impact on the Lives of Black Men and Boys," Social Science Literature Review, The Opportunity Agenda, 2011.

18 Indeed Career Development, "Work Ethic Skills: Top 8 Values to Develop," Indeed, 2020.

19 Discover more about Asmau Ahmed here: www.asmauahmed.com.

20 Taylor, E., Guy-Walls, P., Wilkerson, P., et al. "The Historical Perspectives of Stereotypes on African-American Males," Journal of Human Rights and Social Work, Springer, 2019.

21 Rosette, A. S., Leonardelli, G. J., & Phillips, K. W. "The White standard: Racial bias in leader categorization," Journal of Applied Psychology, APA Publishing, 2008.

22 On March 11, 2020, the global outbreak of COVID-19, a new coronavirus disease, was declared a pandemic by the World Health Organization (WHO), which led to governments around the world placing restrictions on movement and travel, often described as a "lockdown."

Chapter 2

1 Christine Comaford-Lynch, 2021.

2 Gale, Porter, Your Network Is Your Net

Worth, Atria Books, Simon & Schuster Inc., 2013.

3 Vukova, Christina, "73+ Surprising Networking Statistics to Boost Your Career," *Review42*, 2021.

4 Bulao, Jacquelyn, "17+ Eye-Opening Networking Statistics for 2020," TechJury, 2021.

5 "Average Private School Minority Percentage," Private School Review, 2021.

6 "The pros and cons of private school education," Study International, Hybrid, 2019.

7 Moss, Paul, "Why has Eton produced so many prime ministers?", BBC News, 2010.

8 Elfring, Tom, & Hulsink, Willem, "Networking by Entrepreneurs: Patterns of Tie-Formation in Emerging Organizations," *Organization Studies*, SAGE, 2007.

9 Ibid.

10 Harvey Wingfield, Adia, "Being Black—but Not Too Black—in the Workplace," *The Atlantic*, 2015.

11 Association of Event Organisers, "Economic Impact of Exhibitions in the United Kingdom," 2019.

12 UFI, "Global Economic Impact of Exhibitions," 2020.

13 Vukova, Christina, "73+ Surprising Networking Statistics to Boost Your Career," *Review42*, 2021.

14 Rock, David, & Grant, Heidi, "Why Diverse Teams Are Smarter," *Harvard Business Review*, 2016.

15 Ibid.

16 Knowles, Solange, *Seat at the Table*, Saint Records, Columbia Records, RCA Records, Sony Music Entertainment, 2016; and Beyoncé, *Lemonade*, WB Music Corp., OBO, Oakland 13 Music, SONY/ATVRCA Records, Sony Music Entertainment, 2016.

17 Association for Psychological Science, "Familiar Faces Look Happier Than Unfamiliar Ones," *Psychological Science*, SAGE, 2017.

18 Datareportal, "What is the overall popularity of social media compared to internet use globally?", *Digital 2020 July Global Snapshot*, 2020.

19 Donne, John, *No Man Is an Island*, Souvenir Press Limited, 1988.

20 Keith Ferrazzi, 2021.

21 AZQuotes.com, 2021.

22 Davis, Tchiki, "Develop Authenticity: 20 Ways to Be a More Authentic Person," *Psychology Today*, 2019.

23 "First Impressions," *Psychology Today*, 2021.

24 Nelson, Trevor, "Trevor Nelson: My Life in Media," *Independent*, 2007.

25 RoAne, Susan, "Insights for Savvy Networking," *Inc.*, 2010.

26 Discover more about Adrian Grant here: https://www.baronetentertainment.com/adrian-grant.

27 Ibarra, Herminia, "Why Strategic Networking Is Harder For Women," *Forbes*, 2016.

28 Larson, Erik, "New Research: Diversity + Inclusion = Better Decision Making At Work," *Forbes*, 2017.

Chapter 3

1 Washington, Denzel, "The Mentors He'll Never Forget," Guideposts, 2007.

2 Zimmermann, Allyson, "Sponsorship: it"s not who you know, but who knows you," *Guardian*, 2013.

3 Kram, K. E., & Isabella, L., "Mentoring alternatives: the role of peer relationships in career development," *The Academy of Management Journal*, 1985.

4 Block, Betty Ann, & Tietjen-Smith, Tara, "The Case for Women Mentoring Women," *Quest*, 2016.

5 "Race in the workplace," *The McGregor-Smith Review*, 2016.

6 Wood, Claudia, & Wybron, Ian, "Entry to, and progression in, work," Joseph Rowntree Foundation, 2015.

7 Fagenson-Eland, E., Marks, M., & Amendola, K., "Perceptions of Mentoring Relationships," *Journal of Vocational Behavior*, Elsevier, 1997.

8 Inzer, L., & Crawford, C., "A Review of Formal and Informal Mentoring," *Journal of Leadership Education*, SAGE, 2005.

9 Discover more about The Curve Catwalk here: www.thecurvecatwalk.com.

10 Farmer, Betty, "Mentoring Communication," *Review of Communication*, Taylor & Francis, 2005.

11 Ball, Kelsey, "Cultural Mistrust, Conspiracy Theories and Attitudes Towards HIV Testing Among African Americans," *Journal of AIDS & Clinical Research*, Hilaris, 2016.

12 Benkert, Ramona; Peters, Rosalind M.; Clark, Rodney; Keves-Foster, Kathryn,

"Effects of Perceived Racism, Cultural Mistrust and Trust in Providers on Satisfaction with Care," *Journal of the National Medical Association*, 2006.

13 Johnson, W. Brad, Smith, David G., & Haythornthwaite, Jennifer, "Why Your Mentorship Program Isn't Working," *Harvard Business Review*, 2020.

14 Brown, Mike, "Comfort Zone: Model or metaphor?", *Australian Journal of Outdoor Education*, Springer, 2008.

15 Knowles, Mathew, *Racism From the Eyes of a Child*, Music World Publishing, 2017.

16 Nelson, Thomas, "Ecclesiastes 9:10," *The Bible* (New King James Version), 1982.

Chapter 4

1 White, Gillian B., "Black Workers Really Do Need to Be Twice as Good," *The Atlantic*, 2015.

2 Ibid.

3 Ibid.

4 Howe, Catherine Q., & Purves, Dale, "The Müller-Lyer illusion explained by the statistics of image–source relationships," Proceedings of the National Academy of Sciences, 2005.

5 Cherry, Kendra, "Figure-Ground Perception in Psychology," Very Well Mind, 2020.

6 Harman, Jason L., Zhang, Don, & Greening, Steven G., "Basic Processes in Dynamic Decision Making," *Frontiers in Psychology*, Frontiers Media S. A., 2019.

7 Güss, C. Dominik, "The Brain and Thinking Across Cultures," Frontiers for Young Minds, Frontiers Media S. A., 2015.

8 Knowles, Mathew, *The DNA of Achievers*, Music World Publishing, 2015.

9 Gino, Francesca, "Why It's So Hard to Speak Up Against a Toxic Culture," *Harvard Business Review*, 2018.

10 Ibid.

11 Ibid.

12 Cooper, Melody, Twitter @ melodyMcooper, May 25, 2020.

13 Harrison, Lisa A., & Willis Esqueda, Cynthia, "Race Stereotypes and Perceptions about Black Males Involved in Interpersonal Violence," *Journal of African American Men*, Springer, 2001.

14 Doggett, Jolie A., "Imposter Syndrome Hits Harder When You're Black," *Huffington Post*, 2019.

15 Ibid.

16 Hopper, Elizabeth, "What Is a Microaggression? Everyday Insults with Harmful Effects," ThoughtCo., 2019.

17 Montañez, Rachel, "10 Microinsults And 5 Microinvalidations Women Of Color Are Tired Of, Are You Guilty?", *Forbes*, 2020.

18 Smith, Anna, "What to know about microaggressions," *Medical News Today*, 2020.

19 Morrison, Carlos D., "Code-switching," *Encyclopedia Britannica*, 2017.

20 McCluney, Courtney L., Robotham, Kathrina, Lee, Serenity, Smith, Richard, & Durkee, Myles, "The Costs of Code-Switching," *Harvard Business Review*, 2019.

Chapter 5

1 Maxwell, John C., *Failing Forward*, Harper Collins, 2007.

2 "Availability of Credit to Small Businesses—September 2017," Board of Governors of the Federal Reserve System, 2017.

3 Williams, Wallis, "Half of black Britons experience workplace racism, finds survey," *Financial Times*, 2020.

4 King, Martin Luther, Jr., "'I Have a Dream,' Address Delivered at the March on Washington for Jobs and Freedom," Washington, D. C., The Martin Luther King Jr. Research and Education Institute, Stanford University, 1963.

5 *Christian Work: Illustrated Family Newspaper*, American Theological Library Association, 1987, New York Public Library, 2021.

6 Sujan, Harish, Barton A. Weitz, and Nirmalya Kumar (1994), "Learning Orientation, Working Smart, and Effective Selling," *Journal of Marketing*, 58 (3), 39–52.

7 Hamilton, A., "From Bootstrapped to $1.15B IPO—Therese Tucker of BlackLine" Backstage Capital Podcast, Backstage Capital, 2018.

8 Phil Jackson was the head coach of the Chicago Bulls during their most successful era, 1989–1998, and guided the team to six NBA Championships.

9 Maume, David J., "Glass Ceilings and Glass Elevators," Research Gate, University of Cincinnati, 1999.

10 Discover more about Ray J here: www. RayJ.com.

11 Jameson, Robert C., "Be Careful of Your Thoughts: They Control Your Destiny," *Huffington Post*, 2014.

12 Spalding, Dee Poku, "How Black Female Founders Can Finally Break Through the Fundraising Gap in 2018," *Forbes*, 2018.

13 Finley, Taryn, "Like Issa Rae, I'm Also 'Rooting for Everybody Black,'" *The New York Times*, 2017.

14 "The Black P&L Leader: Insights and Lesson from Senior P&L Leaders in Corporate America," *Korn Ferry*, Korn Ferry Institute, 2019.

15 Ibid.

16 "Step into the Shade Room: Where Culture Meets Scale," The Shade Room, 2020.

17 Nelson, Thomas, "Romans 12:2," *The Bible* (New King James Version), 1982.

Chapter 6

1 Munson, Natasha, *Life Lessons for My Sisters: How to Make Wise Choices and Live a Life You Love!*, Hachette Books, 2005.

2 Miller, Stephen, "Black Workers Still Earn Less than Their White Counterparts," The Society for Human Resource Management, 2020.

3 Molomo, Khanyi, "The Unique Challenges Faced By Black Business Owners," Big Cartel, 2020.

4 Forbes, Moira, "How Arlan Hamilton Harnessed Silicon Valley's Most Overlooked Investment Opportunity," *Forbes*, 2019.

5 Mahmood, Basit, "Why Are Black People Still Paid Less Than Their White Counterparts?", *Newsweek*, 2020.

6 Ibid.

7 Ibid.

8 Nelson, Thomas, "Psalm 128:2," *The Bible* (New King James Version), 1982.

9 "The Colour of Money," Runnymede, 2020.

10 Discover more about Bola Sol here: www.bolasol.co.uk

11 Bounds, Andy, "Black-owned businesses struggle to find investors," *Financial Times*, 2020.

12 McIntosh, Kriston, Moss, Emily, Nunn, Ryan, and Shambaugh, Jay, "Examining the Black-white wealth gap," Brookings, 2020.

13 Ibid.

14 Ibid.

15 "The Colour of Money," Runnymede, 2020.

16 Ibid.

17 Mackay, Holly, "Holly's top picks: 6 great mobile-first investment services and apps," Boring Money, 2019.

18 Adams, Riley, "Opinion: What is generational wealth and how do you build it?", MarketWatch, 2020.

19 Wilson, Kimberley, "Why It's Important For Every Black Person To Have A Will," *Essence*, 2019.

20 "Family Owned Businesses," *Inc Magazine*, 2021.

Chapter 7

1 "Mahatma Ghandi's Greatest Quotes," Business Blogs, 2020.

2 "Mental health conditions, work and the workplace," Health and Safety Executive, 2020.

3 Ibid.

4 Ibid.

5 PA Media, "'I will be a happier man': Marvin Sordell retires from football at 28," *Guardian*, 2019.

6 FourFourTwoStaff, "Sordell retires due to mental health struggles," *FourFourTwo*, 2019.

7 "Dual Diagnosis: Substance Abuse and Mental Health," Help Guide, 2020

8 "Discrimination in mental health services," Mind, 2019.

9 Morris, Natalie, "Black and ethnic minority employees 'need more mental health support' in the workplace," *Metro*, 2020.

10 "ADAA Board of Directors Statement: ADAA Stands Against Racism," Anxiety and Depression Association of America, 2020.

11 Ibid.

12 Bido, Tatiana, "The Shocking Ways Stress Directly Affects Our Appearance— And How to Beat It," The American Institute of Stress, 2019.

13 Lewsley, Joanne, "What are the effects of racism on health and mental health?", *Medical News Today*, 2020.

14 Center for Workplace Mental Health, American Psychiatric Association Foundation, 2021.

15 "Understanding Racial Microaggression and its Effect on Mental Health," Pfizer, 2020.

16 Ibid.

17 Ma, Lybi, "The Reality of Imposter Syndrome," *Psychology Today*, 2018.

18 Nance-Nash, Sheryl, "Why imposter syndrome hits women and women of colour harder," BBC.com, 2020.

19 Loehr, Jim, and Schwartz, Tony, "The Making of a Corporate Athlete," *Harvard Business Review*, 2001.

20 Ibid.

21 Nelson, Thomas, "Proverbs 10:22," *The Bible* (New King James Version), 1982.

22 Queen, Douglas, and Harding, Keith, "Societal pandemic burnout: A COVID legacy," *Int Wound J.*, Wlley, 2020.

23 Deloitte Touche Tohmatsu Limited, "Big demands and high expectations: The Deloitte Millennial Survey," 2014.

24 Mental Health Foundation, 2021.

Chapter 8

1 Baldwin, James, *Nobody Knows My Name: More Notes of a Native Son*, Dial Press,1961.

2 *Oxford Dictionary*, Oxford University Press, 2021.

3 "Inequalities and discrimination likely to be playing a significant role in higher rate of black and minority ethnic COVID-19 deaths", The Heath Foundation, 2020.

4 Cohen, Li, "Police in the U.S. killed 164 Black people in the first 8 months of 2020. These are their names. (Part II: May-August)", CBS News, 2020.

5 Friedman, Gillian, "Here's What Companies Are Promising to Do to Fight Racism," *New York Times*, 2020.

6 Holding, Michael, "West Indies legend Michael Holding breaks down discussing racism in the UK", Sky News, YouTube, 2020.

7 "The Black P&L Leader: Insights and Lesson from Senior P&L Leaders in Corporate America", Korn Ferry, Korn Ferry Institute, 2019.

8 Goodwin, Jazmin, "Apps highlighting black-owned businesses see a surge in support during pandemic and protests," CNN, 2020.

9 Ibid.

10 Discover more about Black Pound Day here: blackpoundday.uk

11 Brooks, Khristopher J., "Blackout Day draws national attention to Black spending power", CBS News, 2020.

INDEX

SHINING
IN THE DARK

*Celebrating Twenty Years
of Lilja's Library*